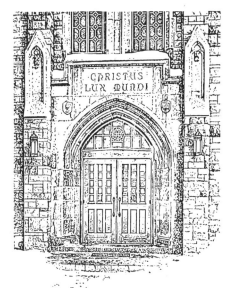

MUIRHEAD LIBRARY OF PHILOSOPHY

An admirable statement of the aims of the Library of Philosophy was provided by the first editor, the late Professor J. H. Muirhead, in his description of the original programme printed in Erdmann's *History of Philosophy* under the date 1890. This was slightly modified in subsequent volumes to take the form of the following statement:

'The Muirhead Library of Philosophy was designed as a contribution to the History of Modern Philosophy under the heads: first of Different Schools of Thought—Sensationalist, Realist, Idealist, Intuitivist; secondly of different Subjects—Psychology, Ethics, Aesthetics, Political Philosophy, Theology. While much had been done in England in tracing the course of evolution in nature, history, economics, morals and religion, little had been done in tracing the development of thought on these subjects. Yet "the evolution of opinion is part of the whole evolution".

'By the co-operation of different writers in carrying out this plan it was hoped that a thoroughness and completeness of treatment, otherwise unattainable, might be secured. It was believed also that from writers mainly British and American fuller consideration of English Philosophy than it had hitherto received might be looked for. In the earlier series of books containing, among others, Bosanquet's *History of Aesthetic*, Pfleiderer's *Rational Theology since Kant*, Albee's *History of English Utilitarianism*, Bonar's *Philosophy and Political Economy*, Brett's *History of Psychology*, Ritchie's *Natural Rights*, these objects were to a large extent effected.

'In the meantime original work of a high order was being produced both in England and America by such writers as Bradley, Stout, Bertrand Russell, Baldwin, Urban, Montague, and others, and a new interest in foreign works, German, French and Italian, which had either become classical or were attracting public attention, had developed. The scope of the Library thus became extended into something more international, and it is entering on the fifth decade of its existence in the hope that it may contribute to that mutual understanding between countries which is so pressing a need of the present time.'

The need which Professor Muirhead stressed is no less pressing today, and few will deny that philosophy had much to do with enabling us to meet it, although no one, least of all Muirhead himself, would regard that as the sole, or even the main, object of philosophy. As

Professor Muirhead continues to lend the distinction of his name to the Library of Philosophy it seemed not inappropriate to allow him to recall us to these aims in his own words. The emphasis on the history of thought also seemed to me very timely: and the number of important works promised for the Library in the very near future augur well for the continued fulfilment, in this and other ways, of the expectations of the original editor.

H. D. LEWIS

MUIRHEAD LIBRARY OF PHILOSOPHY

General Editor: H. D. Lewis
Professor of History and Philosophy of Religion in the University of London

Action by SIR MALCOLM KNOX
The Analysis of Mind by BERTRAND RUSSELL
Belief by H. H. PRICE
Clarity is Not Enough by H. D. LEWIS
Coleridge as Philosopher by J. H. MUIRHEAD
The Commonplace Book of G. E. Moore edited by C. LEWY
Contemporary American Philosophy edited by G. P. ADAMS and W. P. MONTAGUE
Contemporary British Philosophy first and second Series edited by J. H. MUIRHEAD
Contemporary British Philosophy third Series edited by H. D. LEWIS
Contemporary Indian Philosophy edited by RADHAKRISHNAN and J. H. MUIRHEAD 2nd edition
Contemporary Philosophy in Australia edited by ROBERT BROWN and C. D. ROLLINS
The Discipline of the Cave by J. N. FINDLAY
Doctrine and Argument in Indian Philosophy by NINIAN SMART
The Elusive Mind by H. D. LEWIS
Essays in Analysis by ALICE AMBROSE
Ethical Knowledge by J. J. KUPPERMAN
Ethics by NICOLAI HARTMANN translated by STANTON COIT 3 vols
The Foundation of Metaphysics in Science by ERROL E. HARRIS
Freedom and History by H. D. LEWIS
G. E. Moore: Essays in Retrospect edited by ALICE AMBROSE and MORRIS LAZEROWITZ
The Good Will: A Study in the Coherence Theory of Goodness by H. J. PATON
Hegel: A Re-examination by J. N. FINDLAY
Hegel's Science of Logic translated by W. H. JOHNSTON and L. G. STRUTHERS 2 vols
History of Aesthetic by B. BOSANQUET 2nd edition
History of English Utilitarianism by E. ALBEE
History of Psychology by G. S. BRETT edited by R. S. PETERS abridged one volume edition 2nd edition
Human Knowledge by BERTRAND RUSSELL
Hypothesis and Perception by ERROLL HARRIS
A Hundred Years of British Philosophy by RUDOLF METZ translated by J. H. HARVEY, T. E. JESSOP, HENRY STURT
Ideas: A General Introduction to Pure Phenomenology by EDMUND HUSSERL translated by W. R. BOYCE GIBSON
Identity and Reality by EMILE MEYERSON
Imagination by E. J. FURLONG
In Contact with the Physical World by JOHN PENNYCUICK
Indian Philosophy by RADHAKRISHNAN 2 vols revised 2nd edition
Introduction to Mathematical Philosophy by BERTRAND RUSSELL 2nd edition

Kant's First Critique by H. W. CASSIRER
Kant's Metaphysic of Experience by H. J. PATON
Know Thyself by BERNADINO VARISCO translated by GUGLIELMO SALVADORI
Language and Reality by WILBUR MARSHALL URBAN
A Layman's Quest by SIR MALCOLM KNOX
Lecturers on Philosophy by G. E. MOORE edited by C. LEWY
Matter and Memory by HENRI BERGSON translated by N. M. PAUL and W. S. PALMER
Memory by BRIAN SMITH
The Modern Predicament by H. J. PATON
Natural Rights by D. G. RITCHIE 3rd edition
Nature, Mind and Modern Science by E. HARRIS
The Nature of Thought by BRAND BLANSHARD
Non-Linguistic Philosophy by A. C. EWING
On Selfhood and Godhood by C. A. CAMPBELL
Our Experience of God by H. D. LEWIS
Our Knowledge of Right and Wrong by JONATHAN HARRISON
Perception by DON LOCKE
The Person God Is by PETER A. BERTOCCI
The Phenomenology of Mind by G. W. F. HEGEL translated by SIR JAMES BAILLIE revised 2nd edition
Philosophy in America by MAX BLACK
Philosophical Papers by G. E. MOORE
Philosophy and Illusion by MORRIS LAZEROWITZ
Philosophy and Political Economy by JAMES BONAR
Philosophy and Religion by AXEL HAGERSTROM
Philosophy of Space and Time by MICHAEL WHITEMAN
Philosophy of Whitehead by W. MAYS
The Platonic Tradition in Anglo-Saxon Philosophy by J. H. MUIRHEAD
The Principal Upanisads by RADHAKRISHNAN
The Problems of Perception by R. J. HIRST
Reason and Goodness by BLAND BLANSHARD
The Relevance of Whitehead by IVOR LECLERC
The Science of Logic by G. W. F. HEGEL
Some Main Problems of Philosophy by G. E. MOORE
Studies in the Metaphysics of Bradley by SUSHIL KUMAR SAXENA
The Subject of Consciousness by C. O. EVANS
The Theological Frontier of Ethics by W. G. MACLAGAN
Time and Free Will by HENRI BERGSON translated by F. G. POGSON
The Transcendence of the Cave by J. N. FINDLAY
Values and Intentions by J. N. FINDLAY
The Ways of Knowing: or the Methods of Philosophy by W. P. MONTAGUE

Muirhead Library of Philosophy

EDITED BY H. D. LEWIS

THE ABSOLUTE
AND THE ATONEMENT

THE ABSOLUTE
AND THE ATONEMENT

BY

ILLTYD TRETHOWAN
MONK OF DOWNSIDE

LONDON: GEORGE ALLEN & UNWIN LTD
NEW YORK: HUMANITIES PRESS INC

© *George Allen & Unwin Ltd 1971*

ISBN 0 04 231003 2

U.S.A. SBN 391-00177-9

PRINTED IN GREAT BRITAIN
in 11 on 12pt Barbou
by W & J Mackay & Co Ltd
Chatham, Kent

To Louis Bouyer

PREFACE

Absolute Value (1970) represented the first half of a course of lectures entitled 'From Philosophy to Theology', given in the Department of Religious Studies at Brown University, Providence, R.I., in 1969; and here I must reiterate my gratitude to its Chairman, Professor Ernest S. Frerichs, and my other kind colleagues. The second part of the course (but with a number of additions and subtractions) appears in the present book. In order to make it as far as possible self-contained, and independent of its predecessor, I have rearranged the material so that the first section ('The Absolute') may provide such information as may be required about the conclusions previously arrived at; the reader must be referred to *Absolute Value* for the analysis which leads to these conclusions. This first section is a series of critiques of recent works about natural theology, not discussed in the previous volume, and is thus an addition to it rather than a repetition of it. The first chapter was a lecture given in the Divinity School at Yale University and published in *The Downside Review* (January 1970); I am grateful to the Editor for permission to use this and other material which has appeared in his pages.

The contents page should provide a sufficient clue to the movement of thought which is developed in these chapters: it hinges on the self-guaranteeing apprehension of God as revealed in Jesus Christ. As in the previous book, I have quoted copiously from contemporary writers (translations into English are my own unless otherwise described). This was the method of the lectures because I wanted to indicate the existing state of traditional theology on the questions at issue and to compare my own conclusions with it. It was particularly necessary to retain this method in the present volume because I am here trespassing on the ground of dogmatic theologians, and I must show that I am not indulging in speculation which can claim no support from the professionals.

This may provoke the comment that theological conclusions should be supported in the first place by reference not to contemporary theologians but to the primary sources. 'What is the use', it may be asked, 'in writing about theology without reference to the Scriptures?' It is true and (on the face of it) must indeed seem scandalous that there is very little reference here to the Scriptures. The reason is that I am concerned simply with the *interpretation* of fundamental doctrines, acknowledged by all to be essential to the tradition, and my question is, in every case: on what conditions is the doctrine thinkable? It will be clear, then, that I am not offering an 'instant' dogmatic theology but considering certain problems which arise in dogmatic theology—and from a particular angle. Here I should point out that I am using 'atonement' in the older (etymological) sense; but the topic of expiation, to which, primarily, the word nowadays refers, will receive some discussion in due course.

There may be the further comment that this is in any case the business of professionals. I am an autodidact in theology. What business have I to embark on such a project? If there is a satisfactory answer to this, it must be found in the pages of the book. Here I can only say that the question is one which I have often put to myself, but that I see possible advantages in my non-professional status. The difficulties which I find in certain theological theses may be shared by other non-professionals, and it might even be that the language I use will seem rather clearer than that of most professionals. But it is only fair to add, for the prospective reader, that if he finds metaphysics unintelligible he is unlikely to get much help from me. I do avoid technical language so far as possible, and that has (I believe) sometimes proved helpful, but one does need, apparently, a certain type of mind to see anything in writing of this sort. Perhaps it will be some reassurance to say that metaphysical theology means for me, not the systematization of abstract notions, but the intelligibility, the meaningfulness, of Christian experience, to which we are all called and to which, therefore, we must all have some clue.

I am grateful to the publishers concerned for permission to quote at some length from the following original or translated works: *The Philosophy of Gabriel Marcel* by Kenneth Gallagher (Fordham University Press, New York); *Logique de la Foi* by Henri Bouillard (Aubier, Paris); *The Resurrection* by F. X. Durwell (Sheed and Ward); *Introduction à la Vie Spirituelle* by Louis Bouyer (Desclée, Tournai); *The Two Sources of Religion and Morality* by Henri Bergson (Doubleday and Co., New York). These books, taken in that order, will shed further light on the development of my conclusions, and I have been anxious to make them better known; even the last, famous though it is, seems to be little read at the present time. I have also to thank Mr I. P. Sheldon-Williams for his kindness in reading the proofs and many others, too numerous to mention here, for the help and encouragement which they have given me; the chief of these debts is recorded in the dedication.

CONTENTS

I

THE ABSOLUTE

I. THE REJECTION OF THE ABSOLUTE

Anyone who wants to talk about the Absolute will find himself at once confronted today by certain stock objections. They are conveniently summed up in Professor Antony Flew's *God and Philosophy* (1966), and to offer some answers to them at the outset will enable me at the same time to give a rough sketch of the positions which I took up in *Absolute Value* and which I shall continue to discuss in the first Part of the present volume.

I shall not discuss Flew's treatment of certain arguments for God, commonly and rather misleadingly referred to as the 'traditional' arguments, not only because others have claimed to find misconceptions in it but also because the fundamental issue, as I see it, lies elsewhere. In my opinion, as in that of pretty well everyone today except certain Thomists, there is no proof of God to be found in the conclusion of a piece of syllogistic reasoning which begins with what is supposed to be acceptable to everyone and moves to its conclusion in virtue simply of a logical process of which everyone, presumably, but a fool is capable. Nevertheless the traditional arguments have their use, I would say, as 'pointers' to God, and it is perhaps worth noting that the late Austin Farrer's *Finite and Infinite* (London, 1943), the most impressive presentation of this view in our own time, is not included in the extensive bibliography of Flew's book. Before I begin to discuss what I regard as the fundamental issue I shall mention certain features of the book which have not, perhaps, received already the attention which they deserve.

The first, which has indeed been insisted upon by at least one critic, is that Flew attributes to Christianity an anthropomorphic conception of God. Reflective Christians down the ages have rejected such conceptions, and, if we are interested to know whether Christianity makes sense, we should consult those who think about it, not those who do not. Flew admits of course that some Christians eschew anthropomorphism, but the God of whom he speaks is regularly an anthropomorphic one. I add incidentally that the principle that one should judge something by its best, not by its worst, when it is a question of discerning values, is one which needs to be borne in mind at a good many points in Flew's book.

There is another general consideration in regard to his procedures which seems worth mentioning. There would be very wide agreement among thinking people that the human situation provides us with a good deal which we cannot fully explain, whatever our interpretation of it. For example, it would seem to be flying in the face of the facts to reject the notions of moral freedom and spiritual failure. Yet the acceptance of them leads to conclusions which may well seem disconcerting. Moral freedom involves, for me, the possibility of our rejecting God in a definitive way. The doctrine of hell is frequently produced by Flew as a sort of trump card which can always win the game for him in any circumstances, but he never stops to consider (and this is my point) whether his own position about moral freedom is intelligible. He glances[1] at the objection that the ethics of secular humanism, if it is to be consistently secular, must reduce to a system of self-interest (we just *like* to make people happy in point of fact)—unless of course it is prepared to accept moral obligation as just another fact (it is immoral to ask why we ought to do certain things—we just *ought*). Here Flew thinks that the best form of defence is attack and remarks that 'to the extent that Christianity, like Islam, offers more or less enormous rewards and punishments, these religions seem to leave no room for any but the most temporary self-sacrifice by their faithful'; he goes on to describe the Christian view of sacrifice as a 'nasty and dangerous doctrine'.[2] Christianity does not indeed teach self-sacrifice as its fundamental principle of morals (and why should it?) but rather self-fulfilment in union with God, although it also teaches that in certain circumstances we may have to give our lives for the brethren because they are our brethren—because we cannot love God without love for his children. But on what ground does Flew hold that we may have to do this? His only reply, so far as I can see, is: 'no desires or motives are as such either rational or irrational . . . self-sacrifice . . . is one of the many things which people may want to do, or which they do because they think they ought'. But surely we must ask why they should

[1] 114. [2] 116.

want to act thus, or why they think they ought to act thus, at any rate if they are philosophers. Flew criticizes Christianity on what purport to be high moral grounds, but one does not discover what in fact they are. 'Fine things are hard', he quotes.[1] Yes, but why *ought* we to aim at them if we don't *want* to?

The last of my general comments on Flew's procedures is that he encourages an all-too-common confusion about the meaning of the word 'faith' in certain philosophies of religion. He assumes that it must always refer to something not only beyond reasoning processes but also beyond knowledge. What it sometimes refers to in fact is an apprehension of God. Marcel, for example, uses this language as well as that of *intuition boucheé*. I prefer myself to keep the word 'faith' for faith in the Christian Revelation, but this is simply a matter of convenience. I am in substantial agreement with Marcel on the facts. Flew's account in this respect is further complicated by passages in his first chapter which seem to suggest that belief in God is made somehow less reasonable by the existence of rival 'historic faiths', also by a misconception— a very widespread misconception—about the First Vatican Council's statements on the evidence for God: in fact the Council says nothing about syllogisms and is simply laying it down that it is possible for man to have knowledge of God without benefit of special or historical revelation. Flew's claim to have invalidated 'the whole system of the Roman Church' must therefore be rejected. This, I confess, is a digression. Now that I have embarked upon it I might also remark that Flew shows a general tendency to confuse Christian doctrines with theological opinions, in particular with regard to sexual morality. But that is excusable in that theologians have so often fallen into the same confusion.

I now turn directly to the fundamental issue, the question, namely, about an awareness of God. Flew does not give much space to it, and it arises in a curiously incidental way, not in the discussion of natural theology which occupies the first half of the book but only when he has turned to the credentials of revelation. He devotes a chapter to religious experience in that connection. It begins with references to experiences claiming to substantiate particular religious notions, visions of saints and so forth, and, when Flew eventually mentions the suggestion that there could be a form of religious experience which is nothing less than

[1] 114.

19

an apprehension of God himself, we shall find that he simply dismisses it as obviously ridiculous. This cavalier treatment of the issue would raise even agnostic eyebrows in France or Germany. It will be worth while, I think, to consider his remarks on the subject in detail since they are typical of a highly influential attitude among English-speaking philosophers.

In his approach to the topic Flew asks what he calls the 'basic question': 'How and when would we be justified in making inferences from the facts of the occurrence of religious experience, considered as a purely psychological phenomenon, to conclusions about the supposed objective religious truths?'[1] He is not yet facing the fact that philosophers of religion who, if I may put it so provocatively, know their business, do not try to develop an argument on the lines which he describes but are making a claim that an awareness of God, available in principle for everybody, is to be found at the heart of our specifically human experience. When he is led to mention what is in fact such a claim in a passage which I shall proceed to quote, he regards it as simply illustrating a failure to distinguish between 'a purely psychological phenomenon' and evidence for God, such evidence being, necessarily, in his eyes, the upshot of inferential processes based on a 'purely psychological phenomenon'. The passage begins as follows: '. . . it is most remarkable that those who consider religious experience to be evidence so often fail to appreciate the fundamental distinctions and hence fail to address themselves to the basic question'. I break off the quotation to emphasise that Flew's basic question is a question about inferential processes. He goes on: 'This weakness is not confined to the most popular levels of discussion. For instance in a recent volume of the proceedings of a conference of professional philosophers and theologians it is only on the fifty-seventh of sixty pages on "Religious Experience and its Problems" that anyone presses our sixty-four dollar question: "Suppose it does seem that we are 'encountering God', how can we tell whether or not we really are?" and the outline answer given offers as a criterion "the difference between the inner experience of acting and that of being acted upon".'[2] The reference is to the Princeton Symposium of 1962 edited by Professor John Hick under the title *Faith and the Philosophers* (London, 1964), and the 'outline answer' was proposed by Father Norris Clarke, s.J., in the discussion which fol-

[1] 129. [2] 131.

lowed Professor H. H. Price's admirable introductory paper. Flew comments: 'This suggestion is breathtakingly parachial and uncomprehending. It is parochial in that it takes no account of the inordinate variety of religious experience. . . . It is uncomprehending in that it has not seen that the question arises precisely because it is impossible to make direct and self-authenticating inferences from the character of the subjective experience to conclusions about the supposedly corresponding objective facts.'

As we shall see (I hope) more clearly in a moment, Clarke is not in fact relying on an inference or even proposing a criterion in the ordinary sense of that word. First I must clear up an incidental confusion generated by part of the sentence last quoted. 'The question arises', Flew said, 'because it is impossible to make direct and self-authenticating inferences' of a certain kind. Flew's *question* has been *whether* it is possible to make such inferences, and he has said that it is not. What he must mean, then, here, is not that Clarke has failed to see what the question is but that he has made a mistake in supposing that it can receive an affirmative answer. I now turn to the question whether Clarke is in fact proposing a self-authenticating inference, and I must quote from him at greater length than Flew has done. Clarke begins by referring to the situation described in Price's paper in which a man instead of just praying to God *as if* he were there becomes convinced that he *is* there. 'What kind of evidence', Clarke asks, 'can I find within this experience which gives it intellectual respectability, the sense of being objectively grounded and not merely arbitrarily projected?' He answers: 'It seems to me that the crucial element is a certain awareness, elusive and intangible though it be, that I am no longer experiencing merely my own *activity* of pondering and reaching out for God, but also a new strand of *passivity*, as though I am *being* acted upon . . . being awakened and drawn by some hidden Presence. . . .' In an attempt to give some clue about the nature of this 'Presence', he speaks of it as 'just "beyond" my own profoundest centre' and of a 'pull on my soul from some greater force beyond', and he adds that this 'is not an abstract deduction but a responsible intellectual (though not necessarily conceptual or self-consciously analytic) weighing or estimation of an experience and its implications'.[1] Now the word 'implications' in that last sentence could be taken to mean, if we are not sufficiently attentive

[1] *Faith and the Philosophers*, 59–60.

to its context, that an inference is drawn from the experience here described or some subsequent judgement passed upon it and that there is no satisfactory evidence for God in the experience itself. But it is surely clear that what Clarke is really doing is making a claim to an objective certainty about the presence of God. An inference drawn from a religious experience or a subsequent judgement passed upon it could make sense only before such an experience has declared itself as fully objective. Such an inference or judgement cannot prove that the experience is objective. The most it can do is to suggest that the experience may declare itself to be objective if it is further attended to. It would be a 'pointer' to the awareness of God, but it can neither substitute for it nor of itself produce it. The evidence lies in the awareness. So Clarke has been offering not what is ordinarily meant by a *criterion* but an attempted *description* of the experience.

If we now return to Flew's text we find that he cannot entertain the notion of an objective apprehension. So far he has been objecting that people like Clarke can produce no satisfactory inferences to prove what they want to claim and that therefore their claims are invalid. 'It is impossible', he has said, 'to make direct and self-authenticating inferences from the character of the subjective experience to conclusions about the supposedly corresponding objective facts'; apparently it now occurs to him that some of his scapegoats have views on epistemology quite different from his, since he does at this point give us his reasons for rejecting the principle of objective apprehension, which is in fact the basic principle presupposed by claims like Clarke's. 'The impossibility here', Flew goes on, 'is logical. It is not . . . that it just so happens that as a matter of fact there are not in any subjective experience any distinguishing marks the presence of which necessarily guarantees that the particular experience must be veridical. It is rather that there necessarily could not be such marks. . . .'[1] This is one of those denials of absolute certainty which I have been contesting for a good many years. It seems to me that unless we accept our own experience as veridical in and of itself we are condemned to a self-refuting scepticism. I cannot here go into particular questions which arise about sense-experience, but to give some illustration of what I mean by experience I would say that we are simply aware of what is not ourselves. The fact that we *can* always make mistakes if we fail to take certain precautions, if we go

[1] 131–2.

beyond our evidence, has nothing whatever to do, logically, with the fact that I am not making one now if I now claim, for example, that something other than myself is acting upon a part of my body. I should venture to describe it as the floor of this room. To this fundamental and highly controversial topic I shall return. For the present I want to complete my commentary on this chapter of Flew's book.

He is now arguing that there can be no such thing as a self-authenticating experience of something on the ground that no characteristic of experience can be 'an infallible sign of the presence of something altogether different',[1] and at this point he does at last explicitly recognize that claims are made by philosophers of religion to a self-authenticating awareness of God, referring to well-known statements made by Professor H. D. Lewis and Professor H. H. Farmer which contain precisely that claim. Flew considers that he has ruled them out of court. He adds that what they are doing is making an assertion 'which would at one and the same time fulfil two logically inconsistent specifications: first, that of involving only their own experience, without any falsifiable reference to anything beyond, and, second, that of entailing the truth of the essentials of their religion'.[2] What they are claiming, I must repeat, is an awareness of God. The fact that this claim cannot be directly falsified is nothing against it. Nor can Flew's falsification principle show that the claim is without content. Elsewhere Flew tries to show that the claim could be indirectly falsified because a world which contains evil could not be the creation of the Christian God. As to this I can only say in passing that the problem of evil is indeed, to my mind, the ultimate problem, but that the theist who employs what is called 'the free-will defence' is involved in no contradiction, only in an obscurity[3]—the obscurity to which I have already referred in speaking of moral freedom. Flew here remarks that 'all assertion must involve a theoretical possibility of error proportionate to its content'. As I have already remarked, a theoretical possibility is no logical rebuttal of the *fact* that we actually know things. Knowledge of the truth is always self-authenticating in the sense that it is always a matter in the end of my *seeing* something. We ask for proof only when we do not see something and in order to see it. Flew does glance in a later passage at the contention that the question of proof cannot arise about everything. All he can say is that when a man's

[1] 132. [2] 133.
[3] I have discussed this in ch. 10 of *Absolute Value*.

observations of an object at close quarters are confirmed by other people he has 'all the good reason which anyone could possibly want'.[1] This evades the issue.

Flew, speaking of 'pretensions to a knowledge of God grounded incorrigibly in immediate acquaintance', now tells us that 'such pretensions . . . are so common nowadays among Protestants that it may be useful . . . to add some supplementary points'.[2] He would be surprised, it seems, to learn that they are also common among Catholics, although a Catholic theologian will reserve an immediate acquaintance with God for the Beatific Vision and is likely to say that our knowledge of God here and now is direct but mediate, a knowledge of him, that is, *in* the world and especially in ourselves. The supplementary points which Flew adds consist in the assertion that Dr John Baillie's claims in his book *Our Knowledge of God* (London, 1959) are only of 'biographical and sociological interest', that Cook Wilson's parallel (at the end of *Statement and Inference* [Oxford, 1926]) between acquaintance with God and acquaintance with our friends is vitiated by a crucial difference between the two cases (Cook Wilson in fact is only claiming a certain directness for our knowledge in each case) and that belief in a person presupposes the truth of the proposition that this person does objectively exist. Obviously it does, but my belief that you exist is founded not in the truth of a proposition but on my awareness of your presence. I can find nothing further in the rest of this chapter which is not a ringing of the changes on what has been already said (there is a reference, for instance, to 'the Cartesian delusion that knowledge can and must be self-certifying').[3]

But I may seem to have left something out. It will be remembered that when Flew was objecting to Clarke's so-called 'criterion' he objected that 'it takes no account whatsoever of the inordinate variety of religious experience'. How, in other words, is Clarke proposing to identify the object of his experience with the Christian God? Perhaps the first thing to say about this is that he is not committed to satisfying all enquirers that this evidence of God, if they accept it, must commit them to belief in Christianity; they may accept it simply as evidence of God. Then, of course, Flew will ask: 'but *what* God?' I realize that to many minds there does seem to be a great difficulty about identifying the object of an experience with God, even if it is granted objective

[1] 167.   [2] 134.   [3] 137.

validity, but I suggest that this may be due, sometimes at least, to a rather vague feeling that 'people have such different ideas about God'. In fact the name 'God' has a standard meaning in the English language, one which has been imposed on it by Christian experience, and the notion of the Christian God can be entertained by an agnostic or an atheist: he is the creator of the world, the source of being and man's final good. Clarke's claim is compatible with this notion. It does not appear to be compatible with notions of a non-creative or a finite or an indifferent god, which I take to be the other possible notions. And it seems to me pretty obvious that when those who accept the Christian tradition talk about God they are all talking about the same God. It also seems to me pretty obvious, when non-Christians worship the God whom they call infinite, transcendent and strictly indescribable, that they are worshipping that same God. To someone like Flew, who does not realize that the transcendent God is strictly indescribable, this may well seem an odd claim. But that should not disturb his worshippers.

There are two topics discussed by Flew in the course of his book on which I should like to say something very briefly. Like so many writers on ethics, he assumes that a theistic account of morality must be making an ultimate appeal to God's commands, so the question arises: does God command something because it is good or is it good because God commands it? We must say that he commands it because it is good, and then the good becomes a sort of absolute independent of God.[1] Such is the familiar argument. The mistake here is surely very plain. What a theist will say is that God is our good and that his commands are statements of the way by which we may reach him. It is an extraordinary thing that so many modern philosophers think of the Christian God as an autocrat issuing arbitrary orders. The second topic, on which I have said something already, is that of moral obligation. Flew touches on Bishop Gore's argument in *Belief of God* (London, 1921) that the recognition of moral claims which override individual wishes is illogically combined with explicit atheism. He is content to say that 'it is hard to discern what was for Gore the precise nerve of the whole argument'.[2] I would myself say that this is not strictly an argument but a 'pointer'. It is a question of apprehending absolute good which makes its impact on us under the form of absolute obligation. A man's duty to make something of himself, to be honest with himself (however mistaken he may be about par-

[1] 109.   [2] 110.

ticular duties), can appear to him, if he cares to look at it, as absolute, irreducible. On this view the absoluteness of truth and the absoluteness of good are the absoluteness of the source of existence showing itself to us as our goal. To sum up my position as briefly as possible, the basic evidence of God is his action upon us; he is evident *in* his action on us. The cause is evident *in* its effect. I suspect that we should not apprehend him in the world unless we apprehended him, in the guise of absolute truth and absolute goodness, in our own spiritual being.

I must now make some further remarks on the topic of absolute truth, for this aspect of theism seems to arouse increasing opposition at the present time, more especially perhaps in America. A thorough-going sociological relativism will sometimes prove to preside over the meditations even of religious people, of people, I mean, whose interest in religion is not purely academic. I cannot see how such a position is reconcilable with religious *belief*. The logical conclusion to which it leads is, I think, a Rylean behaviourism. That is to say, although we are not machines, we have no spiritual functions. If it is impossible for us to transcend our historical conditioning in any way, then we are different from the other animals only in the degree of our complexity. There would be no evidence that we differ from them in kind by virtue of a spiritual destiny. If on the other hand we do transcend our historical conditioning in any way, we must in doing so make contact with what is absolute. It is impossible for any reasonably mature mind not to see that the conclusion of the simplest sort of syllogism follows from its premises. If the owner of such a mind tells me that he cannot help performing this process of thought *because* he is caught up in a certain sort of sociological web, he is suggesting that in other historical circumstances some other conclusion about that syllogism might be incumbent upon him. I cannot see how he can avoid the ancient objection to all such attempts at relativizing truth. For if he is to be consistent he will have to say that this theory of his about historical conditioning is itself historically conditioned. To say that it is a true theory is only to say that it is one which he cannot help holding. To ask whether it is *really the case* is meaningless. And the ancient objection to this is (in modern dress) that if nothing is really the case then philosophy is a mug's game and we must all be just sociologists. It is, of course, a genuine option. We are free to turn down the notion of absolute truth if we want to. The sociologist will no doubt remark that if we do not turn it down it is because we happen to be conditioned by a religious upbringing or acquired metaphysical prejudices. By speaking of prejudices he can only mean that this is not his way of thinking, that he finds it alien to him and therefore deplores it. It is surely obvious that in those circumstances we cannot engage in any rational discussion of our differences.

I have claimed that a part of my body is now being acted upon by the floor on which I am standing. A relativist may tell me that in speaking of a floor I am exposing myself to all sorts of hazards. How can I claim absolute certainty about so complex a matter? What do I mean by a 'floor' and what right have I to insist on whatever meaning I do give it? It seems to me very difficult to take this seriously. If I ask myself whether I can really cast doubts on my present awareness of some thing other than myself or whether it might be incorrectly described in English as a floor, I find that my claim is irrefutable. Knowledge in the strong Platonic sense is a fact.

If knowledge is a fact it is obviously a metaphysical one, and in a time of philosophical decadence we must expect to find odder and odder attempts to get round it. That it is not describable in any ordinary way ought not to scandalize us. Metaphysics is the sphere of the unique. Knowledge or certainty is at the heart of our experience, which we cannot jump out of so as to inspect it objectively and impersonally. All we can say is that subject and object are found to be, not confused with one another, but *united* with one another. Our objective knowledge of our environment is doubtless very small. We know it only in its activity upon us, as the cause of this activity, present *in* its effects. Sense-qualities in themselves are purely subjective, and we know the things which cause them only as doing so. We know, or think we know, a good deal about ourselves. But we have not the sort of objective knowledge of them which we can have of God. *Solus Deus illabitur animae.* Mysticism? The principle which underlies classical mysticism and all religious awareness is to be found in the fact of knowledge itself. Unless we are going to say that the notion of truth is dispensable, we shall have to say, I believe, that when we claim to know the truth we claim that this truth is available for all other minds. But truth is not constituted as such by general agreement. What is true is what *is*. And what is, is what it is because it is constituted as such by the source of being. To know something as it really is, that is, really to know something, is to encounter it as constituted by this source, as a real *thing*, and to realize this is to encounter the source. This insight may begin in the form of a mere suspicion—the paper of Price's to which I referred seems to me very good on this. It makes a demand upon us that we should fulfil ourselves and for a start that we should be honest with ourselves. This honesty is an absolute. If we accept this, we are already praying. One cannot reverence an abstraction. If we no longer pretend to prove that God exists by sheer force of logic we must either drop the subject or take seriously the claim that he is found in all our specifically human experience. This is indeed an enormous claim, as Flew very properly points out. But unless we are prepared to make it, it seems to me that there is nothing very interesting about religious studies.

2. THE SECULARIZING OF THE ABSOLUTE

A year or two ago Dr Norman Pittenger, writing in *The Times*, gave it as his opinion that 'death-of-God' theology was moribund in the land of its origin and that interest had shifted, promisingly, to the application of 'process-philosophy' to the theological field, that is, to speculation about some sort of process of development which is supposed to be going on in God. From my point of view that might just as well be called 'death-of-God' theology. 'God', in the English language, means the Christian God, unless notice is given to the contrary. Nor is a 'God' who is still, as it were, growing up, a secularized God, a proper object of worship for anyone. To that I shall return at the end of the chapter. Its purpose is to consider the shift of interest and to ask why it should be considered a promising sign by a Christian theologian. But first, what is it a shift *from*?

'Death-of-God' theology will suggest to many people's minds Dr Robinson's *Honest to God* and Dr Paul van Buren's *The Secular Meaning of the Gospel*. Each would reject such a description of his work. Dr Robinson is certainly entitled to do so if only because so many of us find it impossible to pin down what was really in his mind (his subsequent writings seem to indicate, on the whole, a move in an encouraging direction). Van Buren rejects the label, I gather, because he dissociates himself from the extravagant views of some writers to whom it is attached. He is, however, a professing atheist. This should be clear to any reader of *The Secular Meaning of the Gospel*. If it is not, there is

Professor E. L. Mascall's *The Secularization of Christianity* to put it beyond doubt. One cannot therefore talk about 'death-of-God' theology without reference to van Buren's very considerable influence. But I must say here that I should not myself call him, any more than I should call Dr Robinson, an atheist. He must suppose himself to be such, but his commitment to the person of Jesus Christ seems to have an absolute character about it which, in my view, indicates the active presence in a man's consciousness of the Word and so of the Three-in-One: but it is not recognized by him for what it is. Father Robert L. Richard in his book *Secularization Theology* suggested at one point[1] that van Buren's insistence on silence about God should be understood only as referring to the *word* 'God'. I wish I could think that there was something in this. If one adds inverted commas to indicate that the word 'God' is being used to refer to an idea of a transcendent God who is not also an immanent one, then I should be ready indeed to say that 'God' is dead. And, if 'secularization' means only that we should not expect God to do our work for us, then I should be all for it.

For a detailed examination of *The Secular Meaning of the Gospel* Mascall's book must be consulted; this has been considered, not altogether without reason, as more unsympathetic to the writers criticized than it needs to be, but its analyses seem to me, in principle, irrefutable, and it makes very clear the tendency of these writers to canonize modern attitudes of thought simply because they are modern. Even Richard, who goes to great lengths in endeavouring to do all possible justice to van Buren, acknowledges that van Buren cannot rightly claim that 'modern man' uses only the language which he calls 'empirical'[2] (Harvey Cox, as Richard points out, makes the same criticism in the last chapter of *The Secular City*). The fundamental trouble with van Buren, however, is his rejection of metaphysics: he talks a good deal about 'experience', but he recognizes only sensory experience. Mascall refers to 'the amazingly naïve confidence which van Buren appears to have in the permanence of the linguistic analytical doctrine of philosophy'.[3] And he draws our particular attention to the following passage in van Buren's book:

'We reject the cognitive approach to theological language not primarily because it is logically puzzling, but because of certain theological commitments out of which this study has arisen. That approach

[1] 43.   [2] Richard, 260.   [3] 103.

builds its case on a natural sense of the divine and a natural revelation. The history of theology, seen from the perspective of modern kerygmatic theology, suggests that this is a road leading into the wilderness. Within the Protestant tradition, that road has been clearly charted and firmly marked with a "dead-end" sign by the work of Karl Barth, and we see no reason to ignore the warning.'[1] Van Buren, who was a pupil of Karl Barth's, is simply asserting that there is no philosophical evidence for God. He gives no sign of having read any of the numerous books on that topic which have appeared in recent years.

It has become widely recognized that 'secularizing' theologians have made unjustifiable use of certain passages in the writings of Bonhoeffer. Van Buren is one of them. In his opening paragraph he quotes Bonhoeffer's famous remark that we cannot be honest without recognizing that we must live in the world as if there were no God. Richard points out that Bonhoeffer was enunciating a paradox and that 'he continued to pray up until his final hour to the God he believed did exist', whereas van Buren 'drops the paradox completely. God is henceforth systematically excluded.'[2] Richard follows this up with the remark that Bonhoeffer's words seem to mean that we have to live in the world as we would have to *even if* God did not exist (the word in the Latin tag employed by Bonhoeffer is *etsi* not *quasi*)—in other words, he is simply telling us that we must not shuffle off our own responsibilities.

'A loose way', writes van Buren, 'of characterizing these analyses of the language of faith is to say that "God-statements" have been translated into "man-statements".'[3] This seems to me a precise way of saying what he has done: in *The Secular Meaning of the Gospel* God has been abolished. But, according to Professor J. A. Martin writing on van Buren's Christology in *Lumière et Vie*,[4] some more recent utterances of his suggest that his thought may be evolving towards a belief in a limited God. When we turn to Dr Harvey Cox we shall find, eventually, that he provides us with a definite instance of such a belief. But before we leave van Buren, it will be of interest to note, with Mascall, that in his last chapter he seems to go back on the conclusions which he had so emphatically stated. 'When we say that contemporary thought is secular', he writes there, 'we are calling attention to certain characteristics of the way we think and speak today. We have not argued that ours is

[1] Van Buren, 98.   [2] 119.   [3] 103.   [4] Autumn, 1968, no. 89.

a better or worse mode of thought than that of ancient times.'[1] Mascall's comment on this is: 'Any idea that historic Christianity might itself be the criterion by which contemporary modes of secular thought should be judged, and their deficiencies exposed and corrected, never seems to have entered his head.' My further comment is that the passage suggests the view that there is no absolute truth but that truth is always relative to the age in which we live. This view is at the back of a great deal of talk about the application of 'process-philosophy' to theology.

Harvey Cox is not a professing atheist, and, as in the case of van Buren, the absoluteness of his commitment to his fellow-men persuades me that it would be wrong to call him an atheist. That is not at all to say that commitment to one's fellow men is all that is required of a theist. It might be called a life-line connecting one with the God who is anonymously known. But it is a profoundly unsatisfactory position—and, one is bound to add, full of danger, for the lifeline is tenuous. And what Cox seems to have in mind when he *writes* about God does not deserve, in my opinion, to be called theism. I am not concerned here with his interpretation of the Bible or with the sociological questions which are the chief content of *The Secular City* but only with its last chapter in which he sets out to explain to us what can be properly meant, in his view, by the use of the word 'God'—but it is largely a question of what, in his view, can no longer be meant by it.

Cox begins this chapter with a reference to Bonhoeffer's proposal that we should speak of God in a secular fashion, remarking that 'the word *God* means almost nothing to modern secular man'.[2] I speak of God 'in a secular fashion' by referring to the moral absolute in which, as I hold, the supposedly non-existent God is at work in secular man. In this way (but of course not only in this way) God is immanent in the world: he makes contact with *us* (this does not mean that he ceases to be transcendent—only a transcendent God can be immanent in all things). The root of the trouble is that Christians have so often thought of God as being transcendent in such sort that they have banished him for most practical purposes from the world—hence the massive prejudice in the minds of modern men against the Christian God, who appears to them irrelevant, a gratuitous supposition. Cox then considers Bonhoeffer's distinction between speaking about a concept of

[1] 193. [2] 241.

God and naming God as the Bible does, and he points out that 'theologies and languages grow out of a socio-cultural milieu'.[1] Certainly they cannot be understood without reference to such a milieu. He also points out that 'the liberating activity which we witness in the Exodus and Easter' is to be detected in the world so that 'speaking of God in a secular fashion is also a political issue'. There is truth in this also in so far as God's activity should be discoverable in the activity of good men. But Cox recognizes that the fundamental question is not just sociological or political, and he puts it in the form given to it by Miguel Unamuno: 'Is man alone in the universe or not?' It is a question, Cox tells us, of deciding for ourselves 'whether the God of the Bible is real or just a rich and imaginative way man has fashioned to talk about himself',[2] and he adds that in the last analysis 'it is not a matter of clear thinking at all . . . '. That is surely disastrous. What he should have said is that it is not *only* a matter of clear thinking, of an awareness of God, but also one of committing ourselves to him.

When Cox turns to the sociological aspect of the question, he points out very truly that 'the God of the Bible must be carefully distinguished from the cultural avenues of perception through which pre-secular man met Him'.[3] But there seems to be a pre-supposition that 'the cultural avenues of the past' can have no value for us; I hope that with the spread of education some of them will come in time to have a greater value for us. According to Cox, what has to be done is to get rid of the academic humanism in which clergymen and theologians indulge, realizing that it is only a 'sub-culture',[4] and then we shall also succeed in getting rid of 'metaphysical talk of God' which, he says, 'has been made equivocal both by historical change and social differentiation'[5] (here again the question arises about the relativizing of truth). We must first plunge ourselves, Cox continues, into the 'emerging technical and political era' and then we shall find a new way of talking about God. He seems to think that 'metaphysics' can refer only to certain exploded metaphysical systems. His excuse is that Christians have so often connected the God of the Bible only with particular forms of human thinking that our basic metaphysical awareness has been disregarded.

After telling us that 'metaphysics provided the lexicon for the age of the town' and that we should now adopt a 'political' idiom, Cox con-

[1] 242. [2] 243. [3] 245. [4] 247. [5] 248.

siders two rival suggestions, the first that we should go back to a pre-metaphysical stage of thinking (here he refers to Heidegger), the second that we should adopt existentialist categories (here he refers to Bult-mann).[1] He remarks that Heidegger does not say much about 'the socio-cultural collapse which underlies the passing away of metaphysics' and that existentialist theology registers a reaction to an outmoded cultural epoch ('it needs some ultimate explanation for reality . . . urban-secular man . . . does not feel this compulsion to find some inclusive and overarching meaning').[2] These remarks illustrate very neatly a differentiation between Cox's position and mine. It is the disregard of metaphysics, in my view, which leads to 'socio-cultural collapse'. And it is, in my view, the virtue of 'existentialist theology' that it does try to find an 'overarching meaning' for the world. But what does Cox mean by 'existentialist theology'? Has he any acquaintance with the Blonde-lian tradition in theology? Does he know anything about the 'spiritual' tradition in French philosophy? The preoccupation of American theologians with Heidegger and Bultmann gives to their work a surprisingly parochial flavour. Cox does not stop to ask whether urban-secular man is justified in his attitude, and Mascall in his book *The Future of Theology* shows how, in Cox's work, the natural world, no longer seen as a manifestation of God, loses its 'true mystery and nobility'[3] and is cut off from God and from man, who thus enters upon it as an alien intruder. By regarding nature as autonomous, Cox makes it absurd and so allies himself with the existentialist philosophy of Sartre.

What does Cox mean by talking about God 'politically'? We do this, he says, 'whenever we give occasion to our neighbour to become the responsible, adult agent, the fully post-town and post-tribal man God expects him to be today'.[4] This does not take us very far, but there is still the last section of the book, entitled 'Speaking of God as a Theological Question', so one's hopes revive. It begins, indeed, promisingly enough: 'The hidden God . . . of biblical theology' is not to be confused with 'the no-God-at-all of nontheism';[5] the biblical God is 'at once different *from* man, unconditionally *for* man, and entirely unavailable for coercion and manipulation by man'. But it is supposed to follow from this that God is not 'the king-pin in an ontological system'. Does this mean that he is not to be thought of as the Source of all

[1] 249.   [2] 253.   [3] 166–7.   [4] 255.   [5] 257.

beings? To call such thinking the construction of an 'ontological system' makes it sound rather nasty, but this is not to show that there is anything wrong with it. God, Cox continues, remains hidden in Jesus: 'He does not "appear" but shows man that He acts, in His hiddenness, in human history . . . in Jesus God is teaching man to get along without Him.' It seems to me remarkable that a student of the Bible can make that last statement, apparently as a summary of New Testament teaching. But Cox now asks the fundamental question: 'Is this responsibility something which man himself has conjured, or is it *given* to him?'[1] and he seems to give it the right answer: 'It is his experience of the transcendent which makes man man.'

But what does he mean by 'the transcendent'? What is it that we find when we find it? He allows that poets and artists may help us to find it. But what he is concerned to suggest is, as he puts it here, that 'God comes to us today in events of social change, in what theologians have called *history*, what we call politics.'[2] That, he explains, includes all social contacts. 'Thus', he goes on, 'we meet God at those places in life where we come up against what is not pliable or disposable, at those hard edges where we are stopped and challenged to move ahead. . . . He meets us in the wholly other.'[3] So indeed he does, but is he, after all, only a name for 'moving ahead'?

Moving ahead to what? In earlier phases of society, Cox's argument now runs, God was symbolized in terms appropriate to them. In our society the typical activity is that of a scientific work-team in which the relationship between the members is one of 'alongsidedness'. This must influence the way in which we symbolize God. The Bible supports the idea of a partnership between God and man. Man's business is not with God himself but with the work in which God calls him to share. It does not seem to occur to Cox that there could be a knowledge of God which would determine which symbols point towards him (more or less inadequately) and which are merely misleading. It becomes plain that the 'biblical God', whoever he proves to be, is not to be identified with the Absolute.

'God', Cox goes on, 'wants man to be interested not in Him but in his fellow man',[4] and we may have to drop the word 'God' if we are to make this clear; 'the meaning of the word *God* will be altered or a new name will emerge as we encounter that presence in events which draws

[1] 259.   [2] 261.   [3] 262.   [4] 265

them into the history of which we are a part, the history of God's liberation of man'.[1] Cox has affirmed the transcendence of God, but he has nothing more to say about it than this. If we can find the transcendent God, how can it be right for us to take no interest in him? How could that be his will? What are we to be liberated from—and what for? From sin—and for God? There is no suggestion of that. Richard, in the book referred to above, is enthusiastic about a good deal of Cox's work. But he has to conclude that 'what Cox himself would like would be a sort of "sociological" or "socio-historical" concept of God. But he is blocked by not knowing what to do with what has always been called the divine transcendence.'[2] That is, he is not prepared to give it up, but he is unable to fit it into his system of thought. Richard points out also that Cox speaks of the Christian's life in this world 'as though he were to live here forever', although an 'affirmation of immortality' hereafter is to be found in his work,[3] and that Jesus of Nazareth is described as 'the Man for others' but 'without attention to his divinity'.[4] (As Mascall has remarked, the Jesus of the Gospels is first and foremost 'the man for God'). In *The Secular City* then, it seems, Cox's theology does not in fact get us beyond van Buren's, despite his occasional moves in a more hopeful direction. The overall effect of his recommendations would be to promote the disappearance of God from the minds of men.

I have spent so long over the positions adopted by Cox in this book, not only because it has made so deep an impression in so many quarters and because it is important to realize the arbitrariness of its presuppositions, but also because they lead him to a conclusion which may fairly be called an example of 'death-of-God' theology. We may now find an example of the shift of emphasis toward theories of a developing, limited God in his more recent pronouncements.

In the Afterword to *The Secular City Debate* he has admitted with his usual candour that he is dissatisfied with the conclusions which we have just been examining. In his book *On not leaving it to the snake* he revises them. The word 'God', he now tells us, has become, not indeed meaningless, as van Buren would say, but ambiguous.[5] How, he asks, can we have an idea of God which is not relative to historical circumstances? How can we affirm transcendence when once our culture has turned away from it? My answer to these questions would be, in brief, that it is not very profitable to ask *how* we in our historical circumstances can

[1] 266.   [2] Richard, 160.   [3] 171.   [4] 172.   [5] 5.

have knowledge of the Absolute (what we should ask is *whether* in fact we have it), and that (if we have it) the apparent absence of it in other people's minds does indeed present us with problems of communication but has nothing at all to do with the fact of our having it. Cox's answer begins with the statement that he proposes to go on avoiding any 'spatial symbolization of God' and 'all forms of metaphysical dualism'.[1] It ends with the suggestion that if theology would only stop talking about a God who 'is' and would envisage a God who 'will be', then it might have a most exciting future.[2] There is a good deal in this which demands investigation.

First, why should spatial symbolizations be so undesirable? Presumably because they can mislead. But so can all such symbolizations. I wonder whether Cox has read Edwyn Bevan's chapter on 'Height' in *Symbolism and Belief*. It is often supposed nowadays that the disappearance of a certain cosmology, of the notion of heaven as existing literally somewhere above the clouds, has some vital importance for the philosophy of religion as though it affected what St Thomas, for example, writes about God's transcendence. Has Cox ever pondered over St Thomas's account of it? It is extraordinarily naïve to suppose (as theologians out of touch with the great tradition in theology so often seem to do) that our modern conception of a 'one-storey world' (insisted upon in the last chapter of *The Secular City*) constitutes, in itself and not just for the ignorant, some sort of threat to one's belief in God. The dismissal of any sort of 'metaphysical dualism', like that of the word 'ontological', is also, I fear, naïve. The phrase is often used as a sort of smear-expression without any concern for what it stands for. It may stand for a belief in the existence of two opposed principles, benevolent and malevolent, in the universe, or for a doctrine about mind and body; but it may also stand for a belief in God as altogether distinct from man (a belief to which, it may be remembered, Cox has subscribed at one point—he has also rightly insisted that God is not an object among other objects). If there is this clear distinction, it is obviously a matter of metaphysics, and it is hard to see why we should not speak of a 'dualism' in this connection.

But my chief concern here is with the notion of a God who 'will be'. To introduce this notion Cox suggests that a way out of the 'miasma' of the death of God is a world-vision which he connects with Teilhard

[1] 6. [2] 11.

de Chardin and the ex-Marxist thinker, Bloch. He seems not to recognize that Teilhard de Chardin's Omega point is Christ in God, but to be interested only in his belief in man. Bloch raises the question about the identity between man who hopes and the nature of the reality which grounds his hope. This might sound promising, but Bloch calls himself an atheist and considers that the Christian God belongs to a 'static ontology'. Here we meet the depressing misconception that a changeless God must be an inactive one. And it may be remarked, in passing, that the concentration on 'hope' which has been going on for some time among theologians is so often accompanied by a failure to realize that you cannot hope for anything unless you know something about it. It seems to emerge that what Cox is substituting for the 'dead' God is not the Father of Jesus Christ but that conception of Progress which one had supposed totally discredited but which is now reappearing in fresh forms—some sort of living force drawing us onwards to ever-fresh heights which are wrapped in a pious obscurity. That is quite extraordinarily depressing. This force is obviously a finite one. It is engaged in developing its own existence. 'Death-of-God theology' in its original form did at least avoid this sort of metaphysical muddle.

I shall now refer very briefly to another writer as an illustration of the temper of mind to which I am drawing attention. Dr Dorothee Sölle, in her book entitled (in the English version) *Christ the Representative—An Essay in Theology after the 'Death of God'*, may seem at first to be only rejecting that anthropomorphism in theology which writers like Dr Robinson suppose to have been practically universal until the other day. But, in fact (if I have understood her) she, like van Buren, is recommending a secular humanism which sees a particular significance in Jesus Christ. Unlike van Buren, however, she has no wish to do away with any and every idea of God and uses the word 'God' with the greatest frequency. What she means by it is obscure to me, but I offer the following quotations as possible clues: 'Christ makes himself dependent on us—if we say "dependent on God" this simply means that Christ is radically surrendered to men';[1] 'What does it mean to assume responsibility in God's stead and to represent him? It means so to assume responsibility for the irreplaceable identity of others that it remains possible for them to attain identity';[2] 'Christ identified himself with God and thereby made himself dependent on God's attaining

[1] 129.   [2] 134.

37

identity himself. . . . In a world whose characteristic is the inter-
changeability of all men, God's identity is still in the future';[1] 'God
suffers by reason of his unrealized, or only partly realized, existence in
the world.'[2] It is difficult to see how God is being distinguished from
man except in that he has not yet come into existence, or not much.

The reader may perhaps be asking himself why we should be wasting
our time on this sort of thing. The answer is that deeply (but perhaps
not widely) read theologians, people of very considerable influence,
take it quite seriously. Light is shed on the situation when we realize
that Dr Sölle's philosopher is Hegel (she quotes with apparent approval
the view that God is 'self-differentiation and its removal by reconciliation').[3] So we are prepared to be told that 'for long enough God was
known as absolute immediacy more certain than one's own self',[4] but
that nowadays 'Christ stands in God's place, stands in for the God who
no longer presents himself to us directly'[5] and that we must not hand
over to 'the self-assured smugness of those who simply *know* that there
is no God and that Christ is dead; or, worse still, to those who are equally
sure that God exists and that Christ is therefore alive'.[6] We must have
'certainty in uncertainty'.[7] I shall maintain, on the contrary, that we
ought not to hand over to those who are thus, in effect, counselling despair. We must not, indeed, pretend to a certainty which in fact we do
not possess. But if it has ever been possible to have it, it is possible still,
unless we are to take up with the relativism which Dr Sölle appears to
be advocating. It is symptomatic of the confusions in the theological
world at the present time that a learned writer, capable of great
penetration and in many ways profoundly impressive, should be content
to conclude (as in the words last quoted from her) with a flat contradiction.

Her book makes clear a line of division among Christians which has
appeared only in our own time, cutting across all previous divisions.
'Any direct surrender to God', we read, 'such as the saints of the great
religions exemplify, is no longer possible for us in this post-theistic age',[8]
and again: 'the new and progressive reality of the represented God,
who is himself absent, shows that a retreat to God, experienced as
present, is simply a private affair with no claim to authority'.[9] There is a
sort of iron curtain here, a definitive turning away from the Christian

[1] 147.   [2] 149.   [3] 82.   [4] 130.
[5] 132.   [6] 134.   [7] 139.   [8] 128.   [9] 142.

tradition. It is perhaps reasonable that Dr Sölle should refer only (among the moderns) to German writers, but it is sad to find that, for her, people like Hans Urs von Balthasar, Joseph Pieper and Karl Rahner seem just not to count. In considering the *theologia crucis* with which this book ends and the conclusion that we must look for nothing in this world except 'the way of alienation into existence for others',[1] a 'traditionalist' thinker has to bear in mind those traumatic experiences, both national and personal, in which our century has been so prolific. It is a conclusion which must command sincere respect even if we regard it as betraying a most lamentable misunderstanding. It illustrates a tendency among radical theologians to pick out a strand from the New Testament record and concentrate on it to the exclusion of everything else.

Our theology must certainly be a 'theology of the Cross', as Professor Hans Kueng has recently reminded us in his little book on truthfulness in the Church, in the sense that it must not be a glorification of the Church as though the Church were an end in itself and not a people waiting for the Kingdom, called upon to give up everything which hinders the coming of it. But our theology must also be a theology of glory in the sense that the Kingdom, although still to come in its final form, is already among us. That is what the traditional doctrine of grace fundamentally means: that God is active in us and so present to us. Christianity is not a religion of suffering, but a religion of joy in and through suffering. 'Death-of-God' theology is a natural consequence of our unwillingness to face that most searching and necessary form of asceticism in which we stop ourselves talking and arguing, acquiring and disseminating information, and in general getting things done, so that God may be able to communicate with us (this is in fact the *conditio sine qua non* for getting things done properly, although it is not the *immediate* object of this exercise).

In the second volume of his *Theological Soundings*, entitled in the English version *God and Man*, Father Edward Schillebeeckx makes some remarks which are here highly relevant:
'No one will deny that unconditional love for one's fellow men is real Christianity, even when someone remains outside the Church or does not acknowledge Christ. The question, however, is whether this is the only way in which the Christian himself is called upon to love God. But

[1] 146.

39

for the Christian this would mean a return to the pre-Christian stage of anonymous sacramentality in the community of mankind as a whole . . . the solidarity of mankind does not have the last word; this is reserved for consciously experienced human communion with Christ and, therein, intersubjectively with the living God.'[1]

Schillebeeckx, whom nobody could call a 'reactionary' theologian in a pejorative sense, goes on to say that Christian life 'has a separate, sacral sphere, set apart from secular history and culture: a domain in which we pray and are simply together in Christ . . . silence-with-God has a *value in itself* and not only in our dealings with our fellow human beings. . . . To fail to appreciate simple passive communion with God as the Beloved is to take away the very core of Christianity.'[2] Later he writes: 'The appeal of values, as an "oblique" self-testimony and self-affirmation of God, takes place in a world in which God personally encounters us in generous love. God is not merely the foundation of all human values . . . he is the God of salvation, who summons us in grace to a personal communion of life with himself.'[3] But Schillebeeckx is equally insistent that this grace 'presupposes man as a person . . . living in a world of people and things'; our 'openness to grace' lies in our capacity for 'self-donation to others', and this is the 'indispensable basis of the Christian view of life'.[4] Here is the true balance between individualistic piety and a relapse into a pre-Christian humanism which has been so much disturbed by those violent swingings of the pendulum which are characteristic of our time.

The only possible answer to 'death-of-God' theology—and to the theory of a secularized God which seems to be succeeding to it—must consist in pointing to the way in which men have been led to speak of 'God'. The evidence for God, in my submission, is that we find him in and beyond his creatures and, in the first place, in and beyond our own minds, in which he is active as the standard of truth and as the goal of our endeavours. His 'beyondness' is translated in its first impact upon us, so it seems to me, into our obligation to respond to the summons which it addresses to us. It is on this 'beyondness' that we must concentrate so as to discover what can meaningfully be said about God and what must be denied about him. We find him as our transcendent good, on which we totally depend. That is our ultimate ground for calling him the First Cause or the Infinite Cause—and these expressions are a

[1] 201. [2] 202. [3] 260-1. [4] 269.

way of saying that we find him beyond the objects of our immediate awareness, not limited as they are. That will have no meaning for those whose experience does not seem to put them in contact with him (such contact, although itself direct, can be easily obscured by our immediate objects: it is possible to confine attention to *them*). But for a theist 'infinite' has a positive meaning which one tries to indicate in ways which will vary with the capacities, interests and dispositions of one's interlocutors.

In calling God changeless and eternal we are trying to indicate something about our positive knowledge of him just as we are when we call him infinite. The claim that he possesses these attributes is one which our knowledge of him involves as a matter of fact—it is not a matter of abstract argument. We find him as being beyond limitations, and we find time and change as being bound up with them. To say that the infinite can be changing and timeful is therefore nonsense, even if this is supposed to be the case in some quite peculiar way. For to say that there is something about time and change which need not involve limitation must mean, if it means anything at all, a return to the thought of pure Act as lying behind time and change. What is positive, though limited, about time and change is that something is happening, some-thing is in act. We find God as infinite, eternal and changeless seen 'across' limited act. If a theologian denies that God is properly to be 'pointed to' by speaking of him as pure and changeless Act, then I cannot help wondering whether he and I can be said to worship the same God. And to talk of a limited God, it follows, is to abuse language.

What lies behind such talk very often, I believe, is a widely pervasive despair about the possibility of any *awareness* of the transcendent God, a mood rather than a philosophical or a theological position, a spiritual *malaise* which, when it does not lead to a loss of interest in the subject altogether, does lead to mere theorizing *in vacuo* or to the indulgence of mere feeling, 'squads of undisciplined emotion'—sometimes to a conjunction of the two which makes rational discussion difficult or even impossible. It is likely to be accompanied by a hatred of the past (based largely on ignorance) and a pathetic trust in a future which remains completely vague. That is not to deny that there is a revival of genuine idealism among the young or that they have good reason for protesting against the state of things into which they have been born (this is a topic to which I shall return). The point at the moment is that the absence, real or apparent, of a positive awareness of God seems to be at the bottom of these fashionable modes of thought and of feeling, not only on the popular level but also on more sophisticated ones. The only thing to be done about it is to insist that such awareness is in fact available to us and to attempt some account of it. It is the absence of this awareness which leads people to say that nothing is just 'given', that everything in our experience is historically conditioned in the sense that it is never just *true*. And it is the influence of such attitudes of mind which leads so many professing Christians to downgrade or even to abandon the worship, the adoration, of God in favour of politics and sociology. These attitudes have not been without their influence upon certain experiments in the liturgical field and upon the notorious unrest in communities of religion.

So there is no need for elaborate argument when one considers such views about the nature of God as those of Professor Charles Hartshorne, who appears to be the authority most often appealed to by the advocates of 'process-philosophy'.[1] Mr (now Professor) H. P. Owen in his recent book, *The Christian Knowledge of God*, has subjected Hartshorne's central assertions to a careful examination. It will be sufficient to quote briefly from this book. Referring to Hartshorne's *The Logic of Perfection* (1962), he writes as follows: 'There he *identifies* God's necessity with his "infallible power to harmonize relativities in himself, to respond to diverse stimuli" (pp. 136–7). Later (p. 262) he affirms that "God is individuated by containing the world within himself". According to these statements God's individuality and necessity do not merely co-exist with his dependence on the world, they are constituted by it. If this is not a self-contradiction I do not know what is one.'[2] Owen goes on to remind us that in *Philosophers Speak of God* (1953) Hartshorne has said that when God acquires a new mode of perfection 'through such self-excelling the most excellent being changes, not into a more excellent being, but into a more excellent state of the *same* being'.[3] 'God can be necessary', Owen concludes, 'only if we can say, in a straightforward and unqualified sense, that he

[1] Harvey Cox, referring to 'the only constructive work that has been done in recent decades in American theology' mentions Hartshorne in the first instance (*On not leaving it to the snake*, 6).

[2] 106.

[3] Hartshorne, 10.

possesses spiritual attributes in an unchangeable form. Furthermore it is precisely because he is thus unchangeable that he can enter into a saving relationship with his creatures. From St Augustine onwards, Christians have found hope and peace in God because, not in spite of the fact that, he is changeless and self-sufficient Love.'[1] But the meaning of 'necessity' will not be apparent to us unless we are *aware* of God.

3. APPROACHES TO THE ABSOLUTE

There has been a gradual revival of metaphysics and natural theology among English-speaking philosophers during the last twenty years or so, and in the course of this chapter I shall be considering some philosophical works which have appeared in English in the recent past, and which approximate, in varying degrees, to the positions which seem to me the right ones; when one's positions are likely to be unfamiliar to many readers, it should be helpful to relate them to others which are perhaps better known.

Metaphysics, in my view, does not come into its own until it is concerned with an awareness of what is 'absolute' (which proves to mean: the Absolute). To put it in another way, a metaphysician who does not concern himself with this awareness cannot be doing more than skirmishing on the frontiers of what I mean by metaphysics. So I ought to begin by recognizing the fact that some people mean something else by it. They mean by it only a certain way of *describing* the world which is not also a way of revealing more in it than we saw before. That is, there is no question of seeing 'through' it, of finding the transcendent in the immanent. To do that is to embark upon what Mr P. F. Strawson calls 'revisionary' (as opposed to 'descriptive') metaphysics. Professor W. H. Walsh, in his very usefully informative book *Metaphysics*,[2] has this to say when he gives us his own view of the matter: 'There is no such thing as a special stock of knowledge accessible only to metaphysicians, nor is it the case that some metaphysicians have a grasp of fundamental truths of fact which are unaccountably lost sight of by others. We all confront the same world, but we differ in our ways of taking it.'[3] And he also writes: 'To say that the spirit alone

[1] 107.
[2] Hutchinson Universal Library, 1963.
[3] 169.

43

is real, or that in the end everything is swallowed up in the Absolute, is evidently not to imply that chairs and tables are imaginary, or individual things fictitious; it is to suggest that we must think of the world in a certain way if we are to understand it.'[1]

But a metaphysician who talks about the Absolute is saying that there is a 'fundamental truth of fact' which he claims to be aware of and which he hopes to make others aware of: it is the fact that the Absolute is present in the world. Whether or not he realizes that it is also 'beyond' the world is a further question, but if he does not realize this it is difficult to see how he can avoid one of two conclusions, either that the Absolute is only *part* of the world, in which case it is difficult to see why he should call this 'the Absolute', or that tables and chairs are really only *parts* of the Absolute, in which case they cease to be individual things. Walsh, however, continues: 'The Absolute is not the sort of thing one could meet with, anyway; it is not a constituent of the world, familiar or unfamiliar. And the same perhaps goes for God as he figures in metaphysical theories, if not for the God of religion.' This is to take a very short way with dissenters. The Absolute is not indeed to be described as a 'constituent of the world'. But it does not follow that one could not 'meet with' it as present in the world. The vagueness of the last sentence quoted must suggest that Walsh does not think it worthwhile to consider at all seriously the identification of the Absolute with the 'God of religion'.

That Walsh does not consider the 'God of religion' to have anything to do with metaphysics emerges clearly from the sentences which follow: 'Individual metaphysicians have not always appreciated these points . . . Plato was committed by his theory of knowledge to the view that the Forms are actual existents, though they did not exist in space and time, whilst for Aquinas the search for metaphysical understanding was too closely bound up with religious practice for him to be willing to accept anything but an existential account of God.' Plato and Aquinas, it might appear, are isolated exceptions, of no great significance, to one's generalizations about the history of metaphysics. And Walsh then tells us that 'if we remain at a level which is at once theoretical and rational we shall see that the claims about existence made by metaphysicians are subordinate to their pretence to comprehend the scheme of things entire'; what they are really doing, he goes

[1] 164.

on to explain, is to 'adopt a series of categorical principles', and a principle of this sort is not a statement about facts but 'functions rather as an ultimate presupposition'—to illustrate this he here remarks that 'for Aristotle it was out of the question that things should not serve a purpose'.[1] It was also out of the question for Aquinas, but this was not just a 'presupposition'; he thought he had evidence for it. What Walsh has in mind when he speaks of Aquinas's 'existential account' of it I am not at all sure. Nor am I clear why we should have to remain 'at a level which is at once rational and theoretical' if we are talking about metaphysics. An account of our awareness of God is certainly an 'existential' one in the sense that it is about what happens. Must it not also be a metaphysical one?

Let us now consider what some modern thinkers have to say about the Absolute, metaphysicians who do make 'existential' claims in regard to it, and let us take first Mrs Pratima Bowes. Her book *Is Metaphysics Possible?*[2] is a very effective attack on positivism in general (and not just on the logical positivist interlude) and a well-argued claim for the necessity of metaphysics. She maintains that there is an ultimate metaphysical principle; it is true that she sometimes refers to it as a 'postulate', but it is certainly not, in her eyes, a mere 'presupposition'; she certainly regards it as a truth, or rather *the* truth, about the world. Nevertheless she is at the same time an example of a metaphysician of the sort which Walsh had in mind, for she also maintains that the discovery of the ultimate principle is the discovery of a 'unity of form' in the world which is 'a functional unity and not a structural one'.[3] She goes on to say that 'neither common sense, nor science, nor morality is left behind when we enter the sphere of ultimate reality, but all these are found to have a new depth and an added dimension, as seen to be the expressions of an eternal spiritual (i.e. absolutely free and inexhaustibly creative) principle'. And the conclusion follows that 'we may call our encounter with reality from partial points of view, appearance, and define reality as the eternal creative principle, the source of all that there is, can or ever will be'. In other words, Mrs Bowes explains, it is only if we fail to regard the 'appearances' as 'manifestations' of the creative principle and regard them instead as the only realities that they may be called 'unreal' or 'false' (but such a judgement should surely be called not 'false' but 'inadequate').

[1] 165.   [2] Gollancz, 1965.   [3] 196.

Mrs Bowes now declares that metaphysical reality is not 'transcendent'. It could be supposed, nevertheless, that her position might be acceptable for a theist. For if the ultimate principle is creative (and everything else, we must conclude, created), then the rejection of transcendence should mean only that it is not cut off from its 'appearances'. And this may seem to be supported by what Mrs Bowes proceeds to say: reality is not 'to be put in a transcendent realm beyond the reach of appearances'.[1] The passage, however, continues: 'For this source is an eternal creative principle which has no reality apart from its created function. . . . Its transcendence of appearance is no spatial transcendence, for a principle of capacity is not an object to be housed in some area, but a characteristic way of functioning—it is only transcendence in possibilities . . . infinitude is a way of being, of being inexhaustible in possibilities, and not a particular object . . . it has to be conceived as the form that gives reality to all finite phenomena, so far as finite phenomena are the working out of an infinite potentiality.' God (it should not be necessary to remark) is not confined to being a creative principle; nor is he a 'capacity'. And Mrs Bowes seems to suggest that any alternative to her proposals must postulate a 'particular object', transcending the world in a spatial sense. It would appear that she has indeed approached the Absolute, but retreated at the critical moment into the meaningless theory that the source of reality is a purely potential Infinite, not the real one.

But here we have to consider the difficulties which the Western mind has in coming to terms with the conceptualizations of the Eastern one (Mrs Bowes's address is Calcutta). To my mind, an infinite creative principle which is simply an inexhaustible *power* to create and has (apparently) no *actual* characteristics is simply unthinkable. But it must presumably mean something for Mrs Bowes. I can only suggest that in her valuable critique of Western tendencies in philosophy she is prevented by Eastern habits of thought from envisaging transcendence as both 'in' and 'beyond' the world in a non-spatial sense of the prepositions. When the Absolute is not recognized as the indescribable source of all activity, as super-active, and in *that* sense without limitations, then the result seems inevitably to be confusion. But when Easterners speak of the ultimate principle in negative language, and when they are unwilling to allow that this is an attempt to 'point to' an

[1] 197.

indescribable positivity, we may perhaps put this down to a deep-seated fear of anthropomorphism rather than to a form of final scepticism or a retreat from reality. And we may find a clue to Mrs Bowes's real mind in her further statements that 'this ultimate principle can only be spiritual' and that this conclusion 'brings home to man with added clarity the fact that he, in his capacity as a spiritual subject . . . is in tune with the ultimate reality on which the universe rests'. This is much more like a stoic acceptance of universal reason than the Christian's love of God. But it does indicate a frame of mind which, although it seems to fall into the same sort of confusions as the secularizing 'theologians' of the last chapter, does differ sharply from theirs, and deserves to be considered as at least an advance in the appropriate direction.

It must be observed that, despite the difference in spirit between the tradition exemplified by Mrs Bowes's book and the contemporary Western interest in a limited, developing God, it is not difficult for some vague minds to envisage some sort of harmony between them as a religion for man in the future. And in view of this tendency to 'cash in' on Eastern traditions, it becomes all the more necessary to note that there are other versions of Eastern metaphysics which are still further removed from Christian theism than that of Mrs Bowes. It will not be out of place, therefore, to make brief mention of a single example in illustration of this, the work of René Guénon. It is beyond my competence to discuss his claim to represent the traditional metaphysics of the East, the authentic *philosophia perennis*, as he considers it to be, but there is no doubt that the influence of his views has been great, that the same style of thinking has persisted and that it appears to be enjoying an increasing popularity at the present time. The first of Guénon's work to appear in English was *East and West* (1941), followed by *The Crisis of the Modern World* (1943), in which he, like Mrs Bowes, made some very telling criticisms of Western modes of thought and Western institutions; no doubt the fulfilment of many of his gloomy prophecies has had a good deal to do with the reputation which he gained for profundity of thought in respectable quarters. I shall confine myself to a very brief reference to his positive doctrine as stated in two later books, his *Introduction to the Study of Hindu Doctrine* (1945) and *The Reign of Quantity and the Signs of the Times* (1953).

In the first of these books, speaking of the Hindu concept of *adharma* he tells us that 'it is not "sin" in the theological sense of the word, neither is it "evil" in the moral sense of the word. It is simply "non-conformity" with the nature of beings.' And he continues: 'Without doubt, in the universal order, the sum total of all particular disequilibriums always goes to make up the total equilibrium, which nothing can destroy; but at each point regarded separately and by itself, disequilibrium is both possible and conceivable.'[1] This is to overthrow the principle of non-contradiction in the most blatant manner, and it is characteristic of the whole book. Things go wrong only in appearance, he is saying, but in reality everything is all right. If we insist that even appearances must be themselves facts of some kind, Guénon's only resource is to write them off as illusions—they do not really exist at all (Mrs Bowes was at any rate clear in repudiating that ostrich-like policy). In fact Guénon goes on to say that 'there can be nothing really outside *Brahma*' but that 'the world, taking the word in its widest possible sense, that is as universal manifestation, is not distinct from *Brahma*, or at least is distinguished from it in illusory fashion only'. Yet this is followed by the statement: '*Brahma* is absolutely distinct from the world.'[2] This sort of having one's cake and eating it is attractive to many minds who take up with the notion of a 'developing God'.

In *The Reign of Quantity and the Signs of the Times* we find a doctrine of fatalism which is perfectly explicit. 'Whereas', Guénon writes, 'the modern world is an anomaly and a sort of monstrosity, it is no less true that, when viewed in relation to the whole historical cycle of which it is a part, it corresponds exactly to the conditions pertaining to that cycle, the phase which Hindu tradition specifies as the final period of the *Kali-Yuga*.' And we find in the same passage: 'It is these conditions, arising as a consequence of the cycle's manifestations, which have determined its peculiar characteristics, and from this point of view it is clear that the present times could not be otherwise than they are.'[3] Even those who deviate from what Guénon calls 'traditional doctrine' are, he says, 'fulfilling a function which must be fulfilled like any other function, so that the Divine plan may be accomplished in the world', although 'their delusion is in truth the worst possible delusion, since it is positively the only one whereby a being can be not merely led more or less seriously astray, but actually, irremediably lost. . . .'[4] One might

[1] 212.   [2] 281.   [3] 8.   [4] 334.

48

suppose it impossible to take seriously the mutually contradictory statements which I have quoted from Guénon's work. But when there is so much ignorance of authentic Christian theism it becomes necessary to insist on the disastrous consequences which can attend attempts to substitute for it. One hears it said, for example, that we can no longer accept 'an ultimate dualism'. If this means only that we cannot accept a God who is simply 'over against' the world, that the world is unrelated to him, then the statement is a correct one. The world *is* God's 'manifestation', but that does not mean that an affirmation of the world is one and the same thing as an affirmation of God.

This unique relationship in which the world stands to God will now be considered in connection with the work of the Russian thinker, S. L. Frank. His last work, published in an English version under the title *Reality and Man* (1965), while still revealing considerable confusion in speaking of this relationship, maps out an approach to the Absolute with which I am in fundamental agreement. The book has not received the attention which I think it deserves, and I shall therefore discuss it in some detail.

In its first chapter Frank speaks of a 'living knowledge'. 'In it', he writes, 'the known does not confront us as something different from ourselves, but is somehow merged with our very life. Our thought springs from the depth of a self-revealing reality, and is carried on within it. That which we experience as our *life* reveals itself to us—to our thought, which is inseparably present in that life . . . by comparison with this primary kind of knowledge, the point of view of objective knowledge involves an artificial narrowing, so to speak, an emasculation of consciousness. . . . Thought in its objectivized form is only a superstructure on the foundation of living knowledge.'[1] This is a theme which appears in various forms in many contemporary writers. Human awareness is more than a mere registration of facts which we then proceed to utilize. The mind does not merely reflect objects like a mirror. On this basis Frank proceeds to what looks like Anselm's 'ontological argument': 'It is', he says, 'precisely the infinite as "the fulness of all" that is primary and is positively given, while the conception of the finite is formed through the negation of that fulness.'[2] This proves to be a claim rather than an argument, for Frank tells us later that 'to be aware of oneself as a reality distinct from the external world

[1] 11.   [2] 25.

49

of fact is to be aware of being inwardly and directly rooted in the all-embracing primary reality'.[1] Nevertheless, he adds, 'the inward path is not an escape from the common objective world into the closed-in sphere of subjectivity. The very reverse is the case. Only through penetrating into the primary reality do we find our true inner bond with the objective world.' Frank is not asserting that God is the first object of the human mind (the error of 'ontologism'); it is in being conscious of myself that I am aware of the Infinite, encompassing, as it were, the finite self. There is a good deal of incidental matter in this and in the following chapters which I should not endorse, but the bases of Frank's metaphysics are, in my view, sound.

In the second chapter there are some remarks about 'negative theology' which may help to make clear what I have been trying to say about God's indescribability. Those who profess this theology, Frank says, 'have a special inexpressible *positive* vision of God, and in saying that God is different from all else, they only want to bring out the truth that their vision is inexpressible . . . to deny with reference to God all positive characteristics simply means to deny them as particular and derivative determinations'.[2] Here I should add that all genuine knowledge of God must involve an awareness, although this is no doubt commonly inarticulate, of his inexpressibility, and that this may be very unlike what we normally call 'vision'. Frank goes on to speak of an 'intuition that the nature of God as the first source and primary basis of being is super-logical and super-rational, and for that reason eludes all logical determinations. . . .' It is a remarkable thing that so many supposedly intelligent people have jumped to the conclusion that because the source of being is 'superlogical and super-rational' we may contradict ourselves and indulge in any kind of nonsense-talk about him. We may use language about him which seems paradoxical, as when we say both that he is perfectly in act and perfectly at rest, but this is only a way of 'pointing to' him as the source both of the value which we find in human activity and of the value which we find in its completion, in perfected achievement. What Frank is saying, although his way of putting it often sounds like mere irrationalism, is that there is nothing in God for our logical processes to operate on since he is beyond all classifications. He therefore concludes: 'All positive characteristics are denied in order to convey the *categorical* difference between God and

[1] 33. [2] 39.

all that we meet in earthly experience.' We know him as different because he enters into our experience as the Value from whom all particular limited values derive, 'containing' them at infinity.

Frank, in his third chapter, seems to consider that the apprehension of God is not an affair of philosophy, for that is 'conceptual knowledge of being'. However, philosophy is 'not separated from religion by an impassable gulf, but is organically connected with it'; there must be a 'philosophical understanding of religious experience'.[1] Such an experience, since it is in principle available for everyone in virtue of his human capacities, should not be regarded, surely, as itself foreign to philosophy. And it sounds odd to say that 'the experience of "the knowledge of God" or, more exactly, of meeting God as a reality has the character of primary self-evidence and, as such, is completely independent of all that we think or know about the nature and structure of the objective world . . .'. But what this proves to mean is that it is 'in no way affected by the possible difficulties of reconciling it with our knowledge about the world of fact'.[2] This I believe to be sound: the evidence of God is self-guaranteeing and cannot be cancelled out by problems about evil and the workings of Providence. Frank now turns to the theme of man as an 'image' of God:

'On the basis of an inner experience, which convinces him that as a personality he transcends the natural world and is qualitatively different from it, man is aware of himself as an "image" or a manifestation on earth of a supercosmic principle different from all earthly existence, primary and absolutely valuable . . . metaphysical experience of God is in the last resort the apprehension of the absolute ultimate ground of the human spirit—of the ground which in its absoluteness transcends man as an empirical entity.'[3]

This leads to the central idea of the book, that of 'Godmanhood', expounded in the fourth chapter, in which true Christian humanism is seen to derive from the 'positive religious value of man as the image and child of God'.[4] And there follows a critique of non-religious humanism which is particularly impressive.

The last two chapters discuss human freedom and, in general, the human predicament. I shall mention a few important passages which I

[1] 89.   [2] 95.   [3] 105.   [4] 124.

find wholly acceptable. 'The idea of sin contains something essentially irrational';[1] philosophical attempts to 'explain' it end by justifying it (it is a fact of experience, a reality, but one of which we can use only negative terms—we can call it only 'the severance from God').[2] It produces 'the illusion that in my self-contained detachment I become for the first time an autocratic master of my own life' but in fact 'I become utterly impotent, possessed by overwhelming external forces'.[3] And finally 'the world's growth in perfection consists not merely in its having fuller and richer content, and in its life becoming more complex and harmonious, but also in spiritual enlightenment, in the development of the Divine principle in it through, so to speak, the ever-increasing "humanization" of the world.'[4] That will suggest Teilhard de Chardin, whose vision of the world is, in principle, no novelty but a rediscovery of traditional Christian metaphysics.

There is, however, the other side to this picture. It has been a characteristic of the Western mind that it splits up our experience into isolated fragments and fails to glimpse the unity to which it tends. It has been a characteristic of the Eastern mind in general to disregard the all-important distinctions which our experience unambiguously presents to us. It seems to be a characteristic of the Russian mind to be dissatisfied with these distinctions, to find itself faced by them but to succumb from time to time to the temptation of blurring them. This is what we find in some passages of Frank's book. Just as many philosophers become misled by using the language of 'Being', so that they find themselves thinking about 'Being' as though it were an *object* somehow embracing both God and man, so Frank is led to speak of 'reality'. Here I must quote at some length:

'That which I call reality is obviously closely akin to what is known in philosophy as the "absolute" (as distinct from the relative). It has been pointed out long ago that the idea of the absolute involves a peculiar dialectic of its own: being other than the relative, it cannot have the relative outside itself, for then it would no longer be absolute or all-embracing, but would merely be a particular alongside of the other, "relative" half of reality. To be truly absolute, the absolute must include its contrary: only as the unity of itself and the relative is it truly absolute. On the one hand the absolute . . . is in principle qualitatively

[1] 164.   [2] 175 n.   [3] 177.   [4] 221.

52

different from everything relative, but it can be such only through in-cluding everything relative within itself. Its peculiarity and uniqueness lie precisely in its being a concretely all-embracing and all-pervading whole.'[1]

This seems to me inextricably confused, and I shall dismiss it in favour of the briefest possible statement of the thesis which a theist must substitute for it. Our experience reveals to us the world around us and (most importantly) our own selves. It also reveals to us, obscurely but (if we care to attend to it) unmistakably, the Source of the world and of ourselves. From our point of view, the Source is first met with as the Other, but the Other is recognized as the Source—that is to say, we recognize ourselves as standing to it in what Frank himself calls an 'inexpressible super-rational relation'[2] (often he refers to it as 'kinship'), which reveals to us that, although we have nothing strictly in *common* with it, nevertheless the relation in which we stand to it is not one of otherness in the sense simply of opposition. It does not follow that we have to ascribe this fundamental dichotomy which we find in our ex-perience to the mind of God. God knows himself as creator and our-selves as created in the undivided, unlimited activity which is himself. His knowledge of us is (so we have to put it) 'part' of himself, although he does know us as different from himself, for this is the truth about us. We have to say, straightforwardly, that we are *not* 'parts' of him. What leads to the confusions in Frank's work seems to be the fact that he supposes an awareness of 'Being' or 'Reality' to be our fundamental experience. I want to say that we are aware of ourselves as derived from our Source. 'Being' or 'Reality' refers to ourselves as so derived—and also therefore to our Source. It is an abstract notion with an irreducibly *double* reference.

If Frank were content to refer to the 'super-rational relation' simply as 'inexpressible', all would be well. But the paragraph in which he does so refer to it opens as follows: 'The gist of the matter is that the super-rational relation between human spirit and God cannot be adequately explained in the simple logical categories of identity and difference. Man is clearly something quite other than God, but—as already pointed out with regard to reality in general—the "otherness" in this instance is quite other than the usual category of difference.' The reference to

[1] 46.   [2] 150.

'reality in general' suggests that he is, after all, trying to *account for* that unique relationship by appealing to this misleading concept. And although our 'kinship' with God is certainly not a similarity in the sense of a difference in one respect and an identity in some other respects, it remains, to repeat, that we must assert *difference* if we are to be theists and not 'emanationists'. We cannot otherwise indicate what we are trying to say. Or, if this seems to canonize a particular locution (for others, it might be suggested, could do our business for us), at any rate we must conclude that something has gone wrong if we are forbidden to claim for it a plain and ultimate meaning. It is obvious that Frank is not an 'emanationist' in the pejorative sense in which I have just used this expression. But he does sometimes sound like one. And it is difficult to know what to make of such phrases as 'the unity of the actual with the potential which constitutes God's being';[1] for the moment we seem to be back with Mrs Bowes. It has to be added that Frank's various excursions into the field of dogmatic theology need to be treated with considerable reserve. The value of the book lies in its fundamental metaphysical insights, subject to the important qualifications which I have just been making, and in its impressive witness to the life of the spirit and the beauty of Christian holiness.

Frank's approach to the Absolute is too abrupt, too uncompromisingly Platonic, to be of much use, in practice, for tough-minded 'empiricists'. They would seize upon the confusions and dismiss the insights. Fortunately there are nowadays plenty of other writers who may guide them by gentler paths. To take one example, Professor Michael Polanyi, a very distinguished scientist who devotes himself nowadays to the writing of philosophical works,[2] should command a hearing when he tries to persuade positivistically-minded persons that the advancement of knowledge, even in the natural sciences, is not just an affair of logical processes performed upon the data supplied by our sense-organs. Nevertheless his recent work *The Tacit Dimension* was written off in *Mind* as of no particular interest for most of its readers. In this book Polanyi declares that the modern mind is torn apart, on the one side, by a materialistic attitude to the whole question of truth, leading to a stultifying scepticism, and, on the other, by moral motives

[1] 218.
[2] His book *Personal Knowledge* (1958) is of special importance for the revival of metaphysics.

such as the desire for universal justice. These forces are irreconcilable, and something has obviously gone wrong with the whole approach to the question about the nature and workings of human knowledge.[1] Polanyi thinks that this state of affairs should begin with the recognition that there is a 'logic of tacit thought'; that is, we can *know* more than we can *tell*, and we know certain things as the meaning of other things, attending *from* them to these other things—we know them 'tacitly'.[2] It would seem that some of Polanyi's paradoxes could be avoided simply by distinguishing within our awareness between what we advert to and what we merely 'enjoy', but in raising the problem of 'intuition' as it presents itself in the field of scientific investigation he has undoubtedly opened up (or reopened) a promising field of philosophical enquiry.

Polanyi refers to the question raised by Plato in the *Meno*: if all knowledge is explicit, how would we ever have a problem and look for a solution of it? The answer is that 'the kind of tacit knowing that solves the problem of the *Meno* consists in the intimation of something hidden, which we may yet discover'.[3] The investigator, Polanyi goes on to say, makes a personal judgement that there is something to be discovered; he *commits* himself to the task, and feels himself under an obligation to pursue what he takes to be the truth. The relevance of this to metaphysical enquiry will be obvious enough. Our knowledge, moreover, is not a collection of bits and pieces (if I may thus roughly summarize the argument which follows) but bears upon 'comprehensive entities', and the principles which control such entities are to be discovered by examining living organisms. In these we are always faced by a problem of relationship between higher and lower levels, the higher ones being inexplicable in terms of the lower, yet at the same time restricted by them.[4] And in the human mind the process of education 'works like the anatomical differentiation of a developing organism which narrows down its area of equipotentiality while offering in exchange the use of a more powerful biotic machinery'.[5] A 'cosmic panorama' is thus suggested. And the principles which Polanyi finds underlying scientific research he finds applicable to 'the cultivation of man's other ideals' which he regards as 'more vital than the truth of science'.[6] 'It is', he says, 'the image of potential thought which I find revealing for the problems of the day. . . . It provides us with the metaphysical ground and

[1] 4. [2] 6–8. [3] 23. [4] 38–9. [5] 46. [6] 84.

the organizing principle of a society of explorers.'[1] That is to say, it can help to show us that man has a job to do in the world, something which may make sense. It is a job which he does not have to invent for himself—it is waiting for him.

This hasty indication of Polanyi's approach to metaphysics can only suggest its usefulness in a vague way. But it may now be sufficiently obvious that he has reached a point at which the question of religion cannot fail to present itself. So we find him saying that if we are to recognize a purpose in our existence it must be one 'which bears on eternity'. 'A religious solution', he concludes, 'should become more feasible once religious thought is released from pressure by an absurd vision of the universe, and so there will open up instead a meaningful world which would resound to religion.'[2] And here again we seem to find a thinker supposing that the evolutionary picture of the world which he is pointing to is something which has found no place in the minds of religious people previous to Teilhard de Chardin.

There was another reason for drawing attention here to Polanyi's views. They have been discussed in a fat volume, *Intellect and Hope*,[3] to which a number of distinguished writers have contributed, evidencing the interest aroused by them in the world at large (as opposed to that of British academic philosophy), and the comments of Professor (now Bishop) I. T. Ramsey in his essay on Polanyi and J. L. Austin are particularly useful at this point. Here he discusses Polanyi's concept of 'comprehension' and relates it to his own concept of 'disclosure' as expounded in his *Christian Discourse* (1965) and other works; he speaks of 'a cognitive situation which breaks in on us as we survey a series of verifiable criteria'.[4] And he proposes that the 'perhaps puzzling phrases' used by Polanyi, 'tacit powers', 'active foreknowledge of an unknown reality', can be dispensed with. 'The disclosures', he suggests, 'which "comprehension" involves, may well precede, even if they more often follow, the spelling out in terms of some particular features or clues.'[5] Here is a principle which needs particularly to be borne in mind when we are considering how the first suspicion of the Absolute arises; it is embedded in our knowledge. Ramsey also claims, just as significantly, that although 'both Austin and Polanyi recognize the ultimacy for

[1] 92. [2] 91.
[3] *Essays on the thought of Michael Polanyi*, Duke University Press, 1968.
[4] *Intellect and Hope*, 177. [5] 182.

epistemology of the personal act of affirmation . . . what Austin does not recognize, while for Polanyi it is of great importance, is that such personal participation in talking and knowing eludes interpretation in terms of empirical "impersonal" data', so that 'there is involved for Polanyi, in talking about the self-involving character of knowledge, a metaphysical claim; and from his view personal participation is pre-supposed by, and never reducible to the scientific, factual "content" or "clues" which only point to the full, personal, comprehension which transcends them'.[1] And finally Ramsey remarks that it is a 'myth-eaten error' to suppose that we ourselves 'make contact with, establish our hold on some "hidden reality"'. The fact is that 'though knowledge is personal it is not subjective . . . something other than ourselves dis-closes itself to us; comprehension and personal knowledge arise as a matching response'.[2] What, in the last analysis, is the self-disclosing 'other than ourselves'?

Another contributor to *Intellect and Hope*, Professor Edward Pols, gives us an answer. He sees the necessity for 'a self-evidential factor' in the act of knowing 'to complete the metaphysical dimension' of Polanyi's philosophy.[3] 'If our grasp of comprehensive entities', he writes, 'is to be a grasp of them *as they are* then it is not so much a tacit *upholding* of their status that is at issue, but a *recognition* or *enjoyment* of them as having that status.' And he concludes:

'An entity *is* a unity in manifold: to confirm our capacity to discern that kind of unity is to confirm our capacity to *recognize* beings as an expres-sion of Being. For the unity we find in recognizing the unity of a com-prehensive entity is not just *its* unity—not just the unity of a particular among many particulars—but a unity which is general or universal. Our recognition transcends the particularity of the entity we recognize: the presence of a particular entity among the Many is the partial presence of the (One) transcendence which it exemplifies.'[4]

Here we have the full metaphysical insight. The Source of being (as I prefer to put it) is discovered to us in its 'manifestations' of itself, the Unlimited in the limited. This is how the 'partial presence' of the One must be interpreted. It is time to consider this apprehension of the Absolute freed from the confusions which have delayed us in this chapter.

[1] 193. [2] 196. [3] 85. [4] 85–6.

4. THE APPREHENSION OF THE ABSOLUTE

In *Absolute Value* I discussed the work of a good many writers who take up, in essentials, the same position as I do about the apprehension of God. I also discussed there the question of an inferential process which is supposed by some writers, Thomists in particular, to be a necessary means to this apprehension. Here, in beginning to pinpoint my own position by relating it to that of other writers not previously mentioned, I shall begin by referring once more to this question about an inference. There has recently appeared a volume entitled *Metaphysics*, a translation from the German of a treatise by Father Emerich Coreth. Father Joseph Donceel, to whom we owe it, explains in his Preface that it employs 'the philosophical method which investigates the conditions of the possibility of our knowledge', and he therefore suggests that this doctrine might be called, in Kantian language, 'transcendental' Thomism. Whether it ought to be called 'Thomism' at all is a question which need not concern us. What Donceel proceeds to say about it I find most satisfactory except that I should not put it quite so baldly: 'every "demonstration" of God's existence begs the question, since it takes implicitly for granted what it tries to demonstrate explicitly. . . . We reach God right away or never at all.' It does not do much to vindicate the apprehension of God merely to add: 'that we reach God right away can be shown by pointing to the fact that we know everything as finite and limited'. But Donceel is not attempting a full analysis of our experience, and there is nothing in his Preface to suggest that there may be, from my point of view, some trouble ahead. (I agree with his verdict that Father Bernard Lonergan's critique of Coreth's work, printed at the end of the volume, does not seem to make any definite point against him.)

I shall now consider as briefly as possible what Coreth tells us. We must always start, he says, with a *question*, even if it be the question about where we ought to start.[1] The fact that man is essentially a questioner itself raises a question: 'Our attention is forced to proceed beyond the explicit knowledge presented by the context into the implicit knowledge contained in the act of questioning itself.' This will remind us of Polanyi. We start from experience, Coreth goes on, and 'this experience is not mere sense experience, it is an intellectual ex-

[1] 38–9.

perience'; he speaks of pre-conceptual knowledge: 'a real existential self-actuation of the spirit, which manifests itself to us as endowed with a pre-reflexive metaphysical knowledge of being'.[1] Talk about 'being' may make one apprehensive, but there seems no good reason for rejecting the conclusion that this pre-reflexive knowledge is *the constitutive condition of the possibility of any question whatsoever*.[2] And it would appear that this is Coreth's way of pointing to the mind's original contact with God.

Unfortunately apprehensions about this talk of 'being' prove well founded. 'Since every question', Coreth writes later, 'turns ultimately into a question about being in its totality, which is thus the condition of the possibility of the question as such, it follows that we know about being in its totality and that we do not know everything about it.'[3] If this means anything, it must refer to our implicit knowledge of God. But now there is talk about an 'act of being', an expression to which I can attach no definite significance, and a little later we find: 'What we have said does not include a demonstration of God's existence. When we showed that the act of being (*esse*) is unconditioned and ultimate, we meant only the act of being in general. . . . From this absolute nature of being in general we can derive the existence of God only by differentiating and distinguishing it from finite and conditioned being.'[4] If Coreth means that we have to differentiate and distinguish finite from Infinite in our experience, if we are to affirm God's existence, then this is clearly the case. But to speak of 'being in general' is, to put it mildly, dangerous, not only because it seems to include God and his creatures within a single bracket, but also because 'being in general' can easily turn into the middle term of an inferential process.

An inferential process which has only 'being in general' in its premisses can never conclude to Absolute Being unless the latter is conceived of as an *instance* of the former, and that is clearly out of the question. God is not a member of a class. And it is of the nature of inferential processes that they bring to our knowledge a conjunction of subject and predicate which was simply *not* known before, even implicitly. An 'implicit knowledge' which required an inferential process for its explicitation would be no knowledge at all. When we are concerned with judgements about the contents of our experience, the only

[1] 42. [2] 57. [3] 63. [4] 65.

way in which implicit knowledge can become explicit is a further examination of the evidence, that is, a further concentration upon the experience and what it purports to reveal to us.

But does Coreth use 'being in general' as the middle term of an inferential process? At the point which we have reached he seems to me to move off into a world of Thomist abstractions where it would be unprofitable to follow him. But we return eventually to the question about God, and we then read: 'In our every act of thinking there is coposited and presupposed the primordial realization of the necessity of absolute being'.[1] That sounds well enough except for the possible suggestion that what is apprehended is not absolute being itself but only its inevitability (it is impossible to conclude that God *must* exist in the absence of any apprehension of him, any direct contact). But that this is not the suggestion seems to emerge from the rest of the passage: 'This is not yet thematically a knowledge of the absolute being of God, since the absolute and necessary character of being is not yet contrasted with the finite and conditioned beings. At first we have only a general and undetermined knowledge, a basic unavoidable assertion . . .' So what is inevitable seems to be the apprehension of absolute being which is not the same as the apprehension of *God's* absolute being. On the supposition that there could be some meaning in this distinction, how is the transition from one to the other effected? Coreth's first answer is that we have now to show that 'finite being is distinct from absolute being'. I should have thought that this had already been done: what point is there in talking about 'absolute being' if it is not contrasted with relative or finite being? But Coreth has a further answer to give:

'The dynamism of our mind proceeds necessarily beyond every finite object . . . it is only through the mediation of the finite beings of experience that we discover that the necessity of being is distinct from them as the absolutely other, as absolute Being . . . the knowledge of God does not really represent a passage of our mind to something wholly unknown, but only an explicitation and development of our knowledge of the necessity of being.'[2]

Whatever may be meant by the 'necessity of being', it is not, then, by

[1] 171.   [2] 174-5.

means of an inferential process but by 'explicitation and development' that it reveals to us 'absolute Being'.

At this point a danger becomes evident which we must note in passing, that of appealing in the last analysis to a 'dynamism' of the mind without adding immediately that such a dynamism can be brought into operation only by the self-presentation of the Infinite to that mind. The danger becomes the more evident when Coreth speaks of 'an unthematic anticipation, through which we unconsciously reach out towards the Absolute'.[1] This shows the weakness of the Thomist approach associated especially with Father Joseph Maréchal, which has had the otherwise beneficial effect of encouraging a more 'experiential' account of our evidence for God.

But we have yet to examine a final move which Coreth now makes. He argues that 'since we may inquire about everything and continue to inquire beyond any possible limits . . . the act of inquiring presupposes the possibility of an infinite answer . . . neither a finite being nor the totality of all finite beings can supply an infinite answer . . . as we have shown, the possibility of the infinite necessarily implies its reality.' From which it would follow that 'the act of inquiry presupposes the reality of absolute, infinite being'.[2] Coreth's proof that the possibility of the Infinite necessarily implies its reality is that the 'real activity of the spirit . . . is possible only if it aims at a really possible end, the absolute being'. And 'the latter is possible as *being itself*' which 'would no longer be possible if it were merely possible and not real'.[3] The whole of this development must rest upon the supposition that, as Coreth puts it on the previous page, the 'dynamism' of the spirit 'makes sense'. It would make sense, he says, only if it is 'directed' towards a goal which is 'the one, unconditional and infinite being'. It looks as though one's suspicion that, in Coreth's account, an inferential process is somehow involved, is, after all, a justified one. For it seems that a general principle of finality is functioning here as a major premiss purporting to justify the claim that the dynamism does in fact 'make sense'. To 'make sense' here must mean to have a purpose. So what would Coreth say to someone who would claim that man is, in Sartre's phrase, a *passion inutile*? He does indeed say, in this same passage, that the dynamism 'reveals to us the final goal', which should mean that the goal reveals itself to us. That is the claim, I hold, which a theist must make, and this show of

[1] 174.   [2] 179–80.   [3] 179.

logical argument has at least a tendency to obscure the real issue. But what Coreth means by 'Absolute Being' is never in doubt, and the book's orientation is, fundamentally, the right one.

People sometimes say: 'how are we to find this alleged activity of God's in our experience?' The short answer would seem to be that it is not a question of looking for it in some special direction, or even of looking for it in our awareness as a whole, because even that may suggest that there must be some special technique by which it can be unearthed, so to speak, from the foundations of consciousness and brought to the surface; the point is that it arises of itself (we cannot make it do so) and what we have to do is to recognize it. It is not at this stage a question of welcoming it or turning away from it, but simply one of discovering what it is in our experience to which a philosopher who thinks as I do on the subject is pointing when he speaks of this activity. To recognize it, then, means to understand what is being pointed to. It does not mean that some fresh object swims into our ken, but that we now realize that something of which we were aware already (although we may not have explicitly adverted to it) is being referred to as God's activity. This can be called either, in Coreth's language, the goal envisaged by our 'dynamism', or the absoluteness of truth and the unconditional demand that we should accept it. And there are other ways of talking about it. . . . But what we come to know is not *this*, for we have always been in contact with it, but that this is what theists mean (or what they should mean) when they talk about the activity of *God* in human consciousness. We are not interpreting our experience in the sense of finding something in it which was not present there before. If we are interpreting anything, it is the language used by theists which we have not previously connected with our experience.

The topic of interpretation has been discussed by Professor J. E. Smith of Yale in his recent book *Experience and God*, with which I find myself in close agreement at many points. Speaking of those who profess a 'so-called empirical theology' he writes as follows: 'On the one hand, it was felt that religion is too intimate an affair to be a matter of rationalistic doctrines supported by a God whose reality is merely inferred without being experienced. On the other, it was believed that the only alternative is to be found in the immediate data of experience . . .'[1] Smith does not accept either alternative, and it will be clear that

[1] 52.

I do not do so either (our *immediate* data being, in my view, our sense perceptions and that self-awareness in which our knowledge of God arises and by which it may be properly said to be 'mediated'). 'Absolute immediacy', Smith continues, 'can never deliver what it promises because some form of mediation—concepts, language, symbols—always intervenes and makes it impossible to pass from the experience to the reality of God; inference . . . means not that God is experienced but that something else is experienced and therefore God "must be" real.' And so he recommends 'a third approach, that of mediated or interpreted experience in which both experience and interpretation are interwoven'.[1] This theme of an interweaving of experience and interpretation has been announced in the Introduction where Smith says most usefully: 'When our language proves inadequate, we return to experience, but we do so in order to criticize our language and improve it, not to force our experience into conformity with a pre-established language'; but he also says: 'Expression is, of course, essential and can be transcended entirely only if the pure immediacy of which mystics speak is a reality.'[2]

Before considering what Smith proves to mean by interpretation in this context, I must remark upon his view that experience is always mediated by 'concepts, language, symbols'. There are, I believe, two exceptions (at least) to this rule, one at each end of the scale: the intuitive awareness of other bodies interacting with our own and the activity of God in and upon our minds. It is true that this latter awareness does not rise explicitly to consciousness until our mental powers have been sufficiently developed through the use of language. But this is a *conditio sine qua non*, it seems to me, not a mediation. Our pre-reflexive, pre-conceptual knowledge reveals itself as mediated by nothing save the mental powers themselves. We become aware that this contact of the mind with the Absolute goes back in time to the first workings of our specifically human powers of knowing and loving. Smith rejects 'an essentially timeless unity that stands beyond all media and forms of expression'[3] as an account of our knowledge of God (or at any rate as a general account of it); this he calls here the '*mystical view*', and he is of course right to reject it, for one should speak of 'union', not 'unity', and there is always that mediation to which I have just referred, restricting knowledge of God to knowledge of him *in* his activity. But,

[1] 53. [2] 12. [3] 81.

in so far as there is knowledge of God at all, there is knowledge of the timeless, the Eternal. This points to the enormity of the claim which the theist must make and which Smith seems to shrink from making. What is known as 'mysticism' has its root in this.

When Smith goes on to explain what he means by 'interpretation', we find that his real concern is with the interpretation of God's revelation of himself in Christ. It becomes a question whether, in his view, there is anything which can be called *knowledge* of God apart from special revelation. He writes: 'From the religious dimension of experience and the grasp of the holy as distinct from the profane, we arrive at the concept of God and the meaning of the religious quest. We understand, that is, the possibility of a ground and goal of life and the need for a supremely worshipful Being . . . we do not yet reach God in the concrete.'[1] We cannot, indeed, reach personal union with God in its initial degree until we have *accepted* him. But God, we must surely hold, makes himself known to men, whether they know anything about a special revelation or not, in such sort that this acceptance is possible for them. The human mind must be capable, apart from such a revelation, of making, somehow and sometime, that option for which it was created. That is why the First Vatican Council declared for a 'natural knowledge' of God, a knowledge of which man is radically capable in any circumstances. The language which Smith uses here suggests that he is not prepared to go so far as this. Could he get round the difficulty by saying that the 'religious dimension' is never in fact found in abstraction from a special religious tradition? Has it to be 'interpreted' in the sense that one must find something *beyond* it if it is to count as a knowledge of God?

This is not Smith's last word on the subject, but we have to wait some time before we find it. On our way, however, we find a discussion, highly relevant to it, of the difference between the Augustinian and the Aristotelian traditions in Christian thought which seems to me wholly admirable, and which is strongly reminiscent both of Blondel and of Marcel. A single passage will sufficiently illustrate it:

'It is no attack upon the power of reason to deny its identity with purely formal logic and to deny the sufficiency of such logic in the sphere of religion. On the contrary, if it is possible to recover the more contemplative conception of a living reason or quest for intelligibility through

[1] 75.

dialectic or dialogue, we shall have restored thought to a place of importance in spheres from which it has been forced to retire. When reason is too narrowly conceived those who perceive this narrowness often conclude that if reason is nothing more than formal logic, it is better to abandon all attempts at rationality in art, religion, and mortality and seek elsewhere for guidance.'[1]

(And at this point Smith, following Pierce and Tillich, makes the point on which I have often dwelt that to speak of God's 'existence' may seem to make him 'part of a system'; he prefers to speak instead of God's 'reality' to indicate the objectivity of a knowledge of God.) The discussion of the ontological argument to which this leads also seems to me wholly admirable until Smith tells us that the 'experiential element', which he rightly claims to be 'primary and indispensable' in it, requires 'a purely logical transition which takes the self beyond the limits of direct experience' to 'the *necessity* of the divine existence', that is, to the discovery that the 'Absolutely Exalted' cannot be just possible but must be real. I should say that this transition is not 'logical' but consists simply in the articulation of what experience gives us. Smith says that the awareness of this necessity 'is not a matter of encounter', but since he adds that it is one of 'developing' the 'meaning and implications in thought' of direct experience,[2] the difference between us might seem to be more apparent than real. There is, however, the suggestion that interpretation is at work, not in the sense that the 'religious dimension' has to be interpreted by Christianity or some 'positive religion' (although Smith quite properly insists that St Anselm's concept of the 'Absolutely Exalted' comes to him from the Christian tradition), but in the sense that an awareness of God is never just 'given'.

We have to read on still further to find that this does seem to be in fact Smith's view and what it implies. After a valuable critique of the 'traditional arguments' for God (the 'Five Ways'), with which I am fully in accord, he turns to the approach 'through specifically human experience'[3] and lays it down as a principle that '*there is no experience of God that is not at the same time experience of something else*'. This 'something else' is a 'sign', and 'the indication or sign of the divine presence is supplied by or found implicit in the inherited religious tradition'.[4] Let us allow that, in practice, a man is always connected in some way with a

[1] 117–18.   [2] 138.   [3] 149.   [4] 150.

religious tradition and will think about religion in terms of it even if he rejects it. The question is whether knowledge of God *must* result from the interpretation of a sign. Smith speaks of 'three marks of the presence of the divine', which are (in summary form) 'the awareness of the contingent character of one's existence', 'the question of, and concern for, the goal and ultimate destiny of life', and 'the awareness of being a responsible being'. The first two, I consider, are found involved, upon reflection, in the third. Smith calls the process of interpretation a 'rational process' in the sense which we have met before, namely that it is a development of intelligibility: 'What is present in experience, though not immediately apprehended as such, becomes clear and explicit through interpretation and understanding.'[1] What he has to say here about unconditional obligation as revelatory of God would seem to me wholly satisfactory were it not for the insistence that there is no knowledge of God until this process of interpretation has taken place. It is important to recognize that a man who acknowledges unconditional obligation is *ipso facto* in cognitive contact with *God*, even though he may be unaware that this use of the word is in fact the appropriate one. God's approach to man's consciousness is registered as a demand because he is the end to which man's nature is, as such, directed.

It may be an unwillingness to allow that we can ever be said to know anything as sheerly 'given' in experience that is the fundamental difference between Smith's epistomological position and mine. As I have already suggested, it seems to me that in our knowledge of what is other *as* other we do find something as just 'given'. Acknowledging the summons to fulfil ourselves (even if quite inarticulately) is acknowledging the transcendent Other; we are in touch with him because he is *present* in it as *Cause*. That is what we mean, in the end, when we say that anything is 'real': it is *grounded* or (in Tillich's language) has a Ground. This direct, though mediated, knowledge of God is the place of objectivity *par excellence*. My perhaps carping or possibly even inapposite criticisms of certain passages in Professor Smith's helpful and important book were largely motivated by the desire to make this plain.

The relevance of philosophical argument to the question about an apprehension of God is emphasized in a particularly valuable way by Mr H. P. Owen in *The Christian Knowledge of God*, but I find in it a recurrent tendency to suggest that this apprehension (which Owen pre-

[1] 154.

fers to call 'intuition') is bound up with processes of ratiocination in a way which seems inconsistent with his claims for it. In his first chapter he states his general position in a way which I find wholly satisfactory:

'If it is asked whether philosophy can *justify* belief in God, the answer must be "partly but never wholly". Philosophy can justify belief in the sense of showing that belief is reasonable in every relevant sense of the adjective. It can show that the theistic postulation explains facts which are otherwise inexplicable, that it coheres with non-religious facts, and that the experience on which faith rests is epistemologically and logically valid. However, it cannot justify belief in God completely; for it cannot prove his existence by purely speculative reasoning or prove that the believer's putative experience of God is veridical. Nevertheless its failure to produce either form of proof is also entirely reasonable. The first form of proof is impossible because God and the world cannot be brought within the single framework of discourse that such a proof requires. The second form is impossible because the objectivity of experience in all its modes must be undemonstrable.'[1]

Here, then, it would seem that we have a straightforward appeal to an objective experience of God which is undemonstrable for the excellent reason that it demonstrates itself: it is self-guaranteeing.

But there is a strand of thought running through the book which may make the reader doubt whether this is the final answer. A self-guaranteeing apprehension, an apprehension in its full form, excludes the possibility of doubt. In so far as it is enjoyed (for of course it can be later forgotten or, as it were, mislaid), it declares to us that nothing can be found to cast doubt on it, that we shall never be justified in going back on what we know. Owen does indeed say, in his last chapter, that 'the theistic postulate . . . is adopted by the believer with absolute certitude on the basis of a purely spiritual experience'.[2] But in his seventh chapter he accepts Professor Ayer's verdict that knowledge does not consist 'in being in a special state of mind'. Obviously it does not consist simply in this: it is also the awareness of an object. But when we ask ourselves what *guarantees* that we are really knowing, we can point only to the nature of our activity in knowing. The fact that we *see* something is the ultimate fact which answers our question. Ayer, however,

[1] 20-1.   [2] 318.

rejects this thesis.[1] And so when Owen tells us in his penultimate chapter that 'we can never say that our certainty is absolute', although the evidence which we have 'entitles us to be sure',[2] we might suspect that he does not, after all, grant us more than a 'practical' certainty. But in this passage he is comparing our present knowledge with the 'immediate vision' of a future life and points out that there must be a difference in status between the certainties enjoyed in the two cases. So perhaps he means only that in this life a certainty can always be *lost*.

Other passages, however, might suggest that an apprehension needs the backing of reason in a way which casts doubt on its self-sufficient validity. Owen's chief concern here is to defend the rationality of the Christian's knowledge of God against the tendency to assert that it results from the arbitrary adoption of a viewpoint, from making a choice of theism rather than of atheism when there is nothing about the universe to suggest that the choice is the right one. The theistic arguments, he is saying, do lead us in a certain direction. This is one of most valuable features in a book which contains very much of great value. But Owen is sometimes led to make claims for rationality which seem dangerously excessive. For example, he writes: 'Neither reason (*ratio*) nor intuition (*intellectus*) is, on its own, a sufficient ground for faith. Each needs the other. Without intuition belief is empty; but without reason it is blind.'[3] Now, if we take this last statement literally, it is obvious that the whole notion of 'intuition' has been robbed of meaning. What Owen must mean is that an alleged 'intuition' which was contrary to reason could not in fact be an 'intuition' at all. Truth cannot contradict truth. But he could be easily understood to mean that an apprehension of God must go hand in hand with some process of argument in such a way that its validity depends, in some measure at least, on the validity of that process. Ratiocination prepares us for the apprehension of God, but our certainty results from our awareness of him and discursive reason has no part in it. I shall be proposing later that it is the same with our awareness of Christ as God, of God in Christ.

I have drawn attention to these features of Owen's book in the hope that this may help to prevent certain possible misunderstandings of it. It would be a great pity if so useful a book were to fail of its purpose at any point by a misreading of it. On the central issue, I believe we are in

[1] I have discussed Ayer's view in *Absolute Value*, 77-9.
[2] 290.   [3] 176.

fundamental agreement, and I have wished to show that such is the case, despite certain apparent indications to the contrary. But there are some disagreements between us, and again they seem to stem from the emphasis which Owen puts on processes of reasoning. What he sometimes appears to overlook (and what may therefore cause a reader some difficulty) is that when we reason with people what we are really doing in the end is drawing their attention to facts which they have failed to recognize. In arguing against a Hindu monist, for example, Owen, when all is said, is really pointing out to him that in saying that he is totally absorbed into the One he is failing to notice that he is *he*. Otherwise, we may add, there would be nothing to be absorbed—but to add this remark is only to draw attention in another way to the fact that we *are* aware of ourselves as individual persons. Owen says, in this connection, that 'the Christian philosopher can point to objective facts and reason objectively from them'.[1] Is he doing both these things when he talks to the Hindu or only the first of them?

It may be worthwhile to suggest at this point that the chief difficulty which the Hindu monist presents for many enquirers is that he claims an apprehension of the all-embracing One just as vigorously as the Christian claims an apprehension of God as his Creator. Surely this suggests that we cannot give credit to any such claims to an apprehension? Owen at this point would argue for the rationality of the Christian claim. It is preferable to the other because it fits the facts. And of course I agree. But it is important to realize that a difficulty remains. Granted that the monist's claim seems to make no sense, we are still faced with the fact that he seems to be just as certain of it as the Christian is certain about his own. Does this not tell against all claims to religious certainty, even those which are not self-contradictory? The only way in which the question can receive a final answer is discovering for oneself, if one can, that the Christian's apprehension of God as his Creator is in fact a valid apprehension, that is to say by attaining to it— for in the last resort a Christian must maintain that his own claim is the right one because he just *sees* that it is so, and he must conclude that the Hindu, although he does presumably apprehend the Absolute, is deterred from admitting his own distinct existence because he is convinced that this involves a disastrous 'dualism' (I have already suggested that there is a Christian 'dualism' which is not disastrous because it relates

[1] 102.

us to God as his 'manifestations' or 'created reflections'). I have no reason to suppose that Owen would disagree with any of this. But it may help to emphasize the important point that all serious differences in the field of metaphysics spring not from disagreement about a logical nexus (which is always capable, in principle at least, of a straightforward quasi-inevitable solution) but from disagreement about what is actually experienced. In the philosophy of religion persuasion is in the end a matter rather of art than of science. It is a question of getting someone to recognize something.

I now turn to the disagreements which stem, so it would appear, from Owen's emphasis on rationality. They concern only certain incidental conclusions at which he arrives in the course of his book, and so they can be mentioned only briefly. It is clear from his discussion of the divine attributes that he regards them as *deducible* from the divine self-existence. In a discussion of analogy he writes: 'God is not entirely unknown before the application of predicates: he is defined as self-existing being, and this definition determines the predicates' reference'.[1] That is, we have an apprehension of God as self-existent being and reach conclusions about his attributes on the basis of our knowledge of his creatures. And this is true, provided that we interpret 'on the basis of' to mean that we discover God as the source of values in and through created values. But it seems to me, to repeat, that in discovering him as the Source of values we must be discovering him as the 'place' where values converge and are identified in an infinite simplicity. This is what it means, I should say, to discover him as infinite and self-existent. There must be a real contact of the mind, however inarticulate, obscure and limited, with God *as he is*. This knowledge of him is not indeed comprehensive, but it must be informative about *who* he is. (And there can be no question of deducing his attributes by processes of reasoning in the *abstract*). But Owen, speaking of the analogy of attribution, tells us that 'we can infer from it that God is personal . . .',[2] and this sort of inference from finite realities leads him occasionally to conclusions which seem to me anthropomorphic, as when he discusses God's timelessness and his impassibility. But I must repeat that such conclusions are only incidental to an impressive and important account of Christian theism.

Finally it may be useful to make clear that the position which I am

[1] 211.   [2] 214.

adopting in this book approximates very closely to that of M. Gabriel Marcel and is indeed substantially identical with it. This might provoke the comment that Marcel does not appear to have a position but only hints at one in various ways. I have pointed out in my contribution to Dom Mark Pontifex's *The Meaning of Existence* that Marcel's horror of system-building does prevent him from making a coherent synthesis of his insights but that it is not really at all difficult to do it for him; and I gave some indication of how such a synthesis might be presented. Since then Mr Kenneth Gallagher's book *The Philosophy of Gabriel Marcel*[1] has presented one (Marcel has contributed to it an approving Foreword). To this I shall turn in a moment, but first it seems necessary to try to counteract current prejudices which hinder the appreciation of what Marcel offers us.

First, there is the question of his style and manner. I should agree that it is irritating. For example, his elaborate reticence becomes comically absurd when, on the last page of *The Existential Background of Human Dignity*, he refers to our need 'to recollect with gratitude all that has been given to us in our brief or long existence by a power which it seems to me unnecessary to name'. But this sort of thing should not blind us to the fact that even his most inconclusive discussions, punctuated sometimes with what look like portentous platitudes, usually contain something importantly illuminating. The occasional freakishnesses, as they seem to me, such as his playing around with the notion of reincarnation, jostle with the most mature and balanced judgements. What is most likely to offend readers of today is, I suppose, his attitude to technology, his 'pessimism'. But he is not really a pessimist, if only because the very idea of a philosopher's prophesying is rejected by him (and with a perhaps unnecessary violence). In fact he is issuing some very necessary warnings, based on our present experience, about the effect which a technological age can have upon the human sensibility and the proper development of the human personality. And here one may note a popular tendency to write off thinkers and men of letters in view of their (real or supposed) social or political attachments. To say that Marcel is only a psychologist and not a philosopher is to betray a rationalistic outlook; he is unquestionably a metaphysician. It is part of the same complaint to say that he muddles up music and drama with philosophy. In fact, I should say, his insistence that they are bound up

[1] Fordham University Press, 1962.

with one another is one of his great virtues. His metaphysic is, as he says, a 'concrete philosophy'.

Gallagher, from whose book I must now quote at some length, gives an excellent account of Marcel's fundamental position. After giving us a 'representative catalogue' of his pronouncements (mostly taken from *Etre et Avoir*)[1] he writes as follows:

'Each statement is a result of a re-seeing that flashes out of his absorption with a concrete situation. The propositions are actually interrelated, and some might even be inferred from others, but that is not the way Marcel comes upon them. Formulas are forgotten every time he begins his reflections anew. The fact that nevertheless the results of these concrete approaches resemble one another is a confirmation of the value of his procedure and an indication of a pervading orientation to his thought . . . underlying everything is the blinded intuition—but this does not function as a premise from which other statements can be deduced. Rather it serves as a light which is shed upon and reflected by every concrete situation into which thought plunges afresh. And what this light discovers is in each case—presence.'[2]

'Blinded intuition' stands here for *intuition bouchée*, which I should render 'blocked intuition'. Marcel tends to emphasize the participle in this phrase rather than the noun, but that he is talking about a genuine apprehension of the Absolute is perfectly clear. Gallagher continues:

'Every one of Marcel's "central concern" formulas brings out in a different way the notion that philosophy is nurtured by an experience of presence. Ultimately this presence can only be an absolute presence. It is true that other persons and even things can be felt as presences, but our experience of presence infinitely overflows them. . . . This means that the real metaphysical question is not "What is being?" but "Who is there?" Metaphysics is the "science" of answering this question.'

This is followed on the next page with another valuable summary:

'Metaphysical reflection, which is a search for the concrete, issues from a source anterior to the splitting of man into separate faculties. There is a unity in the self . . . that is, at the point where it participates in

---

[1] *Being and Having* is the title of Mrs Farrer's excellent translation of this book.
[2] 118–19.

being, it participates in unity. That is why it is erroneous to criticize Marcel's preoccupation with an experience like hope by saying that he gives a virtue of the will supremacy over intellectual knowledge. Hope is not a virtue of the will for him. It is a metaphysical experience which overflows into both intellect and will. . . .'

Apart from this unnecessarily vague talk about participation in 'being', that seems to me a helpful way of talking about the 'suspicion' of God and about the forward-looking character which all awareness of him exhibits. It is this which, as Gallagher puts it, is 'the dynamic principle behind metaphysical reflection'; and 'transcendence is that which gives no hold for abstraction'.[1]

This leads to a passage on certainty. 'Certitude is achieved through a light which proceeds from the subject, and he must continually assent to its radiation.' ('Not that he is the source of this light', a note explains, 'he is more like a screen which reflects it.') Gallagher rightly emphasizes Marcel's frequent references to 'light', pointing out that this is no mere metaphor, and that it is pointing to an ultimate identity of truth and love. 'In so far as I am spirit, I am a certainty . . . I am actually part of a communion whose vital principle is a transcendent act which is identically love and truth. If I could coincide with my own being fully, I would attain to this transcendence.' Nevertheless 'our intuition is . . . not an object of vision, we can only become conscious of it philosophically by embodying it in works which then reflect it back to us'.[2] This may illustrate that emphasis on the 'blockage' of our apprehension which I find rather excessive, but Marcel would agree that there is something in all awareness of God which must be called 'mystical'. And we find Gallagher adding immediately a quotation from *Du Refus à l'Invocation* which is evidence of this: 'It is a question of knowing whether in the last analysis there is a specifiable frontier between metaphysics and mysticism.'[3] As he points out, Marcel regards it as 'the hallmark of the Platonic tradition' that there is no clear-cut division between 'ethical reflection, metaphysics, spirituality'.

Gallagher is also useful in his discussion of Marcel's 'ontological exigence'. It is through this, he explains, that I come to realize my participation in the transcendent. But it seems a pity that one should feel it necessary to speak of the desire for God in this rebarbative way. And

[1] 121.   [2] 122.   [3] 123.

it is important to make clear that this desire is the effect and not the cause of our awareness of God. People are naturally suspicious of talk about a *need* for God, for this may be explained, they feel, in a naturalistic way: it might be only a 'projection'—in other words, wishful thinking. M. Jacques Durandeaux in a book recently published in an English version, *Living Questions to Dead Gods*, regards it as an all-important issue. He sees that in the end the appeal must be to experience and suggests significantly that 'the mystical experience may be the metaphysician's prime concern'.[1] Gallagher regards Marcel's 'ontological exigence' as the basis of 'a kind of "great dialectic" in which his entire philosophy is encapsulated' and refers to the 'rational subtlety and intuitive existential depth'[2] of a passage in *Being and Having* in which Marcel argues that the question 'What am I?' can receive no reliable answer *coming from me* and that, if anyone else supplies me with an answer, I have still to judge it for myself. 'I can, therefore', he continues, 'only refer myself without contradiction to a judgement which is absolute, but which is at the same time more within me than my own judgement. In fact if I treat this judgement as in the least *exterior* to me, the question of what it is worth and how it is to be appreciated must inevitably be asked afresh. The question is then eliminated *qua* question and turns into an appeal . . . the appeal is possible only because deep down in me there is something other than me.'[3] The passage certainly enforces Marcel's contention that there can be no 'objective' demonstration of God. As Gallagher puts it, 'A "someone" whose credentials I could verify out of my own resources would not be the Absolute Recourse to whom I utter this appeal. In other words, the transcendent is given as metaproblematic in and through the appeal in which I invoke him.'[4] In my balder way of putting it, when we start asking the real questions about ourselves, what is happening is that God is offering himself to us, and until we realize this we shall have no answer.

There is one more passage in Gallagher's book which calls for comment here. 'Perhaps', he writes, 'even the voluminous work of Maurice Blondel might be looked upon as a new concrete approach to the ontological mystery. . . .'[5] 'New' sounds odd, since the first *L'Action* appeared in 1893 when Marcel was four years old, and I cannot think why Gallagher should adopt so hesitant a tone in making so obvious a

---

[1] Durandeaux, 127.   [2] 125–6.
[3] *Being and Having*, 124–5.   [4] 126.   [5] 128.

proposal. He is well aware of the close similarities of Marcel's thought with Blondel's and of his kinship with the French 'philosophers of the spirit', in particular with Lavelle. Marcel makes appreciative references to them from time to time and especially to Blondel. In my opinion, Blondel offers us a solider and richer metaphysics than any of his successors. He is still too little read, largely, I suppose, because his works are not only 'voluminous' but written in a style and in an outmoded philosophical vocabulary which are disconcerting for our contemporaries. In turning now from 'natural' knowledge to 'supernatural' knowledge, from the apprehension of the Absolute to the acceptance of the Absolute (both in an anonymous form and in the light of the Christian Revelation) I shall begin with some account of Blondel's *L'Action*, developing the brief account offered in *Absolute Value* along lines which my present purposes mark out for me.

II

THE THEOLOGY OF FAITH: THE SELF-WITNESSING
OF THE ABSOLUTE

5. THE BLONDELIAN APPROACH

The 'natural' knowledge of God, I have been maintaining,[1] is a summons to the supernatural knowledge of him. It is time to begin a more persistent enquiry into what is meant by this supernatural knowledge and how it is attained. To remove certain misconceptions it may be well to say at the outset that, in this way of looking at the supernatural, what is meant by it is nothing more nor less, in the last analysis, than God himself. He is the goal to which man moves. We are said to live a supernatural life only because we are granted a knowledge and love of him, a union with him, which is commonly referred to as a 'participation' or 'sharing' in his life. It is a union without confusion. Union without confusion, the presence of the object to the subject, is the basic character of our experience; the bedrock certainty from which we must start, that we are in the presence of the 'other', of something other than ourselves (even if it be only the awareness of some foreign body, discriminated simply as such), seems to provide us with a preliminary clue to the mysteries of theology. The union of the divine and the human finds its unique perfection in the Person of Jesus Christ. But there is no confusion between the divine and the human. The life of love which is God himself in Three Persons is the primal union. And again there is no confusion of Persons.

Supernatural knowledge may be said to depend upon natural knowledge in the sense that it can arise only on the basis of natural knowledge. To speak of it as if it had no roots in natural knowledge is to make it meaningless. But it does not grow out of it as a mere enlargement of it. It is something as genuinely new as the emergence of human consciousness in the process of our evolution. It is what happens when our Father's love for us has provoked our proper reaction to it. This is what is meant, in the end, by 'grace' in traditional theology: the communion of God and man.

[1] V., in particular, *Absolute Value*, ch. 9.

This relationship between the 'natural' and the 'supernatural' was obscured by post-Reformation polemics and by the general state of decadence into which theology had fallen; it will be generally agreed, I think, that it has been clarified for our time, in the first instance, by Maurice Blondel. I propose, then, to consider what he has to say about it in *L'Action*, a book which is perhaps more talked about than read and which still awaits translation into English. But first something must be said about a suspicion, prevalent in certain quarters, that Blondel must be considered as out on a limb in a general view of Roman Catholic theology. It should suffice to quote some remarks from a little book *Situations et Taches Présentes de la Théologie* by the Dominican writer, Père Yves Congar, best known in the English-speaking world for his outstanding work in the field of ecumenism and one of those summoned as theological experts to the Second Vatican Council. One would not regard him as concentrating especially on philosophical theology, and there can be no question of his riding a hobby horse when he declares that 'Maurice Blondel's philosophical and religious importance becomes clearer with every year which passes'. He goes on to say that 'Karl Rahner seems to have little acquaintance with Blondel, but, in fine, he resumes his programme'. And to show what he has in mind when he speaks of Blondel's importance he quotes with emphatic approval the following passage from a recent article of Rahner's:

'It would be a tragic mistake about the meaning of Vatican Two to consider that the principal task of today's or tomorrow's theology lies in the field of ecclesiology or in that of Mariology or in that of any of the themes explicitly treated of by the Council. Today's and tomorrow's theology must be a theology of dialogue with men who think that they cannot believe. So it will have to reflect, fundamentally, and with radical sincerity, on what it thinks and means when it talks of God and Christ. . . .'

(It is in the hope of contributing in some small way to this all-important task, so seldom undertaken in a constructive spirit, that I, a mere metaphysician, have had the hardihood to embark on a theological enterprise which one would normally leave to the professionals.)

How, then, does Blondel distinguish the natural from the supernatural, or (it comes to the same thing) philosophy from theology, in his seminal work *L'Action* of 1893? Does he succeed in distinguishing between them at all or is his philosophy a theology in disguise? His intention is clear from the start. Nothing is to be taken for granted. We must begin with something which is plain enough for everyone: it is just the case that we cannot help doing *something*. Is there any point in it? Are we in fact moving in some discernible direction? Let us see what happens in practice when we make use of that liberty with which our nature has endowed us (this is how Blondel initiates his enquiry into the 'logic of action' which is to reveal, at long last, the presence of the 'supernatural'). The following often-quoted passage from the Introduction to *L'Action* will make clear that this is a philosophical investigation: 'The most stupid negations and the wildest extravagences of the human will must be probed to their roots to see if there is not one deep seated, initial movement or impulse that persists throughout them all, that is always cherished and craved, even when it is abjured or abused. Each of these various doctrines and attitudes must be probed for the principle that will enable judgement to be passed on it.'[1]

There can be no question even of summarizing here the long account of man's various attempts to fulfil himself (I have said something about it in *Absolute Value*,[2] and the rest of this paragraph will summarize that). These attempts follow one another with the inevitability which the 'logic of action' discloses to us, but there is always some fresh obstacle appearing, and there is always a gap between the will which wills particular finite objects (*la volonté voulue*) and the 'underlying' will (as we may call *la volonté voulante*) which always remains dissatisfied. This 'underlying' will is not being, as it were, held up for our inspection. This is not just a psychological study. The presence of the 'underlying will' is a conclusion which must be drawn from a rational examination of the facts. I am not here concerned with the validity of Blondel's 'logic of action'. The point is that it is based on facts of experience which are held to be at everyone's disposal. The need for the absolute which emerges from all this, combined with the impossibility of attaining to it by any products of human willing, leads to desperate attempts to force the issue, to compel, as it were, some object to provide what is wanted by filling the necessary role. Blondel calls this state of affairs

[1] xx.   [2] 125-8.

'superstition', and the final example of it is 'moralism'—as we should say nowadays 'secular humanism'. So the result of this 'dialectic' of human action is a requirement which is both necessary and impracticable. A complete *impasse* has been reached.

'It is this conflict', wrote Blondel, 'that explains why there must be present in man's consciousness a new affirmation, and indeed it is the reality of this "necessary presence" that makes us conscious of the conflict. There is "one thing necessary". The whole movement of the determinism, of the dialectic, is towards that "one thing necessary", towards that end which is also a source, a source from which springs the very dialectic whose whole purpose is to bring us back to it.'[1] That is to say, it is through this world's values but through their irremediable insufficiency that God is made known to us in practice. But we are still cut off from him until we have made the great 'option'. Blondel describes it in these rather rhetorical terms: 'Is man willing to give ungrudging consent to his supersession by God for the rest of his life, even if it should be, so to speak, the death of him? Or will he go on trying to be self-sufficing, taking no account of God, availing himself of God's necessary presence but not willing it, borrowing from God the strength to do without him, willing infinitely without willing the infinite?'[2] This states the human dilemma and its divine solution in a highly schematic form. Things do not normally work out in so clear-cut a way, for a man may be turned towards God, related to him in the personal relationship of faith, but without being given to him completely as yet; in other words, there can be imperfect acts of faith. Blondel is describing the act of faith in its perfected form. This, he is saying, must be the ground-plan of all human lives. Eventually there must be a definitive choice, either a surrender which is both God's victory and ours, or a refusal.

Philosophy, then, discovers the presence of God and raises the question of a union with him. But only God can answer this question. (And even he can answer it only if we allow him to do so, for we have a genuine initiative of a negative kind—in the last analysis, we can bring nothing into existence, but we can hold things up, turn them from their proper path, pursue policies which will have negative effects.) So when it is said that philosophy makes the supernatural necessary, in Blondel's view, this must not be taken to mean that the supernatural

[1] 339. [2] 334-5.

is evolved out of purely natural resources. It means that the super-natural is necessary to philosophy because philosophy finds itself faced by a problem which only the supernatural can solve. Philo-sophy must, as it were, abdicate in favour of the supernatural. Or rather we should say that as philosophy pure and simple it disappears, but that its achievement (which must be called at the same time a defeat) is not thrown to waste but carried over into a new life. It is the God who has been found present, though unattainable, with whom union is to be won through the option which is our definitive action, our disposing of ourselves so as to be acted upon, our acceptance of reality at its Source.

There has been as yet no talk of Christianity. Despite some opinions to the contrary, it seems quite clear that 'the supernatural', so far, refers simply to God. What is necessary for men at all times is the acceptance of God. The supernatural, then, at the present stage, is the 'point of insertion' for Christianity. It is not until the fifth and last part of *L'Action* that the question formally arises whether Christianity may not prove to be the definitive answer to the human problem. Union with God is possible without knowledge of Christianity, but Christianity offers a way of union for which specific claims are made. The honest enquirer, then, will feel called upon to align the truths taught by Christianity with the aspirations of human nature to see whether it seems capable of satisfying them. It should come to seem what is finally necessary for him. The acceptance of God must be, so to speak, carried forward so that it becomes the acceptance of his revelation of himself in Jesus Christ. The implications of this will be considered at later stages of this enquiry into the theology of faith. At the moment the point is that this is, for Blondel, the final stage of human 'action'. He constantly insists that philosophy, the 'science of action', cannot substitute for action itself and that we cannot think up the Christian truths for ourselves. As he so often puts it, the Christian revelation comes to us 'from outside': it is an historical affair. The desire for the supernatural is immanent in us because God, the supernatural, issues his summons to us. But the supernatural is itself transcendent, and we find it to be such—it cannot be brought within the 'logic of action', the function of which is precisely to bring us to the 'option': we must be willing to receive what we cannot gain by our own efforts.

It may still be felt that this 'logic' is not properly philosophical. Has

it not been excogitated by a Christian with the avowed object of leading people to Christianity? Does it not in fact presuppose Christianity?
Blondel does not deny that his thought arises from within Christianity,
but he sees nothing damaging to his case in this. He distinguishes
between the facts which he finds in human experience, simply as such,
and the further light which is thrown on them by Christianity. He sees
more in them than the non-Christian does, but as a philosopher he
refers only to what everyone can see. The reader may feel also, whether
or not he thinks that claim a legitimate one, that there is nothing very
remarkable about it. It is pretty familiar. If it is, then this is some
indication of the influence exerted on contemporary theology by
Blondel's work.

It will be profitable, I think, to consider some more passages which
should help to bring out the principles of his thought. He has declared
that to dismiss the possibility of a historical divine revelation is to be
'unphilosophical', and he is then led to make some remarks about
miracles (frequently drawn upon by theologians of our time) which
warn us against a certain approach to the question of such a revelation:

'These jolts administered to people's minds are effective only in so far as
they appreciate, not the perceptible marvel, whatever it may be, but its
symbolic meaning. . . . No mere event, however strange and disconcerting it may be, is impossible; the notion that there are fixed laws
in nature is a superstition; each phenomenon is a particular case and the
answer to a unique question. In the last analysis there is certainly nothing more in a miracle than in the most ordinary events; but also there is
nothing less in the most ordinary of events than in a miracle: and that is
the meaning of these exceptional jolts which encourage reflection to
reach general conclusions about the world. . . . Miracles, then, are
only miraculous in the eyes of those who are prepared to discern the
divine action in the most commonplace events and actions. . . .'[1]

An appeal to physical 'marvels', as such, is not to the point. The notion
of revealed truth springs from an 'internal initiative'.[2] Blondel is faithful
to that 'method of immanence' which he has employed throughout
L'Action.

'But how', he now asks, 'can this disposition which is itself purely
subjective discover whether outside itself there is in fact a sustenance

[1] 396-7.   [2] 391.

capable of appeasing its hunger for the infinite? . . . How is one to recognize the authentic answer if it is really uttered?' Suppose, he is saying, that there could be a revelation—what would be the requirements for such a possibility? This is the final question which the philosopher, as such, can (and should) raise. 'If there is a revelation', Blondel answers, 'it must propose itself to us as independent of human initiative. It must demand an act of submission. . . . But this saving disposition of obedience cannot be attributed to the effort of the human will alone. . . . We must conclude that this very drive which carries us on, which promotes the search for God, is itself, in its origin, his gift.' This leads him to conclude that a revelation must be *mediated* and that 'to make God man's end, as our will imperiously demands that he should be, to become his cooperator, to relate the whole of life to its source and its destiny, we must have a helper, an intercessor, a pontiff, to be as it were the act of our acts, the prayer of our prayer, the offering of our offering. It is only through him that our will can become equal to itself. . . .'[1] And so the *leitmotiv* of the whole dialectic, the distinction between *la volonté voulante* and *la volonté voulue*, reappears in the context of Christology.

The passage continues: 'And it is not only in order to believe and to act, it is also to remedy the inevitable failures of action that succour is needed for mankind. . . . To give, to preserve and to restore our life, we need a saviour.' So the conclusion is:

'These are the supreme requirements which man realizes that he cannot himself satisfy: his reason sees their necessity rather than comprehends their possibility; and they presuppose, in order that they may be merely conceived of, an inspiration which does not come from man alone. But further (and this is the last demand of the human conscience) this initial inspiration must be given to all as a minimum, but as a minimum which is sufficient: revelation, if it is a fact, and if it is authentic, must be addressed prophetically to those who have preceded it in time, symbolically and secretly to those who could not know of it; it must be independent of time and place, truly universal and of permanent efficacy; perpetuating itself not as something in the future or in the past but in the eternal present. . . .'

Here again is a commonplace of contemporary theology: 'anonymous

[1] 399.

Christianity' is one of the current slogans (and it is sometimes presented with so exclusive an emphasis as to suggest that the Christian Gospel no longer needs to be proclaimed). God's universal will to save has always, indeed, been recognized as a Christian doctrine. But its implications had been so regularly bypassed and its plain meaning so regularly volatilized that in Blondel's time it was most valuable to insist upon it. It is still necessary to do so today in the framework of his traditional metaphysic.[1]

Another passage on the approach to faith may make his position clearer. Since it is a question, he says, of an 'alliance' with God, there must be co-operation between ourselves and him. We have a 'natural reason' for playing our part precisely because 'nature and man no longer suffice', and we can only discover that there is a divine answer by 'actual experiment'. And in answer to the objection that it is hypocritical to practise what one does not yet believe, Blondel replies that 'this human desire for what seems just and necessary suffices to authorize the act which it requires of us, an act which is natural in its intention; and, in this action, there is perhaps hidden what the mere intention did not yet contain, the presence of the supernatural life which, if it is there, will reveal itself to man and which can reveal itself to him only in this way. If he evades the obstacles which impeded him, if he goes to the limit of his sincerity, he will find, in his freely chosen activity, the certainty which he requires.'[2] So far the passage might make one suspect that Blondel's position is an anti-intellectualist one, and it must be admitted that he does sometimes show a tendency in this direction. But what he means here is indicated clearly enough when he goes on to describe the 'action' as a 'humble waiting upon a truth which does not come from thought alone' because 'it puts within us a spirit which is not our own'. In other words, the activity which is demanded of us might be called, more helpfully, a passivity. But it is an openness of the mind which must be *willed*.

Blondel's 'dialectic' has not yet been fully worked out, and I shall refer to the further stages of it because they, like their predecessors, indicate the lines of thought which I shall be pursuing later on. His next move is to utter a warning against the notion that it suffices to adore in spirit and in truth without incarnating one's religion in religious practices. 'It is', he says, 'by practising that faith develops and is

---

[1] For a general account of this I must again refer to *Absolute Value*, ch. 9.
[2] 402–3.

purified, as it is faith which inspires and transfigures all man's practical activity. Between the letter and the spirit, between dogma and precept, there is a perpetual exchange and an intimate interdependence. The letter is the spirit in action. Dogmas are not only facts and living ideas, but also principles of action. . . .[1] The same movement which constrains us to conceive of a religious action leads us by the force of an inevitable logic to determine the demands and, as it were, the requirements of this necessary conception. So here is a new link in the chain of determinism.'[2] The natural does not require the supernatural, Blondel adds, in the sense of 'determining the content of divine revelation itself'. For 'in its principle, in its object and in its end, revelation, so as to be what it must be if it is to exist at all, must be beyond the grasp of reason; and no effort of man, simply as man, can penetrate its essence'.[3]

At this point there is a long footnote to 'reassure those minds which are prompt to fear that violence is being done either to their freedom of thought or to their faith'. Reason, says Blondel, is sovereign and autonomous in its own domain, and faith presupposes its activity. These fears are due to a failure to appreciate the *essence* of the supernatural. 'Being above everything which we can suspect or hope for, this mystery, far from discouraging the interference of our thought, opens to it a limitless prospect . . . initiating us into the secret of his own life, the hidden God reveals to us the divine processions . . . man is by grace what God is by nature, and the mystery of eternity is renewed in time . . . faith illuminates the intelligence to know the incomprehensible: charity dilates the will so as to embrace the infinite. These operations, since they do not belong to our nature, return to the source from which they proceed. . . .'

A few pages later there is a passage which suggests that the insistence on action and on the interdependence of action and thought, far from being 'voluntarist', is really binding up the will with the intellect and rejecting that sharp division into faculties which characterizes the Thomist (as opposed to the Augustinian) account of the human soul:

'One cannot comprehend at once the manifold aspects of all that there is to know; but one can pass at once to the execution of all that has to be done. To act only within the limits of what is clear to one at the

[1] 404.   [2] 406.   [3] 406–7.

moment and to confine oneself to one's conceptions or one's realization, such as it is, of the divine, without finding in life itself an immediate application of it, is to diminish onself. By its tyranny, thought restricts action: by its submission, action enlarges thought. . . . What is enslaving is to think only in the light of one's own ideas and to act only in accordance with one's own judgement. A man who no longer feels the need to renew and to transcend himself is not really alive . . . to carry in one's heart the anguish of a seeker along with the serenity and trustful docility of a child is certainly the way, not of enslavement, but of enfranchisement.'[1]

Listening to the Word, we may perhaps sum up, is a loving knowledge, an intelligent love, and it grows through obedience.

The 'logic of action' must work itself out in the sphere of worship on the same supernatural principles. We must learn how to worship and receive our instructions from above:

'If ritual acts are not to be reduced to an idolatrous fiction and if they are to be equal to the faith of which they should be the life-giving expression, it is imperative that they should be, not man's invention or the always imperfect effect of a purely natural movement, but the expression of positive precepts and the authentic imitation of dogmatic truth transcribed into definite ordinances. It is not enough that they should be the vehicle of the transcendent; they must contain its real presence. . . .'[2]

Current debates about the Eucharist, with their concentration upon its social aspect, are sometimes in danger of underplaying these supernatural principles on which Blondel insists: the Eucharist is God's gift to each of us. And so in the last chapter of *L'Action* there is the further insistence that 'the only way to gain the all is to begin by being alone with him'. The passage continues:

'One cannot be at home with oneself or with others without being first at home with him . . .[3] Sacrifice is the solution of the metaphysical problem by the experimental method. And if action, in the whole course of its development, has seemed to be a new source of clarity, it must also be that at the end of it the knowledge which follows upon the act of perfect abnegation contains a fuller revelation of being. This know-

[1] 410.   [2] 416.   [3] 441.

ledge no longer sees it from without, it possesses it, it finds it in itself . . . I have need of all the others, and yet, if we are to speak with absolute rigour, there is no real contact in the world save that between him and me.'[1]

These words, which like many others remind us of Newman, might be, as they stand, misleading. So I add another passage in which Blondel comments on the words of Leibnitz 'to love God and to love all men, it is all the same': 'there is nothing lovable in anything anywhere save him . . . one cannot love any man without embracing all in the same charity. They are really united with one another only in the burning heat of a fire which the whole world cannot of itself enkindle.'[2]

In the final paragraph of *L'Action* Blondel writes of the 'option': 'It is the whole interest of life which is here at stake; in all other cases it is possible to be neutral or to shuffle, because these affirmations and negations, always mixed with some alloy, are always relative: but in face of this absolute "yes", and here only, the issue is settled absolutely . . . It is philosophy's business to examine the consequences of one or other solution and to measure the immense difference between them, but it cannot go further and say, in its own name, whether it is so or not so.' And Blondel ends with his own answer, his own act of faith: 'It is so.'[3] Why are affirmations and negations 'relative' in all other cases? The meaning is, I take it, that all genuine certainty is based on the acknowledgement of the Source of being. These affirmations and negations, then, of which Blondel speaks, refer to what is not in the full sense true for us because we cannot really affirm anything until we see it for what it really is, in its derivation from the Source.

Some forty years later in *L'Etre et les êtres* Blondel repeated this doctrine: 'Created spirits have a role quite different from that of being passive receptacles; but the effort which they have to make does not consist in seizing upon God, who would in that case have to defend himself against the power of an intelligent creature: it is over themselves that they have to triumph, it is from themselves that they have to become detached so as to transcend their limitations and to accept the truth that frees them, giving them a consistency which they could not find in themselves and of themselves alone.'[4]

[1] 442. [2] 446. [3] 492. [4] 318.

I must now turn to a certain difficulty which arises in connection with Blondel's 'great option'.[1] Is there only one option? A passage from an article by Père Henri Bouillard will introduce the topic: 'In showing that the human will always goes beyond its own capabilities, Blondel reveals, by way of the inevitable affirmation of the *Unum Necessarium*, the inevitable idea of the supernatural and the ineluctable affirmation of the necessity of the supernatural. This idea and this necessity emerge in two stages. In the first, the necessity is absolute, but the supernatural remains undetermined. In the second the necessity is that of a hypothesis; but this is the hypothesis of the Christian supernatural order. What emerges in the first stage is the absolute necessity of throwing oneself open to the action of God, whatever form that may take. What emerges in the second is the necessity of accepting the positive revelation of God, if it is made known to the subject by means of the Christian preaching. Thus one does not attain to the specifically Christian idea save by the intermediary of the supernatural in an as yet undetermined form.'[2] Bouillard's purpose here is to make clear, in reply to M. Henry Duméry, that this idea of an 'undetermined supernatural' is an essential part of Blondel's thesis. I am not concerned to discuss this here because Bouillard seems to me to have proved his case to the hilt. The passage has been quoted because it makes clear that the 'great option' passes through two stages. Is it, then, a *single* option?

Let us consider what happens. When the necessity for the supernatural, still 'undetermined', becomes clear, a man must throw himself open to the action of God. He must choose God or reject him. If he chooses God, he will enter into a personal relation with him. He will now at last 'possess' him. In order to choose him, he must know him, but he cannot be united with him until his whole spiritual being has become engaged. When he is apprised of the Christian revelation, we must conclude, he will accept it, provided that he does not withdraw from this engagement. He will recognize God in Christ if he has the opportunity to do so. The 'great option' is, so to say, simply carried forward. But, even if he has entered fully into this engagement, it

[1] This complicated difficulty, with which the rest of the chapter deals, does not affect the main argument, but it seemed wrong for me to ignore it. The reader, however, may well decide to do so.

[2] *Archives de Philosophie*, Jan.–March 1964, 115.

remains at risk. It is possible to withdraw from it. (So he may have to renew it before he can accept Christ's revelation.) It would seem, then, that for Blondel the 'great option', although not the last stage in this development, is, if all goes well, the final option.

In practice, these two stages may not be separated in time from one another. The discovery of God in Christ may be the whole story of a man's spiritual awakening. But even so it is a story with two (logical) moments, the moment at which the necessity arises that he should throw himself open to the action of the supernatural, and the moment at which he does throw himself open to it, which is also the moment at which he becomes united with it. He cannot accept the Christian revelation until he is ready to receive God's word for it. This thesis will be worked out in detail later in this book. Here I shall only repeat that this Blondelian schema represents the genesis of an act of faith in its full, absolute, form. How many people have, in fact, an absolute certainty that they are summoned to the 'supernatural' and an absolute certainty that God has uttered his Word to us in Christ?

But we have not finished with the question about the option. There may be only one 'great option' in the process which leads a man to become a Christian, but there seem to be many other options described in *L'Action*. Father J. M. Somerville in his valuable analysis of the book, *Total Commitment: Blondel's 'L'Action'*, writes of them:

'The most important are the following four: (1) the option for or against transcendence, (2) the option concerned with the necessary idea of the supernatural and the practical necessities which follow upon this idea, (3) the metaphysical option, which comes only at the end of the regressive analysis, and bears on the totality, and (4) the affirmative option, identical with the act of faith, which lies outside the province of philosophy.'[1]

I shall try in a moment to clear up what is meant by the 'regressive analysis', and then, I hope, it may be possible to make sense of the notion of successive options. But first we must have before us the rest of the paragraph from Somerville's book: still speaking of the options, he continues:

'The fourth is clearly distinct from the other three, though it is remotely prepared by them. The third embraces the first two and every other

[1] 33.

option; it is the option of options. The second follows dialectically from the first but it is only implicitly contained in it. The first, which involves the necessary idea of an absolute and transcendent Being, must be embraced if we are to found the reality of anything else. But from the point of view of methodology it is not the same as the meta-physical option, which cannot arise until all the conditions for the expansion of human action are made explicit.'

The sharp distinction between the third and fourth options is not irreconcilable with my suggestion that they are, as it were, spanned by the 'great option'. And the reference to methodology gives us the clue to the distinction between the third and the first two: they are distinct stages of the analysis with which we start, but at the end of it they are brought together and made part of the 'metaphysical option'. This would seem to be what Somerville proposes to us.

A later passage from his book[1] will make clear that this is the case. He first quotes a passage from *L'Action*[2] about the 'metaphysical option' in which Blondel says that 'there subsists in thought a necessary presence of reality without reality's being necessarily present to thought . . . depending on whether we receive or refuse the action of this truth in us, our being is totally changed'. This is 'the practical decision to which the whole movement of science leads us by its very nature', and Blondel here refers to it as 'the supreme option from which man's life is suspended'. Somerville then comments:

'Although it is inseparable from them, it should be clear . . . that the metaphysical option is not to be confused with the option that concerns the Uniquely Necessary or the supernatural [the first and second options]. The present alternative bears on the whole and can only be discussed at the end of the regressive analysis, and the question is whether or not man will be satisfied with a purely speculative view of the series of means, with no personal commitment to all its exigencies, or whether he will embrace the total order as a system of ends.'

In other words, only when we look back over the stages of the analysis (the 'logic of action' or the successive attempts of the 'underlying' will to 'equal itself') does the question of commitment arise. And until we

[1] 294–5.   [2] 429.

have committed ourselves to the real, it is not real for *us*. So far we have regarded the 'dialectic', the 'determinism', the 'series of means', with a 'purely speculative view'. We are now called upon to accept 'the total order', make ourselves a part of it and make it an end for ourselves. As Somerville goes on to say, although we can speak of 'objectivity' before this option has been made, 'the being that is encountered is not the existentially real, but only the idea of being', and 'we cannot resolve the problem of *our* being by halting with a conceptual ontology that makes no imperative demands on us'. In a later passage Somerville writes: 'Much has been written on the question of whether or not the Great Option for or against the supernatural is to be identified with the metaphysical option. No more, we believe, than any of the lesser options that have been encountered as alternatives in the series.'[1] It sounds very strange to say that this 'Great Option' is not to be identified with the metaphysical option, which has been called earlier 'the option of options'. But when we are working out the 'logic of action', the option for or against the supernatural is only an *envisaged* option; the option for the supernatural cannot be *made* until, like all the other terms in the 'ideal' series, it is 'embraced' by the metaphysical option. So the metaphysical option is distinct from the other terms in the series, because it arises only at the end of it. But when it is made, the Great Option is *made* at the same time.

To understand Blondel, as Somerville goes on to say, we have to distinguish 'the indirect method of the science of action' from the direct method of 'ordinary men . . . who are able to affirm the absolute reality of the objective order, even though they may be unable to define clearly and make explicit all that is contained in this global assent to transcendence', but 'science justifies the direct method by showing that the whole is in each of its parts and that the particular implicitly contains the whole'.[2] And it thus presents us with the option, the demand for the 'great action'. When it comes to the point of *making* the option, it is always the same option which we have to make whether we reach it by means of the indirect method (realizing explicitly what the 'logic of action' has revealed to us) or whether we reach it by the direct method (realizing only implicitly what is involved in it). When it comes to the point of action, then, there *is* only one option.

[1] 301.   [2] 303.

It is this difference between the indirect method of 'science' and the direct method of 'ordinary men' which causes the chief difficulty in following Blondel's thought in *L'Action*. For even when we are pursuing the 'indirect method' we are still *acting*. And we may choose not to act. That is to say, we may refuse to go along with the 'logic of action'. We may decide that it may lead us to conclusions which we are *unwilling* to reach. In such a case, Somerville would say, we are not yet rejecting the 'existentially real' but only the 'idea of being'. But are we not rejecting something which is offered to us as a *truth*? Has not *the* option, then, arisen? And, if the temptation to reject the truth is resisted, will not the 'good' option be made? Perhaps it is only the suspicion of a duty which is either followed up or neglected. Our responsibility may not be fully engaged as yet. But, as Somerville himself tells us, 'any link in the chain can become matter for an option, and, implicitly, for the option which involves the whole.'[1] We must now consider more closely how this 'great option' is 'carried forward' to embrace God's historical revelation of himself in the Person of Jesus Christ.

6. THE LOGIC OF FAITH

In 1964 Père Henri Bouillard published a little book, *Logique de la Foi*, in which his previous work in fundamental theology is conveniently summed up.[2] His intention, he tells us in the Preface, is 'to bring out the underlying correspondence between the logic of human existence and the summons of the Christian mystery, and, by so doing, to uncover the rational pattern of the process that leads to acceptance of the Christian faith . . .'. He proposes, then, to indicate the *method* of a viable apologetic, not to write an apologetical treatise. 'Apologetics', he continues, 'is not simply a defence of religion against those who attack it. It is a positive activity, a working-out of the logic of the movement of men's minds towards the faith. It is at once a philosophy of Christianity and a fundamental theology.' Speaking in the same place of Gabriel Marcel and of Blondel, he remarks that 'the former will tell us how concrete approaches to the ontological mystery can pave the way

---

[1] 302.

[2] Available in an English translation, *The Logic of Faith*, but one which, I regret to say, is unsatisfactory at critical points in the argument.

for an acceptance of the Christian message, the latter how the logic of action brings us face to face with Christianity and, without making faith inevitable, cannot fail to raise the religious question in its Christian form'. Bouillard is thinking, in particular, of our contemporaries in the Western world who suppose that 'God is dead'. He goes on to emphasize that this logic of faith 'clearly implies that the transcendence of the divinely revealed mystery and its significance for us are both safeguarded. It cannot be reduced simply to the logic which is immanent in human existence, but it cannot be made clear unless one appreciates the close connection which it has with that logic.'

As we have seen, when Blondel says that the logic in human existence brings us face to face with the supernatural, what he means is that it brings us face to face with God, with the acceptance or rejection of God, and also, in practice, with 'the religious question in its Christian form'. He is not saying, as he has often been accused of saying, that the Christian mystery is found, as it were, already wrapped up in human existence as such and that it is simply a question of unfolding its implications. If that were the case, the doctrines of Christianity would be mere symbolization—mythology, in fact. That is the heresy of Modernism, and nothing could be further from Blondel's thought, which Bouillard is here expounding. His Preface, therefore, continues to emphasize the transcendence of the Christian truths: 'No analysis of human experience could conclude to the necessity of the Incarnation or reveal the contents of the Christian message. The spontaneous manifestation of God in history, in the person of Christ, is an event, an absolute novelty. Only by obedient adherence to the historical Gospel message can we get to know its mystery and learn to live by it.' Nevertheless, 'if it is true that Christ has a decisive importance for all men, then Christ's coming must correspond to something congenital with man's make-up which is open to the supernatural and gives rise to an obscure expectancy. Otherwise we should not be able to discern that Christ is the Word of God for us.'

In the first chapter of *Logique de la Foi* Bouillard therefore maintains that 'to make clear our duty to believe, we must show that the Christian faith is the condition which is required for the fulfilment of our human destiny'. 'No apologetic', he adds, 'is valid if it does not adopt this method in one way or another. It would be useless to rely upon miracles and prodigious events unless the Christian phenomenon of which they

form part is shown to be the answer to the question about our existence.'[1] 'On the one hand', he writes a little later, 'we have the finiteness
of man: we have been thrown into existence and condemned to be free
without having wished it; we are doomed to suffer evil, pain, frustration and death. But, on the other hand, we should not be aware of this
finiteness unless we had within us something by which we transcend it.
Within us the presence of "the one thing necessary" asserts itself. This
affirmation has to be brought to light. Then it must be shown that it puts
before every man an inevitable alternative . . .'. This is by now
familiar ground; Bouillard is keeping closely here to Blondel. And he
now reaches the important conclusion which marks the first stage in
this account:

'The dialectic which makes this idea [of the 'undetermined supernatural'] emerge invites a man at the same time to adopt a religious
attitude. This attitude, which is already a foreshadowing of the attitude
of Christian faith, is necessary for the discernment of the divine
revelation . . . When it has been shown what our relationship to the
Absolute is and what it ought to be, it remains to show that Christianity
is the historic definition of that relationship.'[2]

The theologian is thus presented with a twofold task. He has to show
that the doctrines of Christianity are thinkable and coherent and that it
answers man's fundamental question about his relationship with the
Absolute. 'The first task', Bouillard remarks, 'is performed pre-eminently
by the study of dogmatic theology, the second is more proper to
apologetics. Both, however, consist in bringing out the rational
element in Christianity.'[3] Here two comments suggest themselves.
First, 'the rational element in Christianity' is a phrase which may
suggest to many minds the sort of 'rational apologetics' which ultimately relies on supposedly demonstrated facts, the historical evidence
for Christ's resurrection in the first place, and the sort of dogmatic
theology which claims to deduce theological conclusions by water-
tight processes of syllogistic reasoning from a set of supposedly
revealed propositions. But it will have become obvious that this is not
the sort of apologetic which Bouillard is advocating, and I have tried
to show that there are processes of thought which are rational, indeed,
but are not syllogistic, and which are the movements, not just of a

[1] 26. [2] 28. [3] 29.

human faculty, but of the human person. Secondly, it would follow from the position which has now been reached that apologetics and dogmatic theology must be, in practice, involved with one another. Dogmatic theology, in showing the meaningfulness of Christian doctrines, their practical import, is performing an apologetic task; and apologetics cannot present the fact of revelation in any effective way without presenting the essentials of its content. For, in the end, it is the living fact of Christianity, the life of Christ in his Church, which assures one that it is the Church of God.

And that is what Bouillard goes on to say:

'The object of the Christian faith is not the figure of Jesus laboriously reconstructed by the theologians; it is the figure of Christ preached by the Church, Christ whose life the Church lives. The Church, indeed, holds that the Christ of faith is identical with Jesus of Nazareth and that he, having really lived among men, is a historical figure. But she is immediately concerned with Jesus *as* the Christ, the revelation of God. . . . There is no revelation apart from subjects who receive it. The revelation effected in Jesus implies not only the presence of God in him, but also the recognition of that presence by those who were the witnesses of his life. It is in the faith of the apostles and the original Christian community that Jesus has actually become the revelation of God for humanity as a whole.'[1]

And at this point Bouillard adds the important comment: 'Thus a correct view of the relation between revelation and faith places us in the same perspective as that of present-day exegesis of the New Testament: we know Jesus only through the faith of the primitive community.' We have yet to discuss how it is that we can be said to 'know Jesus', to become convinced of his presence in this way. But if it does make sense to say that such a knowledge is possible, then the possession of it would contain the guarantee that the Church has not misinterpreted the evidence at least on the substantive issue: the living Christ is the revelation of God, and the New Testament record of his earthly life is telling the essential truth about him.

Thus one would by-pass the 'hermeneutial problem' which has engaged theologians, especially on the Continent, in such apparently interminable debate. Without involving myself in this maelstrom—for

[1] 34.

94

a non-professional to rush in would be the height of folly—I shall say something later about certain presuppositions which so often seem operative here. For the moment it is only necessary to emphasize (with Bouillard) that, although one may certainly have faith in Christ without delving into the details of exegetical findings, and indeed with only the most general notions about the New Testament record, the Church's claims would be proved invalid if it could be proved that she had in fact misinterpreted the essential Gospel message. Faith in Christ living in his Church is the proof, for the faithful, that this will never happen. But, for anyone who is feeling his way towards faith, disputes among exegetes will matter. He may be held up by the very diverse results which they appear to reach. Is it reasonable, in these circumstances, to suppose that the Church's claims in the matter are plausible enough to be entertained, even in a provisional way?

It is not the business of this book to provide evidence in support of historical judgements. But I am concerned with the way in which some such judgements, when made, are related to our thinking about the question of revelation. So it seems desirable to say something here in a quite general way about the state of the evidence in the hope of counteracting certain prejudices about it which still survive in unexpected quarters. In the first place, then, there is a general consensus of scholarly opinion that the Gospels do represent the faith of the primitive Christian community and that they are intended as records of historical fact, subject to the literary conventions of the time. Secondly, there is nothing to show that this community had misunderstood Christ's message in representing it as a divine message about himself. Theories have been and are put forward about discrepancies between Christ's own message and its interpretation by the New Testament writers. They are no more than theories. The Church's interpretation cannot be ruled out on the ground that it contradicts the facts. To say the least, it is compatible with such facts as we really know. Thirdly, there is no reason to think that biblical scholars must always continue to differ from one another when they approach the biblical texts with different beliefs or presuppositions. Bouillard points out[1] that a Catholic, for example, will claim, in the light of his faith, to find more in the texts than a 'liberal Protestant' is likely to find, but that both *can* settle down to a purely scientific historical investigation of the facts at their disposal.

[1] 36–7.

This is, of course, what the modern Catholic exegete undertakes to do. Fourthly, modern exegetes concentrate so much on questions of detail, and are so anxious not to claim as a fact what cannot be fully established as a fact, that a false impression of the general picture may be given to an inexperienced reader. He may fail to recognize, for instance, that a series of indications, each of them pointing only with some probability towards some conclusion, constitute, when they are taken in conjunction, a very strong argument in favour of that conclusion. He may also fail to recognize that there are questions of great importance for the study of the New Testament which cannot be settled by an accumulation of scholarly details. To decide whether the Fourth Gospel is or is not the work of one who was a witness of the events which he purports to relate one must bring to bear a literary sensibility.[1]

After this digression, I turn again to Bouillard's book: the implications of his Blondelian apologetic have still to be drawn out. At the end of his first chapter he remarks that this apologetic is best called, from a believer's point of view, 'fundamental theology' since it shows us 'the foundation to which dogmatic and moral theology must always return, for it is there that the meaning of dogma and the meaning of the Christian life are found rooted'.[2] As he explains in a later passage, although 'revelation conditions faith as an *event*', yet faith also depends upon the 'rational autonomy of the subject' because this 'conditions it as regards *meaning*'.[3] These formulas, first employed by him in his earlier book on Karl Barth, had been discussed by Père L. Malevez,[4] who saw in them a rejection of 'the notion of a faith which enriches on the plane of meaning itself'. Bouillard therefore explains in a footnote that 'to say "the natural knowledge of God conditions faith in regard to its sense" is not at all to say that it contains all the signification of faith'. There is no question of making the '*a priori* of the natural knowledge of God' (its 'transcendental condition' as he calls it, in the language of Kant) contain the knowledge of the Incarnation or of the Trinity. 'Like all theologians', Bouillard remarks, 'I hold with Père Malevez that "the light of faith brings with it information which cannot be obtained apart from it".' That topic will be our concern later on. At present it is the '*a*

---

[1] As Professor E. L. Mascall has done to such good effect in *The Secularization of Christianity*, 240f.

[2] 37.   [3] 116.   [4] *Nouvelle Revue Théologique*, April 1959, 385–6.

priori' of the natural knowledge of God which must be emphasized. Unless we bring it with us to the question of faith, we shall not find the answer; that is, it will not be *intelligible* for us. This is the all-important conclusion which results from Bouillard's account. To bring this out more clearly I must quote a whole paragraph:

'As Barth has very justly observed, God does not reveal himself in an immediate and direct manner, but through created signs, through his special works: the history of Israel and the human reality of Jesus Christ. We cannot avoid the question which at once arises in our minds: how could the prophets and apostles, how can we ourselves, recognize the manifestation of God in these "special works"? Certainly the history of Israel, the human reality of Jesus, and the Bible that tells us about them, possess a striking originality, distinguishable to the profane eye. But this originality makes its appearance in the midst of our own world; these realities are inserted into our universe and are homogeneous with it. How could we see in them the action of God unless we bore within us, at the very heart of our spiritual activity, the power to know God, if the Absolute which is affirmed in the depths of every mind had no relationship with the God of whom the Bible speaks? It will not suffice to appeal to a miracle of revelation or of grace which takes hold of and subjugates our spirit. For this would again give rise to the question: how can we know that our faith in God is, in fact, the result of a miracle, that is, of an act of God, rather than that of an arbitrary human decision? Unless we had a pre-existing apprehension of God (however implicit) we should have no recognition of a divine revelation in history; nothing could justify us in affirming that the God of the Bible is indeed our God.'[1]

So this is what must be said to the Barthians: 'The natural power of knowing God belongs to man because God creates him in his image. The exercise of this power is the immediate translation of God's seizing upon the mind. We should, then, say with Barth—whose view here coincides with the common teaching of the Fathers—that we can know God only through God; but we must add the essential reminder that it is *we* who know him.'[2] Here it seems necessary to add that what we have to bring to the evidence of revelation is not just a 'natural knowledge' of God but supernatural knowledge in its incipient form—for if 'natural

[1] 115.　　[2] 116.

knowledge' is accepted it becomes, in the Blondelian account of it, *supernaturalized*; and, if it has been rejected, the necessary religious attitude will be lacking.

The implications of all this are obviously of the first importance for one's assessment of 'biblical theology', in so far as this is thought to be a special sort of theologizing which can dispense with philosophical notions coming 'from outside' (all theology must be biblical in the sense that it must be the understanding of the Gospel message). But it must be pointed out that we have to enter the world of the Bible, we come to it 'from outside', and we cannot abolish ourselves in the process. We must bring our own minds to bear and bring with us what they contain. When we are told that there is a 'biblical' idea of man which a theologian must accept, we may indeed agree that a certain idea of man is implied by God's revelation and that the Old and New Testaments are the record of that revelation as it has developed in the minds of God's people. But it does not follow from this that, for example, the idea of the soul entertained by the Old Testament writers is one which we have to accept as the last word on that subject. And, in general, a certain 'demythologizing' of the Bible is manifestly inevitable. This is another subject on which Bouillard's book is illuminating. Before passing on to another aspect of our topic, it may be useful to take note of the contrast between his own method of demythologization and that of Rudolph Bultmann.

There is, as Bouillard points out, a certain resemblance between his starting point and Bultmann's. For Bultmann also holds that a knowledge of God is a presupposition for any understanding of the Gospel message, but his conception of that knowledge is based on the philosophical theories of Heidegger. Here I must be content to record my opinion that this basis is, to put it mildly, insecure. It seems to amount only to the necessity of one's choosing 'authentic existence'. But the real trouble, Bouillard concludes, is that man's relation to God does not seem to be effectively determined, in Bultmann's view, by the historical revelation, which would thus be reduced to being only the occasion for our choice of 'authentic existence'. There is no room in this system, Bouillard points out, for 'a unique relation of the *man Jesus* with God, a relation which would afterwards become, in and through our Christian faith, the mediating agent of our relation with him'.[1] 'God acts in us', he

[1] 141.

98

continues, 'by means of the Christian preaching, when this arouses our faith in Christ; and his saving action touches us only in so far as we have faith. But it is also certain, according to the New Testament's teaching, that God first acted in Jesus Christ, establishing him in a unique relationship with himself . . .' Bouillard allows that the language of the New Testament borrows from Jewish apocalyptic writings and from Hellenistic systems of thought, but he claims that the context itself effects the necessary demythologization. It is plain that this language of the New Testament is used to refer not to a myth but to persons and events presented as historical. Nevertheless, it is perfectly true that the borrowed language of the New Testament is not suitable for our time: it requires to be interpreted with the aid of contemporary thought-forms, and here Bultmann is in the right.[1]

What conditions are necessary if the faith of the apostles is to be effectively communicated to ourselves today? That is the question which we are considering, and Bouillard has provided us with some answers. We have others to find, and we may find some more if we consider the conclusions of another remarkable book which appeared in 1967, Brother Gabriel Moran's *Theology of Revelation*. Let us first consider what he has to say about the exaggerated claims of some 'biblical theologians'. They have tried to make out that the Jews *founded* history. They did not, Moran says, but 'they accepted the thoroughly temporal character of human life believing that the human temporal events possessed a depth of meaning'.[2] More important for our purpose, however, is Moran's insistence that the Bible is not itself revelation: 'It would be better to begin by conceiving of revelation as an historical and continuing intersubjective communion in which man's answer is part of the revelation . . . Unless one considers in all seriousness the human person who is within the revelation and not outside it, all attempts to unite "revealed truths" with "revelatory events" will be unsuccessful.'[3] This reveals the depth of meaning in Bouillard's remark that there can be no revelation without subjects to receive it. It leads to a further criticism of exaggerated 'biblicism': 'It is a remarkable contention in much theological and catechetical writing today that revelation will become relevant to men's lives if only they study the history of Israel and realize that God revealed himself in the events of Israelite history . . . an event in which one participates and a story

[1] 133–4.   [2] 41.   [3] 50–1.

about an event in someone else's past are quite different things . . . how can a revelation of personal events in the past ever be a present revelation ?'[1]

It is at this point that Moran makes his important move. His thesis is that revelation is recapitulated and achieved not in the apostolic community in the first place but in the mind of Christ himself and that 'the fullness of revelation reached at the resurrection cannot perdure in books or institutions but only in the consciousness of the glorified Lord'.[2] Thus Moran's insistence on the personal relationship implied by revelation is combined with an insistence upon the essentially historical character of the Christian revelation. It is in its final phase a developing process in the mind of Christ: 'His awareness of God was embedded in the patterns appropriate to each stage of his life so that there was continuous growth.'[3] Moran explains this as follows: 'Christ's knowledge is a presence to himself which is at once a consciousness of God and a global awareness of all that is related to God. Such a relation in knowledge not only does not exclude a development of knowledge, but demands as its necessary complement the emergence of conceptual and communicable knowledge.'[4] As Moran points out, it has become widely accepted, even among 'traditional' theologians, that a direct knowledge of God in the present life is not at all the same as 'beatifying' knowledge. We need not ascribe to Christ's human knowledge on earth the 'beatific vision' of heaven. It is therefore permissible to see in Christ's human life 'the recapitulation of man's revelational history'.[5]

This is impressively worked out: 'Like other men, Christ knew more than he could say: he was more than he could consciously grasp. His self-expression through word and action awaited the most perfect expression of the Cross. . . . The final action of his life was the event which recapitulated his history just as his life recapitulated the whole revelational history. In that one act there was concentrated the supreme revelation of God's self-gift to the world.'[6] At this point there is, I think, a slight difficulty about Moran's argument. 'Sinful man', he here writes, 'is frightened of God,' and so the manifestation of God in Christ 'could have only one result'. For 'sinful flesh could not endure it and so the Christ had to suffer and die.' So far this is entirely acceptable, but Moran now goes on to speak of the Cross as 'the supreme revelatory action on

[1] 53–6.   [2] 58.   [3] 70.   [4] 69.   [5] 70.   [6] 72.

God's part' and therefore also 'the supreme act of participating receptivity on the part of man', still speaking of Christ himself as the participant. 'There is no revelation', he writes, 'unless there is a human consciousness taking part in it receptively and answering to God. Clearly it was not the apostles who were here the recipients; it was the one who as main participant offered his life for his brothers.'[1] If the argument is that the Cross, in order to be revelatory, requires a human awareness of it which is contemporaneous with it and that Christ must now receive this last instalment of revelation because there is nobody else capable of receiving it, then one might feel that too much is made to depend on this requirement of contemporaneity; the reasons for it do not seem to be compelling. But we need not hesitate to accept Moran's conclusion that in fact revelation 'reached its fullness' at the moment of Christ's death because it was not until then that he achieved his destiny and gained a full understanding of its meaning: 'the reception of Christ into glory is the never to be surpassed event in the revelational process'.[2]

The thesis now moves to its conclusion: 'The resurrection was for the apostles not so much a proof of his divinity as the light of understanding which was cast upon all the facts of his life. . . . At the end of the forty days and then the pentecostal experience, the apostles had received the revelational communion of God's love. They did not receive it, however, in the same way and to the same extent as Christ did (and does). . . . The risen and glorified Lord is the one place where revelation continues to happen in fullness. . . . Christ remains present to his Church as mediator of her revelation and redemption . . . he is *now revealing* God. . . . A faith that is personal, social and historical cannot spring from the acts of God in the Old Testament, nor from the accounts of the historical Christ . . .'.[3]

The consequences which follow are momentous. First, it is easier to understand what is meant by saying that revelation came to an end with the death of the last apostle. After the forty days and Pentecost they 'witnessed to the whole of revelation for the future Church'. But their understanding of revelation 'was obviously not in the form of conceptual expression and explicit judgment, but it was nonetheless a knowing experience . . . it was the indwelling Spirit who made potentially and implicitly present to the apostles the whole of revelation'.[4] They had to

[1] 73. [2] 74. [3] 74-6. [4] 86.

go on reflecting upon their knowledge and putting it into communicable form for the rest of their lives. Secondly, 'there is a very important sense in which every Christian receives (or takes part in) revelation immediately; that is, he receives it not from men or books, but from the indwelling Spirit'.[1] This will be the keynote of our whole discussion of the theology of faith.

But to see this in its proper context we should note a third consequence of Moran's thesis. It is that the apostolic witness preserved in the Church (Scripture and tradition, that is to say) is the '*mirror*' in which God is seen revealing. That, as Moran points out,[2] is the term used in the Second Vatican Council's Constitution on Divine Revelation.[3] And it can now be seen that Scripture and tradition are not two *sources* of revelation. 'The whole, the ultimate norm for the Church', Moran writes, 'is Jesus Christ . . . the Church accepts the Scriptural canon as normative for her teaching, but Scripture itself points beyond itself to the revelation accepted by Christ and shared in by the apostolic community. The Church cannot find Jesus unless she reads the Scriptures, but it is Jesus she seeks when she reads. . . . If the apostles had been the original source to whom revelation was given, we should have understood revelation simply by a scholarly study of the thought-patterns of the apostles as expressed in their writings. . . . The Scriptural words are an invitation by the apostles to enter with them into the mind of Christ. . . . The believer must read Scripture with the same attitude with which it was written, that is, as the expression of a believing individual within the Church. . . . The mind of the believer should already be in harmony with the general structure of revelation; only to the mind living in the conditions of the Covenant does Scripture surrender its meaning.'[4] This seems to me a very valuable statement. But, to go back to the first stage of the 'logic of faith', only a mind in harmony with God, already open to his revelation through its acceptance of his original approach to it, can be brought into the conditions of the Covenant.

Can it be said that such a 'logic of faith' is of interest only to a Roman Catholic reader? I see no reason why this must be so. There will be differing opinions about the nature of the Church, about the criteria for determining what its tradition really is, even about the value of such a tradition (supposing that we discovered it) in showing us the truth

[1] 92. [2] 110. [3] Ch. 11, art. 7. [4] 111-12.

about Christianity. But it does seem that there is nowadays pretty general agreement that a theologian cannot just leave out the Church, whatever exactly he means by it, in discussing Christianity. An emphasis on the ecclesial aspect of faith should not be, in general, unwelcome. In any case the astonishing change in the atmosphere of inter-confessional debate brought about by the ecumenical movement has produced a lively interest on all sides in other people's points of view, and, as a result, areas of agreement have been discovered to an extent which would have seemed incredible not so many years ago. It is hardly necessary to say—but it would be disingenuous not to recognize here—that the upheaval which has followed Vatican II (but which was preparing long before it) has produced a fluid and complicated situation in which the old landmarks and lines of division seem to have undergone a shift. 'Traditional' theologians of different communions may feel closer to each other than to revolutionary ones within their own. Leaving aside these complexities, however, it seems to be true that certain broad tendencies remain evident which do distinguish the theology of the Reform from Catholic theology in the matter of faith, and it is an essential part of the ecumenical task to recognize genuine divergences. Some illustration of what I have in mind may be afforded if I now make some reference to the work of Dr Wolfhart Pannenberg.

It may be noted, first, that Pannenberg's work represents a healthy reaction against the tendencies, encouraged by Bultmann, to play down the historical character of the Christian revelation and to make faith a matter of arbitrary decision. In *Revelation as History*[1] he writes:

'The proclamation of the Gospel cannot assert that the facts are in doubt and that the leap of faith must be made in order to achieve certainty. If this sort of assertion were allowed to stand, then one would have to cease being a theologian and Christian. The proclamation must assert that the facts are reliable and that you can therefore place your faith, life and future on them.'[2]

But this, from the point of view of Catholic theology, makes the knowledge of faith unnecessary. Pannenberg holds that 'the knowledge or

[1] An English version of *Offenbarung Als Geschichte*, published by Sheen and Ward in 1969.
[2] 138.

revelation is not supernatural'. Otherwise, he says, 'the Christian truth is made into a truth for the in-group, and the Church becomes a gnostic community'.[1] I shall be proposing that this knowledge is supernatural on the ground that the life of faith is a *new* life, cognitive as well as conative, the beginning of eternal life. Pannenberg writes: 'Faith has to do with the future. This is the essence of trust . . . The Christian risks his trust, life and future on the fact of God's having been revealed in the fate of Jesus.'[2] This conception of faith not as supernatural knowledge but as trust marks an age-old difference of approach. But both Pannenberg and I are concerned to emphasize that the evidence on which faith rests must be available to all men, and that man's knowledge of God is, in all circumstances, the work of God himself. Moreover Pannenberg's account of what knowledge is fits in with what I have been saying about it: 'True knowledge really occurs only when someone is wholly involved, so that he allows himself to be engaged by the object in the cognitive act . . . to the extent to which the object concerned with its peculiar character can engage the person.'[3] I have described 'supernatural' knowledge in much the same terms. What can 'engage the person', in the last analysis, save God's action, God in his action?

Both the differences and the resemblances between Pannenberg's view and the 'logic of faith' as described in this chapter are shown strikingly at a number of points in *Revelation as History*. For example, we read:

'The logical priority of insight over faith safeguards precisely the gratuitousness of faith, since it includes the awareness that it is justified by something different from itself . . . in what does the truth consist of on which the believer relies *before* his own act of faith? When this question remains without an adequate answer or is even rejected, the decision of faith is required as a work from the person called to believe.'[4]

Faith is indeed justified by this 'insight' in the sense that it builds on natural reason and would be meaningless if it did not do so. But it justifies itself in the sense that it has its own object (it sees further than natural reason) and has its own guarantee deriving from that object. All knowledge of God is 'gratuitous' in the sense that it cannot be built up

[1] 137.   [2] 138.   [3] 188.   [4] 196.

out of the materials already at our disposal. Yet Pannenberg writes also that the believer 'lives always only in the light of a provisional knowledge, in anticipation of the truth finally to be known only in the *eschaton,* but in anticipation too of a knowledge of what is believed that resolves doubts arising here and at the present time'.[1] He has referred earlier to 'the real certainty of faith'.[2] But if faith is just 'trust' and not also union with Christ, the first stage in a new life, what is the justification for this certainty?

Pannenberg discusses in a most interesting passage the need for a 'theology of reason.' It would describe reason 'in its historical structure of sketching and reflecting, but also in its essential (not, however, always factual) openness to a truth always presupposed but never grasped in the act of thinking out the sketch'.[3] And on this basis he insists that 'no one can have valid rational grounds for deciding against the Christian proclamation's claim to truth'. But can one have merely rational (historical) grounds for adhering to it absolutely? Pannenberg goes on to say that his thesis, 'maintained even by Thomas Aquinas in spite of the division between nature and supernature', must be 'an inalienable property of the Christian message . . . because of the unity of truth'. St Thomas, of course, does hold that faith is reasonable and that truth is one. But he also holds that faith is more than an anticipation. And this real difference of approach is evident again in Pannenberg's conclusion: 'The understanding of reason and knowledge here indicated means that both live in anticipation in regard to their relationship to truth. This proleptic structure, which determines the form of all acts of knowledge . . . is proper to the knowledge of the Christ-event also precisely in view of its content . . . Jesus Christ himself is the anticipation of the *eschaton*. That is why this structure will be proper also to all knowledge of his person and history.'[4] What is missing here, from the point of view of traditional theology, is the thesis that the Kingdom to which we look forward has nevertheless come into existence already with the resurrection of Christ and the sending of his Spirit. It is here to be found. The form in which we find it is provisional, but in finding it we are in touch with the eternal.

The Lutheran theologian Dr Robert W. Jenson in his book *The Knowledge of Things Hoped For,*[5] a most illuminating and acute discussion of the 'hermeneutical problem', concludes that 'the statement of the

[1] 197.   [2] 189.   [3] 198.   [4] 198–200.   [5] O.U.P., 1969.

Resurrection *itself*, "Jesus is risen", cannot be affirmed or denied in a report of historical research'. And, he goes on, 'it is this that is, so it seems to me, necessary to make Pannenberg's hermeneutic work'.[1] Therefore 'the proclamation's projection of history as a whole' is not 'that with which historical investigation does, or should work',[2] as Pannenberg would have it. 'Empirical investigation cannot work with this projection', Jenson goes on, 'for to use it is to affirm as having occurred an event that cannot be discerned empirically.' That seems to me the right comment: natural reason alone will not provide us with the fact of the resurrection as a certainly established one. What solution of the problem does Jenson offer? He agrees with Pannenberg that 'appeals to "intuition", "the eye of faith", etc., fail: the believer has the same organs as anyone else'. (But does he have only the same evidences before him as anyone else?) 'We *prophesy* that Jesus is risen,' Jenson concludes. And in answer to the question of our justification for this, he writes: 'We do this in response to a *command* to do so, the command to proclaim the Gospel which is addressed to us in the proclamation of the Gospel when we hear it. Either this command enforces itself on us or it does not. Thus the affirmation of the Resurrection depends upon the *act* of living proclamation. . . .'[3] But must we not, then, *hear* God commanding us? Must we not *know* him in a new way?

A reader of Jenson's book will, I think, see clearly enough that in the 'hermeneutical debate' as discussed by him there are certain presuppositions at work, as Pannenberg has already suggested to us. They may be summed up as follows: the certainty of faith has nothing to do with 'mysticism', which is sometimes referred to as 'gnosticism'; we cannot claim contact, here and now, with the mind of Christ; faith is a looking-forward to a knowledge of him, not that knowledge itself. It seemed right for me, before going any further, to make clear that I shall not be accepting these points of view.

THE ACT OF FAITH

According to traditional theology, an act of faith must have the following characteristics: it must be rational, that is, it must be in some sense based on reason; it must be free, that is, it cannot be forced upon a man

[1] 229.   [2] 230.   [3] 231.

by any irresistible pressure, whether external (obviously) or (less obviously) internal; it must be supernatural, that is, it cannot be achieved simply by the employment of those powers which are our natural endowment; and it must be certain, that is, it must be made with full conviction. The problem of the act of faith (or the problem of 'the analysis of faith', as it is often called) is to reconcile these character-istics with one another. It has caused theologians so much trouble that it became known as the *crux theologorum*. It presents itself very often to non-theologians (although not, as a rule, in this schematic form), and they may have difficulty in coming across anything about it which seems to them to make much sense of it.

In 1948 I published a book called *Certainty: Philosophical and Theological*. It was received, on the whole, with polite incredulity, and is now out of print. Its central theme, however, as we shall see later, is nowadays to be found commonly enough in one form or another in the works of theologians who concern themselves with the matter (it is not treated as often as one might expect it to be). I shall begin this discus-sion of the act of faith with a brief account of the conclusions to which I came in *Certainty*.

It seemed to me, then, that current theology on the subject was still largely influenced by theories of a rationalistic sort. De Lugo, for example, in the middle of the seventeenth century, tried to justify faith intellectually by appealing to evidence of a purely historical nature. The fact of revelation is discovered by a process of discursive reason-ing; we do not have to *believe* it, to discover it *in faith*. And if we go on to say that the truth of the Christian message follows from the discovery that there has been a revelation, the whole process of thought is a discursive one, and there seems to be no good ground for calling faith 'supernatural'. Cardinal Billot, whose views were very widely accepted by twentieth-century theologians, realized that one cannot reduce the act of faith to the conclusion of a merely logical exercise and proposed a theory of non-discursive faith. He pointed out that we must explain somehow that the motive of faith is the authority of God. And he proposed that our motive for believing what God tells us is not the *evidence* that what he tells us is true; it is simply our trust in *him*. Thus, according to Billot, the supernatural character of faith will be safe-guarded. But he still wants to say that we get to know of the authority of God the revealer only through the scientific evidence. And, if we have once *proved* the fact of revelation in this way (which, pretty obviously, we cannot in fact do so as to put it beyond all doubt), then we have no need to and indeed *cannot* 'pin our faith' on *God* in regard to it. Billot stressed the analogy between faith in God and faith in human beings. But we 'pin our faith' on people only when we have no independent evidence that what they tell us is true. If we have evidence already about the fact of revelation, if we know that God has spoken, then we *must* accept what he tells us because we know that he cannot be deceiving us. This is not to 'pin our faith' on God's authority for the truths of Christianity because, in Billot's account, we are discovering these truths by dint of sheer logic. And if the logic is not coercive (as in fact it is not) 'pinning our faith' on God's authority will be just credulity, for, in this account, we cannot claim to know him supernaturally as the revealer.

That was also the difficulty which Thomist accounts of faith's certainty encountered but seemed not to recognize. They were quite clear that the scientific evidence does not justify faith's certainty, that there is a certainty which belongs to faith itself over and above whatever force of persuasion the scientific evidence may be supposed to have, and that this certainty rests on God's authority. How, then, do we make contact with this authority? How do we *know* that God does authorize us to accept the Christian message? To this question the Thomist accounts seemed to give no clear and definite answer. Somehow we have to believe in God's authority without, as it were, actually coming across it. God's authority can only be believed in if we make contact with God, with God *as* authorizing us to believe in his message, but this the Thomists seemed unwilling to allow. Knowledge of God, in Thomist systems, is never direct. So, since he has to make contact with us in some way, we find these theologians appealing, in default of the intellect, to the *will* as the faculty which is primarily operative in the act of faith. It is true that, unless a man keeps his mind open, he cannot receive God's word. He must be willing to receive it. But his certainty must follow from his reception of it, not from anything else. And the suggestion seemed to be, in these accounts, that God could provide us with certainty, by-passing the intellect, by the attraction which he exercises upon the will. Certainty can be somehow injected into us although we have no *evidence* that what we believe is true. Once the contact with God is established in the will, the intellect, it is urged, can observe the effects of it. But this attempt to bring the two faculties together cannot remedy the situation when once the will has advanced beyond the intellect. It is a Thomist principle (and only common-sense) that the will must always *follow* the intellect in the sense that we can will nothing unless we have some knowledge of it. Here this principle seems to be abandoned. And so one may find, in popular apologetics, the notion that faith is an act of the will in the sense that the evidence is not quite sufficient but that the gap can be closed by an act of the will. God will then make us certain somehow (and this is where the 'supernatural' comes in). Faith is indeed a sort of leap—but not into the dark, as this theory would have it. It is a leap into the light.

But what of St Thomas himself? Does he advocate this sort of wish-ful thinking? Has he not been misinterpreted? Does he really accept a 'faculty-psychology'? Is not his 'voluntarism' only apparent? It seemed to me that St Thomas was at any rate not clear about it, that this peculiar emphasis on the will was part of his own teaching. At the same time there were certainly suggestions of something more promis-ing. He does seem to suggest sometimes that there is some special awareness of God at the heart of an act of faith. But these suggestions seemed vague and inconclusive. In the baroque theology (which had largely lost sight of the distinction between *ratio* and *intellectus*) this side of St Thomas's thought remained unexplored. But there was some excuse for it. St Thomas does say that in faith we receive a share of God's own knowledge, that we are in touch with the Primal Truth and so forth, but he is prevented by his basic epistemological views from asserting formally and unambiguously that God presents himself, is himself *evident* to us, revealing himself in Christ.

These conclusions reached in *Certainty* will be the subject of further enquiry. There is one more to be added. I ventured also to criticize the famous thesis of the great Jesuit thinker Pierre Rousselot about the 'eyes of faith'.[1] It seemed to me that Rousselot was saying that faith gives reason eyes to see in the sense that faith merely empowers the reason to see evidence of a historical, scientific, kind which it could not otherwise see. If the historical facts are waiting to be discovered one does not see why reason should not find them. If they are not already waiting, then faith cannot put them there. And I thought that followers

[1] 'Les Yeux de la Foi', articles in *Recherches de Science Religieuse*, 1910.

of Rousselot, speaking of the Church as a 'supernatural sign', also failed to see that what is still required is *supernatural evidence* because they seemed not to realize that to find God's meaning in the Church we must find *God himself* 'meaning' his Church, giving us his own guarantee that he lives in it by manifesting his presence in it to us.

To sum up, then, what emerged from all these criticisms, it seemed that one could only reconcile the characteristic possessed by the act of faith by allowing at the heart of it an apprehension of God himself in his revelatory activity: such an apprehension, though obscure, is capable of conveying certainty; it is free, because it is avoidable; it is supernatural, because it gives us fresh evidence over and above the historical evidence and initiates a new life, the life of grace; it is rational, because reason points in its direction, providing us with a medium, the 'Christian fact', in and through which it becomes available to us.

This view appeared to be present in the theological tradition but only in implicit form. It was possible to quote a number of *obiter dicta* which could point only to this conclusion, and, if the mystical life is the life of faith in its fullest development (certainly a traditional thesis), then, I argued, that apprehension of God vouched for by the mystics must be found embryonically in faith. The clearest statement of what I was looking for came to light at the last stage of my amateur researches, a passage from an article by Père Philippe de la Trinité, and I quote it again here: 'The Thomist and Suarezian position shows a clear discrepancy between its principles and its effective conclusion . . . what is at stake is the ontological realism of the supernatural order, but the realization of this seems very shadowy. . . . To explain the supernaturality of faith by its object we must go beyond the notional level of concepts and the activity of the judgement, while yet remaining in the line of the intelligence, for faith is an intellectual virtue; we must appeal to the ontological and immediate grasp of God as he is in himself. To find a term which is substantially supernatural we must go to subsistent Truth . . . to seize upon this term otherwise than by analogy, the intellect must, therefore, enter into a direct relation with it.'[1] In my view we can never 'seize upon this term' just by the use of 'analogy'; we always seize upon it directly, though mediately. Otherwise this statement of the position still seems to me most satisfactory.

[1] *Etudes Carmélitaines*, April 1937, 175 f.

Canon Roger Aubert's big book, *Problème de l'Acte de Foi*, then reached me, and I added to *Certainty* an Appendix about it which I shall now summarize. This book of over eight hundred pages, dealing with the history of the subject as a whole, is concerned for about half its length with the various theories about the act of faith which had been put forward in the previous sixty years or so. It was reassuring to find that Aubert too could not see how Billot's theory (originally due to Pesch, he points out) justified faith's certainty. How do we find God's authority as the motive of faith? The authority itself is a sure ground of certainty, but 'Pesch and his successors . . . only evade a most real problem by moving over to the objective order'.[1] A footnote makes the significant remark that the problem is a modern one which the thirteenth-century theologians did not directly envisage. Aubert finds also the same difficulty as I found in Rousselot's theory: 'According to him we believe *because the reason perceives the arguments* which prove that God has spoken; for the eyes of faith are only the reason made more penetrating to *see the arguments*. Thus the effective cause of the act of faith remains the perception of the motives of credibility by the reason; the will and grace intervene only to make possible the perception of these motives. Does it not give these too much honour and give to the speculative judgement of credibility . . . an importance which the ancient and medieval traditions had not granted it?'[2] (We shall see later that this interpretation of Rousselot does not go unchallenged.) And Aubert insists that theologians must also be epistemologists if they are to grapple with this problem.[3]

But what I found most gratifying about Aubert's book was the evidence which he produced of far more support for the position which I had advocated than I had been able to find myself. He quotes Karl Adam as saying that 'the majority of Catholic theologians, St Thomas . . . Capreolus . . . Molina . . . and many more, are in agreement that divine faith rests in the last analysis upon an interior and mystical illumination . . .'.[4] Adam, as Aubert points out, minimizes the role of intelligence in favour of a 'sentiment', but his theory of an intuition 'is generally defensible, and constitutes a very attractive though still too vague attempt at a solution of a problem which the theologians usually brush aside in a far too light-hearted manner'.[5] I must quote in this connection one other passage: 'Scheeben was one of the great labourers

[1] 238-9 (References are to the first edition). [2] 510. [3] 445. [4] 523. [5] 153.

in this work of replacing in its position of honour the "mystical" aspect of faith: for him the light of faith is a grace by which God makes himself known to the soul without intermediary, as being himself who speaks. This doctrine seemed sufficiently grounded in the whole Catholic tradition for so prudent a writer as Lebreton to write on the very eve of the Encyclical *Pascendi*: "The Spirit of Christ, which lives and speaks in the Church, lives also in each of the faithful. . . . If you ask one of those truly faithful souls what is the most powerful motive of their faith, they will perhaps have some difficulty about self-analysis. But on reflection they will recognize that their most pressing reason for believing is that they feel themselves impelled by God".'[1]

That there was a steady recognition in the past of the supreme importance of the 'inner voice' for the certainty of faith was something which had been obvious to me for some time (de Lugo's and Billot's rationalistic approach was clearly a relatively modern one). But I had not found in the tradition an explicit recognition of the *intellectual* character of this experience. It appeared from the passages quoted that Aubert was offering the sort of interpretation of it which I thought necessary if it was to be presented as philosophically respectable, as a genuine awareness of God's activity, of *God* in his activity. What else could he mean by his acknowledgement that we must accept the appeal to a 'supernatural perception'?[2] There was further encouragement in the acknowledgement that St Thomas related the act of faith not to the *ratio* but to the *intellectus*, 'that form of non-discursive knowledge which modern scholastics so easily neglect and which has yet such a great importance in the Thomist system'.[3] Nevertheless it did not seem that, for St Thomas, the 'inner voice' spoke to the mind directly but only indirectly through an appeal to the *will*. And further study of Aubert's book forced me to conclude that he was himself still influenced by such notions and had not in fact reached the conclusion to which he had seemed at first to be moving. For he eventually offers us as his solution, presented as a 'working hypothesis', that God 'inspires in the believer, by a supernatural motion exercised upon his will, a strong desire to see him . . . and to love him. . . . Faith appears to him on various grounds as the means to prepare for and to realize already in an inchoative way this union with God . . . there is an imperious

[1] 724. [2] 720. [3] 487n.

inclination which impels him to give his adhesion to God's word.' And it is on this basis that he appeals to 'a supernatural intuition of the fact of revelation' as the basis for faith's certainty.[1]

But Aubert's book revealed that there are also far more *obiter dicta* than I had realized to support an account of this 'intuition' in fundamentally intellective terms (but without overlooking the necessary collaboration of the will and the interdependence of intellect and will). To take just two examples out of many, there are the words of Père Hugueny in his Introduction to Tauler's Sermons: 'Mystical knowledge begins with the supernatural act of faith . . . God, always present in the soul, is made known there by his grace, in the way in which the soul becomes manifest to itself, through the consciousness which it gains of his activity. It is this beginning of obscure consciousness . . . which gives life and conviction to our act of faith,'[2] and there are the words of Peter Olivi in the thirteenth century that 'when it is said that faith relies ultimately on a word spoken by God, this must be understood to mean that it relies on God himself and his light and power, revealing himself efficaciously in that communication . . .'.[3] It is just this frank recognition of the intellect's contact with God himself as revealer which needs to be added to the Thomist account so well summed up in the words of Père Dhanis: 'According to the Thomist tradition, the formal motive of faith is the uncreated Word, which mysteriously guarantees itself at the same time that it guarantees its content.'[4]

Here I wish to say that Aubert's book seems to me a very fine one except in the one particular, just noted, in which he seems to fall short. And it must be emphasized that, despite his tendency to 'voluntarism', one of the most valuable elements in the book is his insistence that the act of faith is the act of the whole person (in this connection it is worth remarking that a writer to whom he gives much praise, Canon F. Mallet, is now known not to be the author of *Qu'est que la foi?*—it was written by Blondel, but it was thought best that Mallet should lend his name to it).

The next stage in this story, which will lead us to a further sounding of the problem, was the appearance of an article-review[5] of *Certainty*

[1] 729–30. [2] Quoted by Aubert, 710.
[3] Quoted by Aubert, 726.
[4] *Nouvelle Revue Théologique*, 1939, 1102, quoted by Aubert, 613.
[5] 'The Certainty of Faith', *The Downside Review*, Spring 1949.

by Père Alexandre Durand, whose premature death not long afterwards was a great loss to Catholic theology. He accepted, at least by implication, my view about our knowledge of God, whether natural or supernatural, that it is a direct awareness through and beyond the knowledge of creatures, and explicitly accepted my main thesis that in the knowledge of faith we have an 'intuition of God in his testifying' (nowadays I should speak of an 'apprehension'). He found himself 'in ready accordance' with my criticisms of the theories of de Lugo, of Billot, and of the Thomists. And what I found particularly encouraging was his agreement with the contention that it will not do to appeal to an action of grace upon the *will*, in order to justify faith, if there is not *pari passu* an action of grace upon the intellect: 'this sort of "voluntarism" . . . is a mere expedient, a timid and rather shamefaced solution of the problem of faith'. But Durand considered that I had quite misunderstood Rousselot's theory of faith. I had concluded, as had Aubert also, that, when Rousselot tells us that the grace of faith offers us no new object for our knowledge but illuminates a new aspect in the object already known, he must be making the perception of credibility by the reason, the judgement passed upon the historical evidences, the effective cause of faith. Durand assures us that Rousselot's view does not exclude from the act of faith an awareness of 'God-in-his-testifying' and that such an awareness is indeed precisely what he was insisting upon. On the question of Rousselot's own mind in the matter, one must bow, I think, to Durand's authority. I can only say that it does not seem to me at all obvious in what Rousselot wrote.

What is important, however, about this for my present purposes is the account which Durand went on to give of the function of signs in the process which leads to faith in revelation:

'It is the nature of a sign not to exist *as a sign*, as signifying . . . except in so far as in it and through it the mind perceives and grasps its relation with what is signified and, within this relation, grasps the object signified itself, in a unique synthetic intuitive act. It can be seen at once why knowledge by signs is *sui generis* and irreducible to any other kind of awareness. It is not *discursive*, i.e. articulated in distinct moments, and in that sense it is *intuitive*. But on the other hand, as the object (God) is attained in a sign, this is not the strict intuition that is given in the beatific vision. . . . In so far as faith enfolds an intuition of God-in-his-testifying, the motive of faith is "seen", intuitively grasped. . . . But in so far as God reveals himself by signs, the motive of faith, descried through and beyond the signs, is "believed".'

This seems to me an illuminating and wholly acceptable account of how we believe in God's authority.

When I objected in *Certainty* to theories about a 'supernatural sign' deriving in one way or another from Rousselot, it was on the ground that they did not make clear that the mind must, as Durand put it, 'grasp the object signified itself' or that they left the nature of this 'object' nebulous. My own tendency has been to go to the other extreme and to insist so much on the 'interior word', God's testifying, as to separate it unduly from the external sign which both points towards it and receives its own meaning from it. And I cannot now understand why, in my reply to Durand,[1] I made some difficulty about agreeing with him that 'the sign whereby God authenticates the Church's claims is the Church herself'. To be effective as a sign, she needs the 'interior word', 'God-in-his-testifying', but Durand had been quite clear about that. I had written: 'A sign conveys the spiritual power of him who makes it, so that in seeing the sign we find his meaning . . . to find God's meaning, then, we must find God meaning. And what he means we shall find to be his Church. Then we shall find him in her—we can only show her pointing to God who will declare it to us.'[2] And I had also written: 'We hear God's voice, but he speaks to us in his Church. The visible Church, her claims and teachings are in the foreground, although God pervades it with his transcendent authority.'[3] The fact that God speaks to us in his Church, in the life of the Church which is the life of Christ, is itself the proof of her mission as the Church. That is what I take Durand to be saying, and that is the conclusion to which, with whatever fumblings, I had arrived.

There are no fumblings in Durand's account, and I shall draw on it for a little longer. The testimony on which faith rests, he tells us, has several aspects. There is 'the mediation of human and created testimony . . . the word of God's spokesman who is a witness who sees what he speaks of'. Then there is 'a further testimony of God, not now in word

---

[1] 'Second Thoughts on Certainty', *The Downside Review*, Spring 1950. I ought to add that I now find this article confused and unsatisfactory at several points.

[2] *Certainty*, 105–6.   [3] 119.

but in action, a language of action . . . the various "signs" with which God accredits his messenger'. Finally there is 'the intuition of revelation and Christianity as a *strictly divine value*' which 'constitutes in its turn a new testimony, a new word of God in me'. All this is 'the object of a global apprehension, a direct and immediate grasp, and in this sense an *intuition*, if by "intuition" is meant an apprehension which excludes all reasoning, all discourse, any dialectical process that culminates in a conclusion, even the most rapid inference. What is the object of this intuition ? . . . *God himself who gives us a sign, God who speaks to me*.' And again:

'Revelation is a supernatural reality made incarnate in facts. It involves, therefore, a double element, or, if you will, presents two complementary aspects which are *inseparable* and *irreducible* one to the other: a pheno-menal and empirical element and an extra-phenomenal, metempirical element. Considered as an empirical element, i.e. as a fact of experience that has made its mark in history, revelation (the fact of revelation) is attained by a *scientia positiva*. . . . But in its metempirical and super-natural aspect revelation claims a "judgement of value". . . . Now it is precisely because it is impossible to separate the two elements in revelation, the "natural" from the "supernatural" . . . that the assertion "a divine revelation exists" . . . is only possible to the believer, i.e. *in and through his act of faith*.'

I have quoted these passages partly because they throw light on some criticisms of *Certainty*, justly made by Durand, which should be mentioned here if only as warnings of the sort of ungrounded assump-tions which an autodidact in theology may make. First, I had accepted the view that it would be possible in theory for a man (in particular, an Apostle) to be wholly convinced by purely historical, 'scientific', evidence that God was revealing himself in Christ, and I had made it a further objection to Rousselot's view that he did not admit this pos-sibility. The passage last quoted from Durand seems to be a sufficient answer to that. Secondly, I was still under the impression that the First Vatican Council, in laying it down that God can be known by the mind's natural light, was concerned to make a distinction between a natural and a supernatural knowledge of God. It was from Durand that I learned that it was concerned to emphasize that a knowledge of

God is possible without the help of Christ's revelation of him. (It is still open to anyone, Durand went on to argue, to say that when there is knowledge of God reason is always aided by grace. That conclusion, however, I am not prepared to accept: there is, I have maintained, a 'natural' knowledge of God which is the *summons* to the life of grace—grace, we may say, is acting on a man but it is not yet active within him.) Finally, I had taken up with a theory about a difference between natural and supernatural knowledge of God in respect of their modes of operation, natural knowledge always involving sense-presented materials and supernatural knowledge being always a direct intuitive awareness of God, this being attested most obviously by the experience of the mystics. There is, as Durand pointed out, no good reason for maintaining such a dichotomy. Nevertheless the reference to the mystics, which he regarded as irrelevant, still seems to me of importance as testifying in a particularly cogent fashion to that directness which attaches to all knowledge of God even in its obscurest forms.

It may be asked whether these discussions of twenty years ago are worth recording in such detail. The answer is that they are not out of date but altogether relevant to the present position of the problem of faith's certainty, as the next chapter will show. Before ending this one, I shall mention certain features in a little book, *Faith Seeks Understanding*, by Father John Coventry which appeared in 1951 and was dedicated to Durand, 'who well knows that this book is already his'.

Coventry's first chapter is an account of the 'preamble' of faith as it used to be set forth (and may still be found) in apologetical treatises. This purports to prove the fact of revelation and the claims of the Church to be its depositary by the ordinary processes of reason; then there is a duty to believe what the Church teaches (this is where faith comes into play), since the Church has God's authority. We have seen already a number of reasons for regarding such an account as unsatisfactory. Coventry gives these reasons and adds some further comments to which I now refer. He points out that the Gospels do not make use of any such preamble: they simply ask us to *believe*. And if the fact of revelation could be proved in this simple and straightforward way why does not everyone accept it? It is true that the Gospels offer us 'signs' of Christ's divinity, but it certainly looks as though faith were something which one needs to have so as to *read* the signs. At this point

I have a slight difficulty about Coventry's statement of his position. 'The point is not', he writes, 'that the argument of the preamble turns out on inspection to be anywhere shaky or invalid' but that faith must 'generate its own (supernatural) certainty from inside.'[1] With the second part of this statement I am, of course, in complete agreement. The difficulty is that Coventry has written on the same page that 'there are questions of history, and about them one could have only historical certainty, the kind of certainty proper to history, which is not always of great weight . . .', which might seem inconsistent with the statement that the arguments are not 'shaky'. It becomes clear, however, that what Coventry means is that the Christian explanation of the fact of Christianity, based on the acknowledgement of the resurrection as a fact, is the only one which makes *good sense*. The difficulty, indeed, is only apparent, but the status of the rational arguments in this matter is so important an issue that the point needed to be made.

Coventry goes on to remark that there could be no question of a free acceptance of revelation if the fact that it has occurred could be fully established on purely historical and logical grounds. To the objection that some people could be unwilling to subject their minds to God, however plain the evidence, Coventry replies that the uneducated have no intellectual pride to provide such an obstacle, so that faith would become, for them at any rate, inevitable.[2] It seems to me that one must simply deny that, if the fact of revelation were fully established on historical and logical grounds, it would be possible to admit these grounds and *at the same time* to reject the fact which they establish (although it would be possible *at a subsequent moment* to dismiss from one's mind a conclusion which proved a disagreeable one). It is important to recognize that one cannot reject evidence in so far as that evidence is actually being seen. One is free to open one's mind to it beforehand or not to do so. And one can be free to get rid of it afterwards or at any rate to disregard it. As Coventry points out, the fact that some people (Newman, for example) have found the historical evidence incontestable but have not yet found it possible to *believe* is not an argument for a 'free' acceptance of a conclusion based on merely historical and logical grounds but rather an indication that the certainty of faith does not rest on such grounds.

And finally Coventry makes the point that millions of people have

[1] 16.   [2] 19.

been certain of their faith who have never heard of the 'preamble' and would have made little of it if they had done so. As he says, it seems to have been thought up to satisfy a certain modern mentality. If it were the true account of faith's reasonableness, he adds, 'we are in danger of being forced to the conclusion that till quite recent times the faith of the Church was not reasonable after all'. For in 'the Church of the Apostles, the Church of the Fathers and the Church in many centuries' the method of the preamble was not adopted.[1] 'The conclusion then follows that 'the true function of the preamble . . . is to make plain to all that faith is already reasonable in its own right'. This must mean that faith has its own evidence, for we have been told that 'it generates its own (supernatural) evidence from inside'. It seems a little strange that Coventry does not employ some such formula here.

This introduces a major difficulty which I find in a passage (in Coventry's second chapter) which I now quote in full:

'All that Christ teaches externally by word and deed and life the Spirit teaches internally by enlightening the soul. It is this that makes faith possible. God can ensure infallibly that he is understood and that the signs are read aright, by joining to the external signs what we may call the interior sign of his grace. Without the latter the external signs would be material indices—pointers into the darkness, vague sketches of a truth we could only inaccurately and uncertainly guess at. But when the internal signs are coupled to and complement the external, then, and then only, can the latter fulfil their function formally as signs. They become meaningful and accurate signs only when we can read their meaning. It is not that God in giving grace injects into the mind a sense of conviction when the external evidence does not warrant it; nor does he infuse into the mind a new and interior type of evidence which is intangible, inexpressible, incommunicable. *He gives eyes to see the evidence that is there already for all to see.* He enables us to see the value of the evidence as evidence, to comprehend its worth and relevance and where it is leading to. It is only when we can thus discern the message that we can appraise the value of the means by which it is expressed and conveyed to us. It is only when we grasp what the signs are signs of, that we can apprehend them as meaningful and authentic signs.'[2]

[1] 17.   [2] 30-1.

The beginning and the end of this passage cause me no difficulty; they say very clearly what I should wish to say. But the middle of it seems to strike a different note. Surely the external evidence, simply as external and apart from the 'interior sign', does *not* warrant absolute conviction? Surely the 'interior sign', the awareness of 'God-in-his-testifying', *does* infuse into the mind 'a new and interior type of evidence which is intangible, inexpressible, incommunicable'? It is true that the external and internal signs are bound up with one another and that the external sign is not properly a sign until it is illuminated by the interior one, but it remains that it is the interior one which provides that absolute conviction which was still lacking when the evidence was viewed simply as a matter of phenomenal history and as matter for rational argument. And when Coventry puts into italics the sentence 'He gives eyes to see the evidence that is there already for all to see', how could this fail to suggest to the reader, if he relates it to the other statements to which I have just alluded, that the grace of faith merely strengthens our powers of assessing historical evidences and of arguing on the basis of them? It is clear that such an interpretation is completely at variance with other statements in the passage, but there is some excuse for wondering, at this point in the book, whether these other statements do really represent Coventry's mind. It was this sort of language in this sort of context which had led me to suppose that what I had loosely referred to as 'the school of Rousselot' did not admit, or at least did not clearly recognize, that there must be an awareness of God himself testifying to his revelation of himself in Christ if the certainty of faith is to be intelligible.

That Coventry does accept that conclusion becomes quite clear as one proceeds. A few pages later he faces the objection: 'You cannot say you merely "believe" you have the authority of God; that is a vicious circle; the process of faith must come to rest somewhere in something that can be called knowledge, a direct awareness of an evident object.' This indeed is the crucial point, and Coventry accepts it; 'there must be', he writes, 'some kind of vision'. And he goes on to say that '*what* we directly apprehend in faith is not the truth revealed but *God-revealing-this truth*'[1] (his italics). When he adds that 'God's grace and interior sign enables us to grasp the exterior sign as conclusive *evidence* of, *making evident*, his revealing of the truth', there can now be

[1] 37.

no doubt that we must have the fresh evidence of 'God-revealing-this-truth' before we can see the exterior sign as evidencing itself. God makes us a sign and we find him in it; only in finding him do we know it as a sign of him. We find him *in* his activity in Christ. And at this point it may be suggested that this language of an 'exterior' and an 'interior' sign needs some clarification. The sign, as a matter of 'scientific' evidence, is only a 'pointer' or 'signpost'. The sign which is Christ is both 'inner' and 'outer'. What we find is both the human life of Christ, which belongs to the 'outer' phenomenal world, and *God's* action in him. When it is said that we hear God's voice authenticating the outward sign, constituting it *as* a sign, what should be meant is that we find him in it. But it has always to be borne in mind that this is (normally at least) a recognition, for the God whom we find is the God who is at work in the activities of the human mind as such. And thus we may say that an 'inner voice' now speaks to us plainly and distinctly. Coventry, I think, would not disagree. He concludes most helpfully that 'it is God we reach and not merely his "external gesture", just as it is our friend whom we encounter, and not some word or action hanging in mid air and unrooted in a self'.[1]

To my mind, there are no further difficulties in this valuable book. It was a great disappointment when, not long after its publication, it was thought proper to withdraw it from circulation. This was because it might have seemed out of harmony with the Encyclical *Humani Generis* of 1950, which included a remark about 'the certainty with which the divine origin of the Christian revelation can be grasped by the light of natural reason alone'. In 1967, however, Coventry published another little book, *The Theology of Faith*, in which I can detect no change in his views on the question which is concerning us here.

8. THE EXPERIENCE OF FAITH

In the early years of the century the reduction of the Christian faith to human experience was rightly seen to be the conclusion to which those doctrines which are, in the technical theological sense, 'Modernist' must lead. And this led to a recrudescence of theological rationalism among the orthodox and to an attitude of suspicion in face of all appeals

[1] 38.

to 'experience' in theology. After the Second World War there were attempts to restore the balance on the part of those who were called, by their opponents, the 'new theologians'. The Encyclical *Humani Generis* was understood to be a disapprobation of them, and some of the most intelligent and best-informed among Roman Catholic thinkers found themselves for the time being in a very awkward position (they are regarded nowadays as pillars of orthodoxy, and spend a good deal of their time trying to curb the extravagances of those 'new theologians' of the present day who seem to be moving back again towards 'Modernism'). Papal encyclicals, despite the peremptory tone which they sometimes adopt, do not claim to settle once and for all questions which are matters of dispute among theologians. But those who are in communion with the Roman See cannot just ignore them. And so, after 1950, the theology of faith did not show that development (along the lines indicated in the previous chapter) which one might have hoped for. That is why the discussions of twenty years ago may claim to be of interest. It is only in the fairly recent past that such discussions have come into the foreground again as a result of the theological revival which we are now witnessing.

Already in the 'fifties, however, Canon Jean Mouroux had published his book entitled (in the English version) *The Christian Experience* in which he accepted[1] the following formulas: 'If I have infused faith, I know with certainty by an intuitive knowledge that I have it, because the reality of the faith implies this reflection upon itself . . . my certainty that I possess infused faith is of the experimental order'. And he went on in the same place to reject the theory of a 'natural faith'. Still more striking were some of his remarks in a little book *Je Crois en Toi, Structure personelle de la foi*.[2] Speaking of the Thomist principle that the object of faith is the 'First Truth', he points out that it has given rise to frequent misunderstandings:

'For us the word "truth" is abstract, and denotes a relation. The adjective "first" corrects it, setting this truth on its own, on the absolute level . . . there remains the danger that the formula will be understood only at the abstract level, which leads to false perspectives, as though this truth were merely something existing in the mind along

---

[1] In the Additional Note to the third chapter (83).
[2] I quote from the English version, *I Believe* (Chapman, 1959).

with other such mental objects, although more noble than the rest, something serving primarily as a logical rule . . . it is nothing of the sort . . . the first Truth is Subsistent Truth . . . it is a Person . . . *God himself under the aspect of First Truth*: this is the explicit and rigorous formula which expresses the object of faith.'[1]

Mouroux demonstrates in detail that this is in fact the teaching of St Thomas, and there can be no reasonable doubt of it. But I am not concerned with this kind of historical question. What matters is that the doctrine makes sense and can find an echo in the believer's own consciousness. Aubert has shown us that it was for long driven underground.

At the end of this book Mouroux emphasizes very properly that faith is not a matter of 'experience', if by this is meant 'religious *feelings*'. It will be accompanied, naturally, with feelings of some kind, not necessarily of a particularly gratifying nature. It is not what is meant by an 'emotional' business, although it is sometimes startlingly 'affective' in tone. It is a matter of conviction, an 'obscure assent in a radical homage to the First Truth; it is the most spiritual, the most pure and the most mysterious act there is'. Mouroux denies that it is a 'vision'. But he writes that 'it enables the soul to glimpse, choose and adhere to its object: it is revealed, not in itself and in its mystery, but in the fruits of its presence and the efficacy of its action'.[2] This I would interpret to mean that the certainty of faith is normally *adverted to* in the way which Mouroux describes: it is or it can be recognized as having been obscurely operative at an earlier stage and as becoming explicit in the present. Mouroux tells us, in the same place, that the 'grace' of faith is 'not a reality apprehended, but a power of apprehension'. I shall discuss later the theologians' opinion that 'grace' cannot be experienced *as such*; for the moment it will suffice to say that the question of what should be meant by 'grace' will receive further examination and that it may be disregarded for immediate purposes—it has been mentioned here only because it has tended to confuse discussions about faith's certainty, and, in my view, should be treated as a separate problem.

'Yet', Mouroux continues, 'we must add that in faith is concentrated an *entire experience of God*, because it is transforming and uniting from

[1] 14-15.   [2] 106.

its very birth in a soul . . .,' and he proceeds to enunciate the traditional thesis that in the knowledge of faith 'the whole contemplative
and mystic life' is contained in embryo.[1] It will be remembered that
Durand regarded this thesis as irrelevant to the question about the act
of faith and that I was not prepared to follow him in this. But Mouroux
also warns us against looking for 'a personal experience of the Spirit
realized in isolation': it must be 'one which shares in that of the Church,
and receives therefrom its certainty of truth'. The Christian revelation,
that is to say, cannot be recognized as such unless it is recognized as
revelation to a society. In this sense, perhaps, one can accept the
further statement that this is not an 'experience whose own light
suffices, but an experience always infinitely mysterious'. It is not the
experience of an isolated individual, but it is nevertheless an individual's experience, and it is self-sufficing in the sense that it can make
him *certain*. One must also add that this reference to its mysteriousness
might seem to detract from its efficacy in that respect. But Mouroux is
not intending this. In his final sentence he writes that 'faith does not
"cut us off" on the human plane, and never allows of that certitude
which would cause it to escape the dangers resulting from time, the
flesh and the world'.[2] I have emphasized already the obvious point that
faith, although not itself a 'risk', is always 'at risk' because, as Mouroux
here remarks, 'we do not walk by sight, but by faith'. The passages
which I have quoted from him make it quite clear that, in his view,
there is nevertheless an element in faith which requires us to use of it
the language of 'sight'.

That this view can be no longer regarded today as an eccentric one
will be made clear by some further references to Père Bouillard's
Logique de la Foi. The coincidence of his conclusions with those reached
in the last chapter seems to be, in all essentials, complete. Once again I
must quote at considerable length from this short but important book,
which is far too little known in the English-speaking world. After an
introductory section on the general idea of apologetics, he turns at once
to the topic of 'the foundation of faith's certainty'. He puts out of
court without more ado the suggestion that the fact of revelation could
be proved by historical arguments. God reveals himself through certain
historical personages, and our knowledge of them has its part to play—
but it is obvious that it cannot *establish* our certainty. The point is that

[1] 106–7.   [2] 108.

the 'divine reality as such is not the subject matter of a mere historical judgement. . . . If we make contact with him in the world or in ourselves, it is because he is revealing himself to us . . . we have no other means of knowing that he reveals himself save his own revelation itself.' The clarity, firmness and conciseness of this exposition seem to me altogether admirable. The question then is: by what means does this revelation get through to us individually? Bouillard replies that it 'reaches us by means of itself'; that is, 'we have the certainty that God reveals himself, by the very fact that he reveals himself to us, to each individual believer'.[1] This is the supreme example of that self-guaranteeing certainty which is the ultimate basis of all our mental operations and which is so strangely overlooked, so it seems to me, by contemporary philosophers and theologians. So I have had to harp on it time and again.

Bouillard then insists, in a way which reminds us of Gabriel Moran, that revelation is not just a matter of 'the objective reality of Christ or the objective tenor of the Christian message'. For 'a revelation which nobody received would not be a revelation'. Christ's words to Peter after his confession at Caesarea Philippi (Matthew 16, 17) tell us that 'it is the heavenly Father who has revealed to Peter the supernatural character of Jesus'. So 'it is God himself who reveals and who reveals himself to the believer within the act of faith which he determines', that is, within the act of faith which he himself effects in the believer.

The two paragraphs which follow are of decisive importance and must be quoted in full.

'This notion is commonly presented in theological teaching in a way which is slightly different. What determines us to believe, we are told, is the light of grace, the inner illumination and impulse of the Holy Spirit, the *instinctus interior Dei invitantis*. But this is sometimes understood in too imaginative a way. People talk as though we were first faced by a revelation apart from anyone's perception of it and then received, so as to enable us to discern it and accept it, a supernatural light in which it becomes visible and a supernatural impulse by which we are drawn or driven in its direction. In reality, there is no objective reality unless it is grasped by subjects, and the divine light in the soul is

[1] 18–19.

just that of the revelation as received. The Word which God pronounces in Jesus Christ becomes, through the Holy Spirit, his word in the believer. And the light of faith is that Word itself in so far as it is present to the believer.'

It may now begin to become clear, as I was suggesting a little earlier, why a certain sort of talk about 'grace' can cause unnecessary and damaging complexities at this crucial point in the discussion. In Bouillard's account we find that ontological and epistemological realism which had seemed lacking in other, more familiar accounts. And the next paragraph reads (after repeating once more that 'God reveals himself to each one of us, at the heart of the act of faith which he determines'): 'Our awareness of this revelation has the character of a direct, personal apprehension, of an experience in depth (*expérience intime*), of a supernatural perception analogous to mystical knowledge. This is acknowledged by many theologians today: it is this experience of God which is the basis of faith's certainty.'[1] It is hardly necessary for me to say with what satisfaction I read that passage when this book made its appearance a few years ago.

To continue with this account a little further will reveal an exact coincidence with Durand's views about knowledge by signs in regard to revelation. For Bouillard issues a warning at this point against 'illuminism': 'God always reveals himself in a mediate fashion, beneath the sign or the veil of objects distinct from himself, and we always know him in an indirect way, across these signs.' This is in formal contradiction of what he has just said about the directness of this knowledge, but it is clear enough that what he means can be expressed by employing that distinction between the 'direct' and the 'immediate' which I have employed here in such connections. By 'signs', he goes on to say, 'we should not understand just miracles of the physical or the moral order, but the whole divine work which is the history of salvation' and 'the supreme sign is the human reality of Jesus Christ'. This reality has its 'prolongations . . . into the past in the history of the people of Israel whose Messiah Jesus is and into the future in the existence of the Church . . .'. And this is where we find God's revelation today. 'But we must note', Bouillard adds, 'that these signs are not the middle term of a discursive process leading us to conclude, by force

[1] 19–20.

of logic, that God has in fact revealed himself. They are the place where we verify, the transparency in which we discern, the revelation which God makes to us. Their mediation is the place of immediation between God who reveals himself and the experience of faith . . .'[1] Again the distinction between 'direct' and 'immediate' seems called for. But the passage excludes in a very clear way that discursive indirect procedure which I had seemed to find in certain accounts of our knowledge of revelation which referred to the Church as a 'supernatural sign'.

Finally Bouillard points out that these signs can hide as well as reveal: 'One can even be scandalized at being asked to recognize the Absolute in a human, an all too human, reality.' The human reality of the Church is 'ambiguous'. And 'God, even in his revelation, remains mysterious, and it is as mystery that he discovers himself to the believer'. Thus he concludes: 'Revelation is such that I cannot prove it as an evident fact, but only recognize it at the cost of an acceptance of its mystery. In a very real sense, I perceive God who reveals himself; but I perceive him in such sort that I am not dispensed from believing that he reveals himself. To perceive the reality of the revelation and to perceive the obligation to believe are one and the same thing. Across the signs, I grasp revelation as a *credendum*. The act by which I grasp it is an act of submission. Experience is here an obedience.'[2] I need add nothing now to these carefully chosen words.

Bouillard makes only indirect reference to that special emphasis on the function of the will in the act of faith which lies at the heart of some theories about it. It is obvious that he has no use for them, and it might be supposed that they have had their day. In fact they are still to be reckoned with, and if we consult one more contemporary writer on our present topic we shall find not only a valuable confirmation of our chief findings but also, in the end, what appears to be a tendency to retreat from a sound position in the direction of some such theory. I refer to Père Léopold Malevez, whose articles in *Nouvelle Revue Théologique* for many years past helped a great deal to make it perhaps the most important theological periodical published by Roman Catholics at the present time. His most recent book, *Pour une théologie de la foi* (1969), contains a number of these articles together with an important new study of the motives of credibility in relation to faith. I shall be chiefly concerned with this new material, but before turning to

[1] 21.   [2] 21–2.

it I want to make brief mention of the introductory paper, *Le Croyant et le philosophe*, which adopts the Blondelian approach to the business in hand.

'The adhesion of faith', Malevez writes here, 'makes determinate reference to the Absolute already implicitly affirmed by the mind. When we declare, in faith, that it is God who speaks in Jesus Christ, we refer this Word to the Absolute already imprinted on our consciousness, we declare that it verifies the characteristics of a God whose existence we have affirmed by the natural light of reason, whose living image we already in some sort bear; and it is in virtue of this relationship to the God implicitly known (*vécu*) that the God of revelation and of faith makes sense *for us* and becomes *our* truth'[1] (and we soon find the expected reference to Bouillard's account of the matter, as described in our sixth chapter). After insisting that a profession of Christian faith is dependent not just on 'a general acceptance of the supernatural' but upon 'an intimate communication of the Word', Malevez speaks of this communication as being operated 'under the form of an attraction exercised by God himself . . . an invitation infused into our souls to unite ourselves with the Beyond in the bonds of intimacy proclaimed by the Christian message'.[2] He adds in a footnote that the 'formal motive of faith' is nevertheless not 'the rational apprehension of the divine witness in the signs' (this referring, I take it, to a discursive process), but 'God himself . . . as inviting and attracting us to himself (and attracting us to the Christian *Credo* as the means of uniting us with him), giving us by the same token witness of himself, making himself present to our minds . . .'. All this appears to correspond entirely with the conclusions which we have just reached.

When we turn to the new material (the book's second chapter) we find more points of agreement. Malevez grants willingly to Bultmann that what is of faith cannot be *proved* in the sense that it is not based on 'coercive rational evidences'. The evidences of themselves can only invite us to make a 'judgement of moral certitude', not the absolutely certain judgements of faith.[3] At this point Malevez discusses the importance of Blondel's views about 'a double affirmation of God'. As we have seen, and as Malevez proceeds to say, Blondel declares that there is an affirmation of God at the heart of our specifically human experience but that it does not give us a 'real' or 'possessive' knowledge

[1] 34.   [2] 38–9.   [3] 54.

of him. That cannot be ours unless we make a 'free option for God'. We cannot be 'in communion' with him unless we accept him as our Creator and Saviour;[1] and here too Malevez makes his acknowledgements to Bouillard. We may apply this doctrine of a double affirmation, he now suggests, to the question about the relation in which the 'proofs of credibility' stand to the act of faith. Fundamentally, I should add, it is the same question which is to be answered in each case. Blondel's 'science of action' shows us that God is addressing a summons to us. If we accept it, we enter upon the life of grace (even though we may not know that this is so). If we reject it, we lose touch with God; that is, his action upon us, according to Blondel, has now a negative, not a positive effect. The 'proofs of credibility' also lead us to the conclusion that God is summoning us—but to the explicit acceptance of him as the Father of Jesus Christ. But it must also be added that our awareness of the summons to the life of grace (as opposed to the specific summons to Christianity) is, for Blondel (if I interpret him aright), a matter of certainty (although a precarious certainty, because, if the summons is rejected, it may be lost), whereas the 'proofs of credibility' are, of themselves, only the 'place' where revelation is offered to us; they do not, of themselves, make us *certain* of anything.

The language which Malevez uses about the 'proofs' seems at first to contradict my last statement. He tells us that 'the judgement of credibility involves an affirmation of the truth of Christianity (and not only of its probability)'. But he goes on at once to say that this judgement does not of itself make possible 'an adhesion which is absolutely and sovereignly firm', but only 'an assent which has merely moral certainty'.[2] In my view, there is only one kind of certainty, and unless we possess it we are not entitled to 'an affirmation of the truth' about the question at issue. But what Malevez has to say about the firmness of Christian faith is unexceptionable. 'Could one conceive', he asks, 'that men can have only a moral certainty of such a doctrine . . .' a doctrine, that is, which makes such demands upon them? He considers that 'Protestant theology would not contest this requirement' (the requirement of absolute certainty) and regards it as obvious that Catholic theology could not do so[3] (this is perhaps rather sweeping, and I shall return to the topic later in this chapter). Nevertheless he holds that 'absolutely firm faith can co-exist and co-exists, in fact, in each of us

[1] 59-60. [2] 63. [3] 62-3.

129

with an "incredulity" . . .',[1] and on the same page he accepts the view that if we had 'strict evidence' of the fact of revelation before the act of faith we could not be free in making this act. Are these various statements reconcilable with one another?

In principle, I think that they are. A man is free in making an act of faith not because he is uncertain about the summons to listen, to dispose himself to receive the revelation of God, but because he can *refuse* this summons (often, no doubt, it is rejected when there is still only a 'suspicion' in regard to it, but I am not now considering that case). This is a fact which a philosopher may find most disconcerting; all that can be said of it here is that it is nevertheless a fact—moral failure is something which we find in our experience. A man becomes certain of the fact of revelation only *in* making an act of faith, only *in* receiving the 'supernatural evidence' of 'God-in-his-testifying'. The act of faith, we might say, is *made in him* when he has freely removed the obstacles to it. Before the act of faith he is still uncertain of the fact of revelation, but he has the certain evidence (the awareness of a summons) which justifies him completely in his submission to God's activity upon him. So long as this attitude of acceptance—this attitude of love, we may call it—is present, there is this certainty. Malevez at one point speaks of a renunciation of 'the whole independence of the reason'.[2] He is speaking of that leap, not into the darkness but into the light, of which I have been speaking. Thus the act of faith is itself incompatible with doubt. There is 'strict evidence' of 'God-in-his-testifying'. It cannot be refused so long as it *is* evidence. It can, however, be *lost*. It can be edged gradually out of consciousness, not by some kind of attempted direct assault, but by neglect (probably it is an assault on the implications of it—or on what are thought to be such—that leads to this neglect). 'Absolutely firm faith', then, cannot co-exist *contemporaneously* with incredulity (but the one could alternate with the other). It can, of course, be accompanied by difficulties (Newman's emphatic distinction between 'difficulties' and 'doubts' comes at once to mind). There may be the most painful obscurities; one may not see *how* the difficulties can be overcome, while remaining convinced at the deepest level of one's thought that in fact they can be.

Malevez is prepared to accept the view that 'the interior summons to the supernatural end is mysteriously involved, from the first instant of

[1] 64n.   [2] 70n.

reason's awakening, with the summons of natural morality', and he adds that this 'supernatural attraction' must illuminate for us 'the values which the evangelical message possesses'.[1] He then considers the suggestion that this attraction 'justifies the absolute and sovereign firmness of faith' and that 'the light of grace directly manifests to us the goodness (*bonté*) of that firmness of assent' which the message itself declares to us as necessary.[2] This exemplifies the 'too imaginative' way of talking about 'supernatural lights' and 'supernatural impulses' which Bouillard was criticizing, and Malevez (very rightly) thinks it necessary to modify the suggestion, which seems so obviously a case of wishful thinking; he gives it the following significantly different form: 'the subject sees this goodness . . . founded upon the divine witness obscurely grasped by him in the attraction: this reveals (*désigne*) to him, in some sort, God himself . . . it is this . . . which is the definitive foundation of the legitimacy and the duty of an absolutely firm assent'.[3] In other words, I take it, it is this revelation which *gives* him his certainty. So here, with a special emphasis on the *desire* for God, which is a natural and proper way of describing part of this process (always provided that it is not divorced from an *awareness* of him), we come back again to our own conclusion.

Later, however, we meet with complications. Malevez is prepared to grant that to the desire for salvation aroused in us by grace 'there is necessarily connected an obscure light'; but both this 'light' and the 'attraction' are said to be 'created effects' through which God is in some sense known.[4] We may wonder whether he is, after all, advocating that epistemological and ontological realism which was so evident in Bouillard's account. He does indeed insist that the created effect is not *what* is known but the medium, the 'sign', in which we know. Now to speak of the Gospel message as a 'sign' in which we know God is surely right. But to make an 'obscure light' and an 'attraction' into 'signs' is quite another matter. If we talk about 'light', as Bouillard has explained to us, in the present connection, we must be pointing to the knowledge of God itself, not to something which could in some way explain or account for it. And an 'attraction' cannot explain or account for an apprehension; it must be the *effect* of an apprehension. What seems to be happening here is that a certain sort of Thomist 'voluntarism' is beginning to show itself, a certain priority of the will over the

[1] 69. [2] 71, 73. [3] 74n. [4] 81.

intellect. This suspicion is confirmed in a passage in which Malevez tries to answer the objection that the divine witness, being communicated only in a very obscure way, cannot be 'the principle of supreme certitude'.[1] He first appeals to the unlimited goodness which we find in the promise of the Christian message. This, he allows, gives rise to the further objection that, although it may explain one's willingness to give a firm assent, it does not explain how there can be *certainty*, which is a matter of the intellect. His reply to this is that God 'does indeed first attract the will, but his attraction, causing confidence in the God who is the guarantor, is communicated as such to the intelligence'.[2]

Does this mean simply that we are aware of God as attracting us? If it does, it seems strange that Malevez does not say so. He concludes (with acknowledgement to his colleague Père Dhanis) that 'the sovereign certitude of faith is . . . the accomplishment of the duty of receiving a gift'.[3] And this is acceptable in a Blondelian framework. For then we should say not that the will itself empowers the intellect in some incomprehensible way but that its exercise—the *attention* to the message—is the necessary condition for the intellect's reception of it, for its receiving the evidence of God-in-his-testifying. The obscurity of this testifying presents, in principle, no epistemological difficulty (although the need for attention may well present a moral one). We can become certain (if we attend) of a good many things of which we have no 'clear and distinct' idea.

I now return to the rather sweeping statements which Malevez made about the acceptance on the part of both Catholic and Protestant theologians of the requirement of absolute certainty for the act of faith. It is surely common enough to meet with the view, even in the writings of the more traditional Anglicans, that faith is a 'risk' in the sense that it requires 'commitment' to doctrines for which one has no complete intellectual justification. Otherwise, it is said, there would be no 'merit' in it. In the view which I have put forward here intellectual justification is complete: God's revelation to us is guaranteed by God himself, although its articulation in the form of particular doctrines may remain obscure, hard to understand or even unintelligible in this or that instance. There is indeed a place for 'commitment' here, as I have tried to show: the moral requirements of faith are all-important.

[1] 96.   [2] 97.   [3] *Ibid.*

But there is no 'merit' in claiming as true what is only probable; considered objectively, it is intellectual dishonesty, and, when people appear to make such a claim, one must suppose there is confusion either in thought or in expression. To do what one sees to be a duty, however, is always meritorious[1]—that is to say, it makes it possible for us to receive God's further gifts (the accomplishment of one's duty being itself God's gift, with our willingness to receive it as its necessary condition). It is perhaps the failure to think this out which is chiefly responsible for the confusions.

And there has been in recent years, it seems to me, a marked tendency among Catholic writers also to speak of faith's *uncertainty*—and not only among those theological journalists who are such a notable and sometimes such an embarrassing feature in the present theological scene. If this meant only that faith is precarious (in the sense that I have explained), then it would be harmless enough or beneficial. But faith is sometimes made into a 'dialectical' business which seems of its nature to involve not just difficulties and obscurities but a suspension of judgement. Durandeaux, for instance, in the book already referred to, asks the question: 'Can the believer draw his belief from one moment in his life, a belief which envelops and determines his whole life?' And he then writes: 'We cannot answer this question in the affirmative unless we realize that our Yes will be subject to doubt at a later time, subject to doubt again and again.'[2] The implication may seem to be that it is not faith's business to give us certainty. It may indeed be the case that many of those who are called 'the faithful' are only in various stages of 'suspicion' in regard to the truth of Christianity, but one does not need, I hope, to be a professional exegete in order to declare that the New Testament writers regarded the gift of faith as providing (if we do our part) an absolute conviction. So far as I can see, the tradition is solid about this. Faith is the beginning of eternal life, not just a working hypothesis.

This chapter will conclude with remarks on some practical implications of these conclusions about faith's certainty. It follows from them that one would not expect faith to develop in the young, at any rate in the later years of the twentieth century, unless they have a habit of

---

[1] And it may be a man's duty to adopt the Christian way of life even if he is not *certain* that it is the true one. This is what is often meant by 'commitment'.

[2] *Living Questions to Dead Gods*, 106.

personal prayer, prayer which is not just a matter of conforming to the habits of the family or of some society but an affair of personal decision, implying some beginning of love of God for his own sake and thus distinguished from mere superstition. Whatever we are to mean by faith as 'a virtue infused at baptism' (and it is increasingly emphasized by theologians that the decrees of Trent must not be understood in too literal-minded a way), it is certainly not something which will grow quite happily provided only that it is not interfered with; it will not grow at all unless it is actively encouraged. There is no need to harp on the evident reasons why those brought up as Christians, if they are possessed of any intelligence, must ask themselves whether what they have been brought up to believe is indeed the truth. The advice which is to be given to them is certainly to study the relevant documents, and in particular the Gospels, but also to consider what faith *is* according to traditional teaching. But unless or until there is an interest in God (which, as we have seen, is not necessarily promoted by a reading of the Gospels) this advice will fall on deaf ears. A process of education has then to be undertaken, an attempt to show that fundamental questions do really arise for the human mind, leading to the suggestion that prayer is, in the end, the only way in which they might find an answer.

For faith is an act of worship, and it can grow only through worship. When people are told to 'pray for faith', the suggestion might sometimes seem to be that faith might be injected into one as a reward for saying prayers. But a willingness to experiment with prayer is itself some beginning of faith: as a theologian would put it, the virtue of faith is already beginning to exert its influence, although its proper act (the act of faith itself) may still be a long way off. It must be insisted upon both that this act is a real contact with God in Christ and also that this contact is obscure and (normally) quite unspectacular, not to be discerned (very probably) in the actual exercise of prayer, which is itself at least as much a shifting of interest in the whole course of one's ordinary avocations as the attempt to transcend them in periods of recollection. (Such periods, however, are today more necessary than ever if Christian life is to develop as it should do.) A man may wake up one morning to find that it is no longer possible for him *not* to believe. There has been, for his mind, in Pauline language, a gradual bringing into captivity to the truth of Christ. But it is to be expected that he should gain from time to time a less negative sort of awareness that God is acting upon him in Christ's Church.

Here I must quote, for the last time, from Bouillard's *Logique de la Foi*. We can apprehend God's revelation, he tells us, in the signs 'in the precise measure in which we can also apprehend in them the meaning of human existence', for otherwise the signs 'will not be signs at all, but disconcerting or irrelevant facts'.[1] And so 'apologetics consists precisely in making explicit through a coherent account of universal application the spiritual act by which God's revelation is discerned in historic Christianity'.[2] The great issue of our time is, manifestly, whether there is any such thing as 'the meaning of human existence'. And the first stage in this process is to realize that there is such a thing as a 'spiritual act'. But what of 'historic Christianity'? How is one to interest the typical product of a technological age in a topic, from his point of view, so unprofitable as the witness of the Christian past? There is the special difficulty at present that the pendulum has swung violently against institutional religion and that the darker side of Church history, by a natural consequence, is insisted upon to the comparative neglect (sometimes, it would almost seem, to the total neglect) of what is really the true history of the Church as such, a history which from the nature of the case is not directly visible, the history of man's love for God and for his fellow men in response to God's love for us. There is a peculiar ignorance among so-called educated Christians today of the witness of the first centuries of the Church, of the medieval flowering (the first Cistercians, for example), the splendours of the seventeenth-century *invasion mystique* . . . But I have said enough at an earlier stage about the secularizing tendency among Christians. To invite non-Christians to read Christian literature is, in many cases, to invite them to enter a wholly foreign world. They *may*, of course, discover a new 'dimension' in this way. But if they are ever to enter this world, it is likely that it will be through their contact, in the first place, with living members of the contemporary Church. This is always the normal way of discovering God's revelation in Jesus Christ. And in the conditions of the modern *diaspora* the opportunities for this are very often lacking. The 'signs' are hard to come by and in any case so often ambiguous. This is another reason why it is so important to realize that they *are* 'signs', not proofs. The limitations of

[1] 22–3.   [2] 26.

merely rational discourse are glaringly obvious in our day-to-day experience.

In conclusion, it is necessary to underline the danger of a rationalistic approach for those who try to help their fellow Christians in their 'religious difficulties'. If people suppose that they are intellectually justified in their Christian belief for certain specific reasons of a historical, sociological or merely logical kind, if in the last analysis this belief is thought to rest on particular events in the past or even perhaps in the Church's visible success in the present, then they may find themselves very much disturbed by the discovery of some fresh piece of evidence which appears to have disconcerting implications, by the sudden appearance of some hole in an argument or even by the behaviour of important ecclesiastics. And if they are argued with on that level, if they are not encouraged to take deeper soundings, then they are unlikely to be helped. But one must not fly to the other extreme and suppose that one can dispense altogether with 'signs'. Since it is in the Church that Christ is found, what the Church is and has been does matter. A Christian must proclaim his belief that the Church is the centre of holiness—not that all holiness visibly proceeds from her, although it would be possible to show that in the Western world spiritual revivals in the last thousand years have always been revivals of one spiritual tradition (or an aspect of it which has gone underground, for the time being, in the 'great Church'). And this spiritual tradition appears as central because there is no other in the West which can rival its claim to authenticity, to a genuine contact with God, and because there is none in the non-Christian East which can rival its claim to combine this authenticity with a genuine humanism, a positive attitude to the whole created world, a sense of proportion and balance, a theology which has as its substratum an intelligible metaphysics, a metaphysics of charity. If life has a meaning, one is entitled to ask, does it not lie here?

9. THE INTELLIGENCE OF FAITH

Some fifteen years ago, in a talk to Catholics at Cambridge, I hazarded the following statement about the light of faith and the conceptual content of faith: 'In theology there is an interplay between the light of faith and the concepts used by the doctrinal statements. Without the light of faith, we know what we are talking about only, as it were, from the outside; without using our ordinary powers of thought to grasp the meaning of the doctrinal statements, we shall not be able to make any advance in our new territory, to bring out the implications of our supernatural knowledge and give content to it, or even to maintain our hold on it, for the light of faith must work on these materials.' This led me to the conclusion that 'thinking about religion and praying require one another, at any rate where educated persons are concerned'. And I then contrasted this point of view with another which seems to go to excess in two opposite directions: 'On the one hand, it seems to regard God as so far beyond the scope of our minds that we can believe anything of him: statements which seem to make him arbitrary or vindictive are considered acceptable on the ground, presumably, that we have no clue to the way in which they apply to God (I would say: we *have* a clue, and it enables us to say what expressions are valid 'pointers' to God and what are not). On the other hand, the view which I am criticizing draws conclusions about God from general principles as though he were an instance of a philosophical rule. You will find scholastic theologians demonstrating that God has a will because all beings endowed with intellect have one. People whose minds work like this tend to think that religion can be based on a knowledge of God which is wholly indirect, beginning with a philosophical proof which gives us a God of whom we know only that he is *not* a creature, and going on to a revelation which is equally uninformative, since its descriptions of God are referring to the "Unknown".' It must be added that the sort of philosophical proof which I had in mind does not really give us anything, and that our clue to statements about God which seem to mean that he is arbitrary and vindictive is that, if they are acceptable at all, they are pointing to the immutability of his plan for us and to the inevitable consequences of failing to conform to it.

These remarks, at the time, occasioned, I think, some surprise, even perhaps some suspicion, on the part of the more theologically conventional members of the Cambridge audience. Nowadays they would be taken for granted by tolerably educated persons in so far as our original knowledge of God is commonly conceded *not* to be the result of merely discursive processes. But there is still a good deal of suspicion on the part of 'traditional' Christians that talk about 'experience' in matters of faith is anti-intellectual or a form of dangerous 'illuminism'. So, of course, it can be. But, if the conclusions of the last chapter are acceptable, we must surely say that the doctrines of faith are the working out of that apprehension of God in Christ which is at the heart of an act of faith. For this puts us in touch with Christ's own knowledge which is the 'place' where revelation occurs, and the development of our knowledge, although discursive processes are useful to it, moves from an apprehension relatively incomplete to apprehensions which are relatively complete. To call dogmas the crystallizations of Christian experience, although not yet by any means always received as theologically 'safe', is a way of talking about them which is in fact common enough today in 'safe' theological circles. Christ's knowledge is communicable to each member of his Church according to his measure. But it is as a member of the Church that he receives it. To put it crudely, he draws upon a common stock. The authority of faith is God's authority, but it is found in a society.

It is time to consider more closely the nature and function of the *propositions* of faith, although still only in general (I shall be discussing specific instances later on). What seems to me a clear and helpful approach is found in an article, 'The Exigence for Theology',[1] by Dom Odo Brooke. 'To many people', he writes, 'the theological world appears as a vast superstructure unrelated to the central Christian experience.' This is because they see in theology 'nothing but the reflexive, conceptual, formulation of faith' and fail to realize that this is in fact based on a 'pre-reflective, pre-conceptual experience of faith'. The fact that theologians themselves have so often failed to realize it is the reason for this widespread misapprehension. And it does not solve the problem, Brooke goes on, 'to shift the object of theology from the classic, Greek, scholastic concern with God in himself to the contemporary concern with God in Salvation History', for that by itself does not make clear that the point of departure, the point from which theology arises, is an experience which lies behind the *propositions* of faith, behind the 'thematization' of faith, as people like to put it nowadays. And Brooke then argues that this 'thematization' is nevertheless, despite its dependence upon the experience of faith, a necessary development of it. He writes: 'Even the most primitive formulations of faith, which are revealed in the Biblical sources, are themselves a thematization of a primordial experience', to which he adds that 'even

[1] *The Downside Review*, Autumn 1968.

if the primordial experience is not necessarily temporally prior, it is always logically prior to an explicit formulation of faith'. He thinks it necessary to insist that the experience of faith 'implies a judgement that God has objectively revealed himself through his actions in history' and that 'subjective experience is realized through objective knowledge'. It is curious that the 'Modernist' tendency to reduce everything to the purely subjective should still fascinate theologians (or rather 'religious thinkers') and require this persistent emphasis.

In developing his argument Brooke bases himself on Karl Rahner, and I shall now quote two passages of Rahner's to which he refers. The first reads: 'Grace, understood as the supernatural self-communication of God, is also light . . . as the older theology had always acknowledged. . . . Hence the simple inner bestowal of grace is already a kind of revelation, even though it only comes to its full being in the form of public and official revelation meant also for others, in the divinely guaranteed objectification of what is already contained in it . . . it is easy to understand that this original process of revelation, which even in Scripture comes before theology, cannot be sought in, and simply identified with, any particular objectification in chosen statements of the New Testament. It lies at the basis of these statements but is not identified with any determined, conceptually objectifying statements, even though these are absolutely binding and properly communicating objectifications of the original event of revelation for us.'[1] In the second passage, Rahner tells us, he is using 'in the field of dogma . . . a natural analogue for an explication other than that of the logical explication of propositions'. It reads as follows: 'The lover knows of his love: this knowledge of himself forms an essential element in the very love itself. The knowledge is infinitely richer, simpler and denser than any body of propositions about the love could be. Yet this knowledge never lacks a certain measure of reflexive articulateness: the lover confesses his love at least to himself, "states" at least to himself something about his love. In this progressive self-achievement, in which love comprehends itself more and more, in which it goes on to state something "about" itself and comprehends its own nature more clearly, the love itself becomes ordered . . . Original, non-propositional, unreflexive yet conscious possession of a reality on the one hand, and reflexive (propositional), articulated consciousness of this original

[1] *Theological Investigations*, V, 40–1.

consciousness on the other—these are the not competing but reciprocally interacting factors of a single experience necessarily unfolding in historical succession. Root and shoot are not the same thing, but each lives by *the other*.'[1]

As Brooke puts it: 'The primordial experience of the lover is presupposed to all that he can say about that experience. But the experience is not about the talk. The talk is about the experience.' He goes on to describe 'the central primordial experience of God's self-disclosure' as 'the connatural affinity given in the initial act of faith', and tells us (with a reference to my own *Certainty*) that 'the theory of the connatural instinct of faith is widely accepted and based on the teaching of Aquinas'. Whatever we may make of that teaching, it is gratifying to find that Brooke seems to mean by this Thomist language what I was meaning. He continues: 'The exigence for thematization is rooted in the very nature of this experience. The Christian community wants to articulate to itself and to others what this experience means. The connatural insight and judgement is not itself sufficient.' The following passage also demands quotation: 'The articulation gives a common meaning and a common language for the Christian community. The experience of Revelation is now given public embodiment. Theology is often conceived as an inward, abstract, cerebral exercise in antithesis to outward, concrete, visible embodiment. But I suggest that theology is the outward expression of an inward experience rather than an inner abstraction from an outward experience . . . Theological thematization is an aspect of the visible structure in which the Church expresses and realizes herself in the world.'

It follows from all this, says Brooke, that 'theology must embody itself in the contemporary historical context'; for 'to be embodied means to be embodied in history'—otherwise 'embodiment' is just an abstraction. And this means, not that we must discard the theology of the past, but that we must develop it by applying it to fresh situations and to fresh insights in the human situation. He points out, again following Rahner, that to reject the development of doctrine as thus envisaged 'is not to "safeguard" God's Revelation but to imprison that Revelation within limited human categories and within a limited historical context, whether of the past or of the present'. This raises questions, to which I shall turn shortly, about the validity, the truth-

[1] *Theological Investigations*, I, 64–5.

value, of theological concepts. Brooke is not directly concerned with them here, but he points out that he is presupposing a correspondence theory of truth, 'not the theory of truth proposed by Leslie Dewart in *The Future of Belief*'.

Before I leave this article, there are two further points in it which merit attention. The first is: 'To articulate and embody a deep, central experience is to expose oneself to the peril of losing touch with the experience in its immediacy. . . . The poet may lose touch with his original creative experience in the very process of his attempt to articulate to himself and others what that experience means. The theologian may lose touch with the immediate experience of Revelation. . . .' To put the point in my own words, an abstract, rationalizing theology must be given life by returning to its sources, and not just in the formalizations of time past, the records and writings of the first Christians, the Fathers and the rest, but in the experience from which they derive, into which the theologian himself must enter, so far as he can. Theology does not only develop; it also contracts and becomes impoverished. And in these circumstances (which are still our own to a considerable extent and in certain respects to a greater extent than in the recent past) the first task is to regain what we have lost. Only then can we see our way forward.

The second point is that 'the potentialities of that experience [the faith experience] are orientated ultimately towards the transcendence of our present human condition and therefore towards the transcendence of discursive thought and linguistic embodiment . . . to know God through the mediation of a sign implies a tension towards the immediate knowledge of God in himself. . . . The Church is totally incarnational *and* totally eschatological. The Church is always in the world and the Church is always moving beyond this world. Therefore, incarnationally there is the exigence for the realization, the expression and the embodiment of Christian experience in history and eschatologically there is the exigence for the Christian community to realize itself in the immediate presence of the transcendent mystery.' I shall be suggesting later that this second exigence is the reason why we must take account of mystical theology, and also of those institutions which promote and bear witness to this exigence, in particular of monasticism.

The question about the permanent truth-value of theological

concepts is at present a burning one. After a period in which the common opinions of theologians were accorded (among Roman Catholics, at least) a status to which they are not entitled, we are now in a period of reaction against this state of affairs which leads to extreme statements in the opposite direction. This sort of thing is a common enough phenomenon in the Church's history, and it is to be expected that an equilibrium will be eventually restored. For a properly balanced account of the situation I believe we should return to Father Edward Schillebeeckx. The theme which runs through *The Concept of Truth and Theological Renewal* is that a purely 'conceptualist' theology is to be rejected (he insists, for example, on 'the experiential aspect of the act of faith'),[1] but that all the same theology cannot dispense with concepts. He is particularly concerned to defend St Thomas against the charge of conceptualism, but he is obliged to admit that even in St Thomas's later works 'unmistakably "essentialist" echoes are discernible',[2] that is, a tendency to look at things from an abstract rather than from an experiential point of view, and before we consider what he has to say on the topic which now concerns us we must briefly consider his quasi-Thomist approach to the philosophical question about our knowledge of God.

Following St Thomas, he tells us that 'our knowledge only comes into contact with God in conscious unknowing'.[3] What he proves to mean is that we come to know God as the 'wholly Other'. He says in the same place: 'We know that God is good, although the conceptual content of this goodness is only a creaturely goodness and the divine mode of this goodness therefore escapes us.' Here I should wish to say that we know God as the source of goodness and that, although its divine mode is profoundly mysterious to us, we are, however tenuously, in 'touch' with God as infinite goodness (otherwise, in my view, we could not say that we were 'in touch' with *God* at all). Schillebeeckx goes on:

'The typical intellectual value of our conceptual knowledge of God is therefore situated in a projective act in which we reach out to God via the conceptual contents. In this we cannot grasp God conceptually, although we do know that he is present in the objective and definite direction that is indicated by the contents of the concept.'

[1] 30. [2] 206. [3] 20.

And here I should say that the concept as *abstract* refers simply and solely to created goodness, but that the *content* of the concept, if we are speaking of 'metaphysical' goodness (not just of 'what one happens to want'), refers both to creatures in their relation to God and to God as their source at one and the same time.[1] Schillebeeckx claims to be employing here the *theologia negativa*, the theology which negates in God the limitations which attach to created values, but it must be emphasized again that this theology must be based on a positive (though strictly inexpressible) knowledge of God. Despite this difference between our approaches,[2] we can agree that the goodness of creatures 'points to' the goodness of God and is informative about his goodness, although it is not simply as the goodness of *creatures* (so I should say) that it so informs us.

We may now see how Schillebeeckx applies this conclusion to the supernatural knowledge of faith:

'If our concepts are, in the case of our natural knowledge of God, naturally open to the transcendent, then our natural concepts are, in the case of the concepts of faith, made open by positive revelation to the expression of supernatural truths. The God who revealed himself in human form has given a new dimension to human contents of knowledge—a new objective perspective which these contents do not in themselves have for our human intellect as such, but which they only derive from revelation and thus from the non-conceptual aspect of our act of faith. This natural intellectual content, which is included in the supernatural act of faith, directs our spirit by virtue of revelation (and thus by virtue of the non-conceptual element in the act of faith) objectively to God's intimate life, which is not attainable by purely human knowledge.'[3]

Schillebeeckx is saying (if I understand him) that the knowledge of faith gives us a fresh knowledge of *who God is*, a fresh non-conceptual inkling, one might call it, of infinite love. The human words in which the Christian community has formulated its faith-experience can be seen to have a true bearing upon God in the light of that experience, shared as it is, in some measure, by all true believers. Each generation of

[1] This thesis is argued in *Absolute Value, passim.* cf. in particular 163.
[2] Discussed in *Absolute Value*, 60f.   [3] 21.

Christians recognizes its experience in these human words (comes to it, indeed, normally, in and through these words).

'Thus', Schillebeeckx goes on, 'the fatherhood and sonship of God, for example, are really an extension of the reality, father and son, of our human experience, but we cannot grasp conceptually the manner in which fathership and sonship is realized in God. . . . We do not in fact apply the purely conceptual representational content of *father* and *son* to God, but we can, by extending that and no other conceptual content (that is, father and son), really reach God. Consequently, God is in himself Father and Son, although in such a way that we cannot form any real conception of this divine fatherhood and sonship.'[1] To put this again in my own way, we know from the formulations of faith, starting of course with the New Testament, that there is something in the life of God which corresponds to the human relationships between father and son and between son and father (although it would be more proper to say that these human relationships correspond to it). Once more I must insist that if we are to claim such knowledge we must have some 'inkling' of what we claim to know, that is, of the divine mode of this relationship, profoundly mysterious though it remains for us. We are now dealing with the content of intelligible concepts seen in the light of revelation. Only through revelation can we discover that there are distinct super-persons, Father, Son and Spirit, in God. Without revelation we might perhaps guess that the value of love between distinct persons is found in a divine mode; but we could not *know* it. But just as we can have no more than an 'inkling' of how the relationship between father and son is found in God, so we can have no more than an 'inkling' of how it is that God *is* three Persons, an 'inkling', moreover, which can only declare itself explicitly when the knowledge of faith has developed to a degree which must be called fully 'mystical'.[2]

Now at last we can consider what Schillebeeckx has to say about the 'reinterpretation of dogmas', the permanent truth-value of dogmatic formulations. He considers that we have now found 'the true perspective within which we can affirm both the absolute character of the truth of faith and the high degree of relativity and thus of growth in our reflection about faith'.[3] Dogma, he tells us, is 'always an expression by the Church of the Church's whole experience of faith as this is made present again and again from the apostles' faith and throughout the

[1] 20–1.   [2] This will be touched on again at the end of ch. 14.   [3] 22.

THE THEOLOGY OF FAITH

history of the Church'. It is 'thus a new formulation relating to a particular situation . . . the experience of faith itself in a particular phase of ecclesiastical expression . . . consent to faith in the dogma does not have the formulation itself as its end, but—via the dogma— the reality of the God of revelation . . . in the dogma the mystery of faith is expressed in human concepts that can never be sufficient to convey the whole mystery . . . the strictly conceptual aspect is its sharply defined intellectual aspect, which is, however, at the same time a part of the wider background of a historically conditioned world of ideas.'[1] The point comes out more clearly in what follows: 'A subtle distinction has therefore to be made in the definition of any dogma between the real essence of the dogmatic formulations—that is, what is necessary if we are to move towards the inexpressible content of faith in a true and authentic way—and the secondary aspect relating to the form in which the definition is couched. . . . Human experience, precise scientific data and similar factors can help to purify the way in which the dogma is presented. An example of this is the idea of Christ's ascension, the representation of which was formerly connected with the ancient [Ptolemaic] view of the world. . . . The dogmatic meaning continues unchanged whenever these older forms of expression are changed.'[2]

Schillebeeckx is well aware that we cannot separate absolute truth from conceptual expressions of it, but we can come to see that one such conceptual expression must give place to another as human thought develops. A conceptual expression, I take him to say, may even reflect philosophical (not merely, as in the example above, cosmological) ideas which can subsequently appear not only incomplete but mistaken; yet while these ideas are the currency of the age it may still be a valid 'pointer' to the truth. What he goes on to say seems to confirm this:

'The reinterpretation of dogma may mean that the fringe of ideas representing the conceptual framework of the dogma in its historical setting is cut off, but also that the conceptual structure—in so far as this truly, if not exhaustively, expresses the reality of salvation—is itself presented in a more subtly shaded manner. . . . What has once been declared a dogma can never be revoked, but it can certainly be inte-

[1] 24–5.   [2] 25–6.

grated into newer insights in which its life really continues . . . the truths seen earlier have been thought out again in the newer insights.'[1]

Schillebeeckx adds that 'these views may be said to be more or less generally accepted throughout the theological world of Western Europe, although there is still a group of scholastic theologians who continue to regard human knowledge in rigidly conceptualistic terms, and who confuse the unchangeable character of truth with a representational view of human concepts.'

The account of the matter which Schillebeeckx has given seems to me perfectly acceptable if we remember that dogmatic formulations refer to the relation in which we stand to God. Since they are *about God*, they cannot exhaustively express what they mean in the language of human concepts. But if they are indeed dogmatic formulations the concepts are genuine 'pointers'. Here we have to remember that they are commonly designed to preserve the faith against some interpretation of it which is seen to be unauthentic, and in this respect their truth-value is a negative one. Can we conclude that there is *any* permanent conceptual structure expressing the faith which can be distinguished from the 'fringe of ideas' which may surround it in dogmatic formulations? Surely this must be so. Our concepts of fatherhood and sonship, for instance, as Schillebeeckx has said, can tell us something about God —they are true as far as they go—but it is only in the light of faith that they reveal this to us.

It is the part played by the light of faith in the intelligence of faith which must now be considered more closely. And there is one more passage in Schillebeeckx which must be mentioned because it might seem at first to deny that faith itself provides illumination. 'Philosophy', he writes, 'seeks the intelligibility of the datum of experience, and in this sense it is not dethroned by faith and theology. Revelation itself does not provide us with any supra-metaphysical truth, but only with explicitations along the lines of salvation history.'[2] Certainly there is no such thing as 'supra-metaphysical truth': theological truth *is* metaphysical. And 'only with explicitations' is at least an odd description of the way in which God reveals himself as Triune. Schillebeeckx, however, promptly removes one's suspicions. 'Pure philosophy', he goes on, 'is concerned with the Christian God, with the God of salvation, in so

[1] 28.   [2] 103.

far as he is attainable by means of natural human thought. But [philosophical] metaphysics does not . . . reach God precisely in his personal, dialogic relationship with man—it reaches in the creature *only* and *precisely* what must be assumed as a possibility for this personal dialogue if man is to be able to engage meaningfully in this dialogue.'[1] (This passage could have come straight out of Maurice Blondel. Schillebeeckx, like Rahner, seems to have little first-hand acquaintance with him.) Clearly this personal dialogue involves *fresh* knowledge of God, so that there seems no good reason for rejecting 'supernatural metaphysics'.

Six years ago I was delighted to discover in an article by Père Malevez, '*Contemplative Theology and Discursive Theology*',[2] a magisterial expression of what I had in mind on this subject. He begins by referring to the many complaints which have been made in our time about a rupture between theology and spirituality, a rupture which is not found in the works of the great medieval doctors (nor, one might add, in those of the Greek Fathers) and which is due precisely to a failure to realize the vital role of the light of faith in theologizing. Can we go so far as to say, he enquires, that discursive theology (theology in its employment of the ordinary powers of human reasoning) must, if it is to be true to its own proper laws, develop itself in the light of a certain perception of the Absolute which is already of a mystical nature? He gives the expected reply that there is an inchoative mysticism in the act of faith, a mysticism in embryo. It is his defence of this position which seems to me so eminently satisfactory.

First he considers the objection that, although the light of faith may be the source of certainty in theology and necessary for its intelligibility, the business of discursive theology is to organize the truths of faith into a coherent system, and it does this by following the laws of human reason and nothing else. In reply to this Malevez refers to the presence of the Absolute 'which moves the mind in all its operations and makes it posit all its objects'.[3] All that is creative in human thought, the burgeoning of symbols, for example, comes from 'the earnest attention of the mind to this presence, summoning to its service all its intellectual, affective and imaginative resources'. There is 'a presence of God at the heart of our regenerated being' which is 'immeasurably more profound than the natural presence of God . . .'. Is it conceivable, then, that

[1] 103–4.   [2] *Nouvelle Revue Théologique*, 1964, 225–49.   [3] 231.

this should 'play no part in the formation of theology'? 'Could theology, having that eminent dignity which one must grant to it, be the only production of the mind which owes nothing in its coming to birth to that presence which is peculiar to it? Could it be, in itself, nothing but the exercise of a mere dialectical virtuosity?'[1] (It is to be observed that in this passage Malevez assumes as a matter of course the acceptance of a Blondelian position in philosophy on the part of his readers.)

A positive argument for the present thesis, Malevez continues, is that 'discursive Christian theology has been constituted historically and traditionally' by the *theologia negativa*, and this implies that it was inspired by the 'great inner presence'. It is the Absolute which has 'given it the impulse to adopt this procedure'.[2] But it has to be made clear that the *theologia negativa* does really have these implications, and so Malevez now turns to its famous exponent, the mysterious Dark Age figure Dionysius the so-called Areopagite, commonly referred to as Denis. According to Denis, the mind in quest of union with God begins by functioning on two interconnecting planes, that of symbols and that of ideas or concepts. The symbols have to be purified and transcended; the concepts must be subjected to a dialectic in which first the intelligible perfections (goodness, beauty and the rest) are affirmed of God (these are the 'divine names'), and then, since this is demanded by the simplicity, the perfect unity and the transcendence of God, there must be a negative moment which eliminates anthropomorphism. But this negation, as Malevez puts it, 'does not bear on the content of the affirmation but on the mode which is attributed to it in the affirmative judgement. . . . So the negation, penetrating to the heart of the affirmation, far from destroying it, in fact preserves it and fortifies it.'[3] This is the procedure which I have constantly employed in these chapters, but I have described it as an increasingly explicit discrimination between the elements of which our experience is fundamentally composed, between created values and Absolute Value, rather than as an affirmative movement followed by a negative movement: the two movements take place together.

In Denis's eyes, Malevez goes on, discursive theology, having reached this summit, has reached the frontier of mystical theology, by which is meant not the science of mysticism but the mystical experience itself, communion with God. There is contact with God himself, with-

[1] 232.   [2] 238.   [3] 240-1.

out the mediation of symbol or concept. And how has this been achieved? The affirmative and negative moments of the dialectic have not achieved it of themselves—they are only the preparation for it. The fact is that the dialectic of discursive theology has been constructed throughout under the obscure impulse of the One, the ineffable God present to the soul of the believer. It must be this which dictates to the mind the necessity for purifying the symbols and the concepts. The process is otherwise inexplicable.[1]

But could it not be objected, Malevez now asks, that in fact it is not a mystical element in the knowledge of faith but rather sacred Scripture which has inspired the negative theology in Denis and his successors? Have not the scriptural *propositions* dictated these purifications and subliminations of our concepts? Our natural powers, it may be said, are sufficient to show us God's transcendence but only in so vague a way that we still need to be saved from the dangers of pantheism by the scriptural witness. We have the necessary equipment for embarking on the 'negative way' without appealing to any 'mystical element' proper to faith itself. In reply to this, Malevez acknowledges that natural theology may discover, of itself, the law of negative theology (God's indescribability) and that Scripture, if one may use the vulgar phrase, 'cashes in' on an awareness of God's transcendence which is native to the human mind. But 'there is in the mind of the believer, in virtue of the light of faith, an infused and "mystical" sense of transcendence which is necessarily much more sure and more effective'.[2] It is to this 'sense' in the believer that Scripture appeals. It has not suppressed but built upon the natural sense of transcendence.

There is a final question. Could it be that this thesis, although valid for our thought about God in himself, is not valid for our thought about his designs upon us? Could we exclude the 'negative theology' from the theology of salvation? Malevez, of course, rejects this curious (but nevertheless current) suggestion. We use the 'negative theology' as a check on the logical manipulation of the concepts in which dogmas receive expression. For example, Malevez points out, we say that the Word of God became man. 'According to the logical form of this judgement, we are saying that humanity is predicated as an act determining a potency, the Word. But in fact this is not so at all'[3] (that will be the main topic of the next chapter). And all the concepts which we

employ to express the mystery of salvation have to be seen as comple-
menting, helping to explain, one another.[1] To put this in my own way,
if we regard these concepts in isolation, we miss their true meaning.
As we can express the dogma of the Trinity only dialectically, stating
the unity of the Godhead and the fact that God *is* Three Persons, but
without comprehending how these truths are in reality one truth, so
with all aspects of the mystery of Salvation. The concepts which we use,
while never contradicting one another, do not add up to a single
comprehensive concept which exhausts the mystery. There is always
more than we can express.

In conclusion, then, Malevez justly claims that to re-animate that
bearing on transcendence which is proper to faith must be of vital
importance for a Christian and a theologian. Otherwise he will miss the
true meaning of his faith. Does this not mean that he must live 'in
the simplicity and silence of a contemplative theology'? It does in the
sense that discursive theology is not only leading to contemplation but
must spring from 'a certain contemplation which is immanent in the
exercise of faith itself'.[2] So here is full confirmation of the thesis with
which I began that there is an interplay between our concepts and the
light of faith.

It seems desirable to mention a concrete instance of the process. To
take one from the monastic theology of the twelfth century, we find in
the work of William of St Thierry the development of theology (in
particular, the theology of the Trinity) and the development of contemplative prayer considered as two processes which not only go hand
in hand but are ultimately indistinguishable from one another. Here I
must refer once more to Dom Odo Brooke, who has expounded the
views of William of St Thierry in a number of important articles; it
must now suffice to quote from the conclusion of one of them:

'The value of William's theology of faith is its dynamic conception of
faith as ascent to God. . . . His contribution is his recognition that,
whatever may be the value of speculative reasons for belief, the situation here and now of the believer is determined largely by his whole
disposition and that the right disposition is given by an ascent from the
"carnal" to the "spiritual" man . . . William sees faith as orientated
towards a supernatural experience . . . William's trinitarian mystical

[1] 247.   [2] 249.

experience appears as a development from the life of faith and as an anticipation of the final vision to which faith ultimately tends. . . . The whole logic of William's thought is therefore towards an intrinsic connection between faith and mystical experience so as to see that experience as developing progressively from the initial act of faith.'[1]

[1] *Recherches de Théologie ancienne et médiévale*, July–December 1963, 200–1.

III

THE ATONEMENT

10. THE INCARNATION

It may be well to repeat here what was said in the Preface that I am using the word 'atonement' in its older, etymological sense (although something will be said in due course about 'expiation'), and that I am not attempting a theological treatise on this greatest of subjects, the definitive union of man with God, but only considering, from a certain point of view, some problems which arise in connection with it. The first of them arises as soon as we turn to the first stage of that history on which the process of atonement hinges, the incarnation of the Word. 'The Word became flesh'—how can the Son of God, God the Son, *become* in any way? Would not this simply contradict that experience of the Absolute without which Christianity is unintelligible? Professor Karl Rahner, as we shall shortly see, brushes aside the difficulty with results which I find most disturbing. But before going into this I want to make clear that I am not mounting an attack upon Rahner's theology in general; nor do I dissent from his main conclusions about trinitarian theology—on the contrary, I am grateful to him for the warning that the word 'person', as applied to Father, Son and Spirit, can be easily misunderstood; I accept his formula: 'the one God subsists in three distinct manners of subsisting' (in explaining it, he shows clearly enough that the doctrine of the Trinity contains no contradiction), and his insistence that we know God as Father, Son and Spirit because they are *as such* communicated to us in our Christian experience is extremely welcome (this is what he means by the formula: 'The "economic" Trinity is the "immanent" Trinity').[1] It is the central difficulty of Christology and this alone with which I shall be concerned.

In the first volume of Rahner's *Schriften zur Theologie* we read:

'. . . the assertion of God's "immutability", of the lack of any real relation between God and the world, is in a true sense a dialectical

[1] His short (but, as usual, highly involved) account of this is to be found in an English version, *The Trinity* (Burns and Oates).

statement. One may and indeed must say this, without for that reason being a Hegelian. For it is true, come what may, and a dogma, that the Logos himself has become man: thus that he himself has become something that he had not always been (*formaliter*); and that therefore what has so become is, as just itself and of itself, God's reality. Now if this is a truth of faith, ontology must allow itself to be guided by it . . . and grant that while God remains immutable "in himself", he can come to be "in the other", and that *both* assertions must really and truly be made of the same God as God.'[1]

The question whether God's 'immutability' means 'the lack of any real relation' between him and the world (and, if so, in what sense) will be discussed later. It is the rest of the passage just quoted which raises the main issue. I took occasion to refer to these remarkable statements in the course of an article in 1962[2] and said that I could not understand them. A few years later, when they seemed to have aroused no protest and still seemed incomprehensible, I wrote an article about them,[3] some parts of which will be reproduced here. An attempt to elicit a reply from Rahner was unsuccessful unless we can count what his former student, Dr Louis Roberts, in his book *The Achievement of Karl Rahner* (1967), has suggested with reference to me, that 'a transcendental system may not be clear to a metaphysician of a different school'.[4] In fact, as I have already indicated,[5] I am not in disagreement with the 'transcendental system' except in so far as it seems to me to involve needless complexities which are capable of causing some confusion. If it leads of its nature to the conclusion that God is not always the same, then, in my opinion, there must be something more wrong with it than I had realized.

I have said that when I wrote the above-mentioned article Rahner's statements seemed to have provoked no protest. Pannenberg, however, had commented in a detached sort of way that, if we are going to allow change in God at all, it will not do to postulate an 'inner being' of God from which change is nevertheless to be excluded; that is what he takes these statements to mean.[6] And there had been certain develop-

---

[1] I quote from the English version, *Theological Investigations*, I, 181, n. 3.
[2] *The Downside Review*, 329 n.
[3] 'A Changing God', *The Downside Review*, July 1966.
[4] 119.   [5] In ch. 4.
[6] v. *Jesus—God and Man* (S.C.M.), 320.

ments. As we shall see later, other writers had followed Rahner's lead. But, more importantly, he had discussed his own views at considerable length in a symposium ('Considérations Générales sur la Christologie' in *Problèmes Actuels de Christologie*).[1] Here he tells us that we must try to effect a reconciliation between God's immutability and 'the Word became man' if we are to be truly Christians. 'The traditional scholastic theology and philosophy', he goes on to say, 'explain that becoming and change are on the side of the created reality which has been assumed, and not on the side of the Logos'[2] but 'the affirmation of God's immutability must not make us forget that what has occurred in our midst in Jesus, in "becoming" and as history, is precisely the history of the Word of God himself, *his own* "becoming". If we consider the fact of the Incarnation without prejudice and without blinking . . . we must hold all this together: God can become something, the Immutable in himself can *himself* be mutable in another.'[3]

So far Rahner has told us nothing fresh. But at this point he discloses to us the workings of his mind. In a long footnote to the passage last quoted he says that whether one is prepared to talk about 'change' in this connection or not is not really the point. 'If we do call it a change . . . this "changing *in* another" cannot be considered a contradiction of God's immutability nor be simply reduced to meaning only the "changing *of* another". Ontology must here be guided by the message of faith without "scholasticizing" it.' Rahner goes on to suggest that the unity of God is in the same position in regard to the Trinity as the immutability is in regard to the mutability. In each case the tendency of the natural intelligence would lead us to a one-sided conclusion if we were not checked by the message of faith. This seems to me, to put it mildly, a dangerous line. Certainly it does nothing to show that Rahner's formula for the Incarnation does not involve a contradiction. But it would appear that this is, in his eyes, too simple-minded a way of approaching the question. We have to approach it in a 'dialectical' way:

'The statement about God's immutability is a dialectical statement, like that about his unity: the two statements do not remain for us—in actual fact—truly accurate, unless our thought at once opposes to them the two other statements (about the Trinity and the Incarnation) . . . the doctrine of the Incarnation reveals to us that the immutability (without

[1] Published by Desclée de Brouwer in 1965.   [2] 24.   [3] 28.

being suppressed, all the same) is not precisely and by itself *what* distinguishes God, but that *the latter*, in his immutability and despite it, can truly *become* something. . . . And we must not consider this possibility in God as a sign of indigence, but as the high point of his perfection, which would be less if, as well as being infinite, he could not become less than he eternally is. One can, one must express oneself so without thereby becoming a Hegelian.'

This may seem an attractive position. Just as the claim to a know-ledge of the Absolute apart from the Christian revelation is a claim to a knowledge of what is strictly inexpressible and can only be 'pointed to' in paradoxical terms, so (we may think) that more intimate knowledge with which the revelation provides us leads us to make further para-doxical statements. It is the inexpressible knowledge of the Incarnation and the Trinity which is the ultimate source of intelligibility, and what we *really* mean by 'immutability' (if we know what we are talking about) can be seen only in its light. A theologian should not deny that what we mean by it will be immeasurably deepened; it will now be seen in its proper context, and there will be now no temptation to regard God as 'static', in the sense of 'inactive', for we know something of the activity in which he subsists. But does our Christian experience require us to say that God 'can truly *become* something' in the sense that these words are ultimate, irreplaceable, 'pointers' to what we are trying to express? Does it make any *sense* to say that God is 'immutable' if we must also say that he becomes 'less than he eternally is'? And would this not *contradict* that ('transcendental') knowledge of God which is the presupposition of accepting his revelation? At the very least, Rahner cannot claim to have put out of court, theologically speaking, that highly authoritative statement of St Thomas's in the sixteenth question of the *Tertia Pars* (a.b, ad 2.): 'When it is said "God became man", no change on God's side is meant, but only on the side of the human nature.'

Certainly there is a sense in which we are dialecticians when we speak of God. That is, the things which we say positively about him have to be denied in their finite sense, so that we may be understood as affirming them in an eminent sense. If we say that God is unchanging, we must not be understood to mean that he is unchanging in the sense in which we might say that someone's habits were unchanging, for this might spell mere inactivity and would then be the very opposite of what in fact we mean. And to say that someone is active in the ordinary sense is to say that he changes. God is unchanging because his activity, being infinite, can never be either less or more than it *is*. When we say (as we do) that God is unchanging in *that* sense, I cannot see that there is anything 'dialectical' about it. If our faith told us that in fact he *does* change, we should have to abandon *either* our previous statement *or* our faith.

To say that God is infinite or active or perfect or whatever is always simply to say that God is the ineffable Other, who can be 'pointed to' but never *described* in human words. This fundamental affirmation of God is expressed in negative terms (he is *Other*), and we know that this negation is true absolutely and without remainder because the affirmation has for us positive significance. It is also true that we are 'reflections' of God—we are in a unique sense 'like' him; but the fundamental 'otherness' remains. We know what we mean by the negative statement, and we know that it is not contradicted by the 'likeness'. There is no sort of parallel in this state of affairs to Rahner's suggestion that we must hold together the notion of changelessness and the notion of change if we are to face God's incomprehensibility in the right way. To say that there is would be to say that God is both the Other and not the Other, both Infinite and finite. It would be to say that he is totally unintelligible.

Rahner restates his formula in the following way: 'The original phenomenon given us in the faith is rather the self-stripping, the becoming, the Κένωσις and the Γένεσις of God, who can become in so far as, positing the other as an effect, he himself *becomes* this effect, without becoming it in himself because he is the principle' [of this process].[1] This adds nothing new. But the report of the discussion following upon his paper contains points of interest. It was not until the end of it that the question of God's mutability arose in a big way. Rahner (in reply to a question) remarked that he did not reach his conclusion by way of an abstract concept of God, 'possessed in advance'.[2] I might remark that my references to the religious consciousness have had just as little to do with an 'abstract concept'. He went on to say that there is truth in the formula: God has no real relations *ad extra*. 'But', he asked, 'what is this God who has no real relation with myself? This is absurd: God really loves me, really became flesh. . . .' This seems to me quite unsatis-

[1] 27.　[2] 407.

factory as an argument for Rahner's thesis. God loves his creatures with an unchanging love—it 'makes no "difference" to him in the sense that it is always what it is; it is not something "added" to him'.

After Rahner's reply he was asked: 'And so what do you now mean by God's immutability in himself?' Rahner's final statement, in answer to this, must be quoted in full:

'Let us take an example: Jesus Christ sat here, then there: I can affirm that of God himself: before God was here, now he is there. All Christians agree about that. Thus God was in a real situation—however you like to express it—in which he is not now. That is what I mean by mutability.

I know that God was defined as immutable by the First Vatican Council. I accept it. And I want to reconcile these two affirmations, at least in my own mind. The way to do so is to say that God is immutable in himself, but mutable in another, since I forbid myself, in the name of faith, to abandon either term. Scholastic theology presents us with an anomaly which is certainly very understandable but which we should try to avoid: certain things which ought to have been said at the beginning of a discussion are brought in only in view of objections. It is only when we come to the Incarnation that we speak for the first time about the mutability or non-mutability of God. Why not plumb the depths of this question at the beginning, for example in connection with the co-existence of a limited and created world with the immutable and eternal God? Furthermore the question of God's mutability and immutability arises for the philosopher too. For he puts more formally the celebrated question: "Why did not God change in creating the world?"—the question whether God would be different if he had not created the world.

For my part I reply that he would not be different in himself but that he would be different in another.'[1]

It seems to me very strange that Père Bouëssé, winding up the discussion at this point, should have commented on Rahner's last words: 'That is equivalently what the great scholastics meant in agreement with St Thomas when they taught that the relation of the world to God is real on the side of the world, because it is on this side that there is change; (a relation) of reason on the side of the immutable God. . . .'

Again Rahner offers no fresh illumination in the passage last quoted

[1] 408–9.

but introduces two fresh topics, Vatican I and the problem of God's freedom in creating. It is surely very odd to interpret Vatican I as saying something compatible with what he wants to say. One might surely expect him to consider the possibility that 'freedom' might be interpreted in a way which does not make God 'mutable'. If Vatican I did not *really* mean 'immutable', just like that, then why must we say that in its condemnation of Guenther (*libertate a quavis necessitate soluta*) (1) it must be defining God's freedom as freedom of *choice*? It does seem to be true that if we attribute to God freedom of *choice* in creating (in any ordinary sense of that expression) then we are conceiving of him as being faced by alternatives and as leaving one of these alternatives unrealized. Thus, if God had not created, his act of creation would remain in him as an unrealized possibility, capacity or potentiality, which is plainly out of the question. If, on the other hand, we say that there is no question of God's not creating we identify his act of creating with himself and it then becomes *necessary*. But this does not make the created world necessary to God or a 'part of God', and those conclusions are all that we must avoid. God does not create because he needs something, but because he is super-generous. That is what we should mean here by calling him 'free'.[1] It becomes obvious, then, that Rahner's final contention (which proves to be a *philosophical* one) is far from plausible. We are asked to accept a God who is partly mutable and partly immutable on the ground that his freedom in creation must be interpreted in a way which would lead to this result. It is certainly not clear that it must be so interpreted.

It remains to consider the suggestion that any other account of the Incarnation will avoid a contradiction only by lapsing into vacuity. If God does *not* change, what can we mean by his 'owning' a human nature? It would be absurd to attempt a full answer to this question here, but it is not very difficult, I think, to show that we can mean something by the formula. We can mean by it that the acts of Jesus Christ are the acts of the divine Word, which is considered to be a touchstone of Catholic orthodoxy. We can mean by it that the sacred humanity is the *instrumentum conjunctum divinitatis*, which is St Thomas's favourite phrase. We can mean by it that our Lord was tried in all respects like ourselves except for sin, which is as far as the New Testament will take us (Hebrews 4, 15). We can mean all these things by it if

---

[1] This has been discussed at length in *Absolute Value*, ch. 8.

we take it as saying that there was no human centre of moral responsibility in the Incarnate Word but that the divine Word acted upon the human will, acted *in* that will without hindrance and without the possibility of hindrance. The human will was always and indefectibly united with the will of the divine Word. That at least we can mean by the truth that there is no human *person* in the Incarnate Word. A human person is exposed to the danger of sin. He is the sort of created reality who has to *choose* his destiny. The human nature of Christ is not that sort of created reality. The divine Word acts in and through the human nature which refers its activities wholly to the Word. In the moral order we can originate nothing but our defects. Everything else is God's gift to us. Christ's human acts are nothing at all but God's gift. These acts are human acts, but there is no defect in them. And in that sense they are wholly attributable to God.

In the moral order, then, there is a difference not only of degree but of kind between our human nature and Christ's. But there is not only a moral difference. There is an ontological difference, and it is to this that we refer when we speak of the 'hypostatic union'; we can describe its effects or at any rate one of them: the absence of a human centre of moral responsibility. But this must be made clearer. By 'moral responsibility' here is meant moral control, the control over a situation which is always, during this life, radically at risk. Our human actions are under our moral control because there is always the possibility that we might have *chosen* otherwise than in fact we did. Thus they are *ours* in a sense in which the actions of Christ's human nature are not his, for these are always entirely controlled by the divine Word. The absence of moral responsibility, thus understood, is not therefore a defect but a supreme privilege. A human personality is *for* union with God; it has to achieve it and by its own free choice. Christ's human will was always perfectly united with the divine will; his soul was never separated from God by the barrier of a human personality. His human nature possesses from the start what gives *value* to a human personality.

There is no need to attribute suffering to the divine Word (supposing that we could mean anything by this) on the ground that a human nature, as opposed to a human person, cannot be the subject of it. Certainly it makes no sense to attempt such a distinction between a human person and a human nature. But nobody is trying to do so; the distinction is between the 'man Jesus' and the divine Word. The lack of

'personality' in the 'man Jesus' is not loss but gain. He is in all respects
like us, save for sin; that is to say, human nature in him is not an unreal
abstraction (we say '*the* human nature', but even so there is always the
suggestion of something unreal about it) but a mind, heart or soul with
all that this normally implies as well as a body with all that it normally
implies. The fact that his human will is indefectibly united with the
divine will does not make him any less of a man (although we might say
that it makes him a different *sort* of a man)—on the contrary, it makes
him, as Rahner has put it, 'the supreme and unique case of the essential
achievement of the human reality'.[1] We can therefore attribute suffering to the 'man Jesus'; there is no reason why he should not be considered as a subject. But, it may be said, if he is to be considered a
subject of suffering, why is he not also a subject of acts?

To this one must reply that he is not the *ultimate* subject of acts, and
not merely in the general sense in which all our actions are God's gifts
to us but in the particular sense that his are 'owned' or 'appropriated'
by the divine Word as gifts which cannot be refused or impaired by the
receiver. But they are received by the human Christ; they are gifts to
him; and in that sense they belong to him. All this seems perfectly
obvious and straightforward if one puts it in concrete terms and avoids
abstract formulas and 'notions'. The sufferings of Christ also belong to
Christ as man, but it does not follow that they are 'owned' or 'appropriated' by the divine Word in the same way as the activities. In some way
they are indeed 'appropriated': the divine Word is in a unique relationship of ownership in regard to the human nature. The human nature
which suffers is the human nature which is granted an inexpressible
sanctity by the hypostatic union and caught up thereby into the
trinitarian processions. But if we are to say 'the divine Person suffers',
we are using a formula which can be given a meaning only through the
'communication of idioms' (and it is all too clear that the risks involved
in this procedure are not always properly appreciated). It is precisely
in so far as they proceed from God that the moral activities of the
human nature are attributable in a special sense to God. The sufferings,
on the other hand, of Christ are due to the malice of men; they arise not
from above but from below.

But if we follow Rahner we shall have to say that 'the divine Person
suffers' *as divine*. And this has been maintained in an article '*Unus de*

[1] Article cited, 21.

Trinitate passus est' which appeared in 1965.[1] The author declares explicitly that it is not enough to say that the manhood suffered,[2] but he wants to say also that the immutability of the 'divine essence' is untouched. He admits, or rather insists, that this is 'from the point of view of human wisdom, pure folly'.[3] And in regard to the Antiochene theologians he writes: 'Not distinguishing properly between the divine nature and the divine Persons, they inclined to believe that to attribute suffering to the Person of the Word leads to the absurdity that the Divinity has undergone it.'[4] I cannot see how he himself avoids this absurdity. Is there something called 'the Divinity' which is *not* the Persons? In any case the literal attribution of suffering to a divine Person seems to me simply meaningless, a contradiction. It is perfectly true, as this writer says, that Christians have regularly used language which, on the face of it, could be taken in this sense and that some of the Fathers seem to have *meant* it to be taken in this sense. He maintains that to take it in any other sense is to be untrue to the tradition. But how can it be denied that the distinction of the 'natures', human and divine, in Jesus is not solidly grounded in the tradition? The Chalcedonian formula may not be the final and perfect *expression* of this truth, but the insistence that the 'natures' are 'unconfused' is clearly traditional. It is astonishing that one should need to say so. And to introduce suffering into the divine Word is surely to confuse it with the human nature. In reply to such objections it is simply repeated that the 'divine Person', not the 'divine essence', is in question.[5]

In his *L'Unité du Christ* Père Galtier has written: 'People imagine a Christ who is accessible even in his divine being to what makes men weak and wretched. That is to return to certain morbid dreams of other days . . . men love to recognize themselves in their Saviour, but a God so degraded could not move them.'[6] Whatever one may think of Galtier's book in other respects, one would have thought that this passage was unexceptionable. But our author goes on to quote it with disapproval. And here he opposes to it Rahner's view which, he tells us, is 'in the logic' of the Incarnation. Once more he insists: 'That is not to believe that God's state is diminished. The objection would stand if we supposed, as some interpreters of the *Kenosis* have done, that the Word, in accepting suffering, lost his essential impassibility. But our faith is

[1] *Recherches de Science Religieuse*, 4th issue, by Jean Chéné.
[2] 547. [3] 564n. [4] 552. [5] 581–2. [6] 326–7.

quite different. The Son of God, St Cyril said, suffered impassibly.'[1]
He then puts the rhetorical question: 'Is it true that such a picture of
God is not likely to move us?' If it does move us, I can only say, it must
do so in a most unsatisfactory way. What can it *mean* to say that the
Word literally experiences suffering *and* is impassible? The passage
from Rahner which is adduced to support this conclusion will be found
in the same chapter of *Theological Investigations (I)* from which my
original quotation came (it is preceded by a discussion of creation on
the lines which we have already traced): 'How many have died
"piously in the Lord" with the thought that this common and general
death must mean something just because . . . the coherent Meaning
at the heart of being, because He—really He himself—died.'[2]

Our author observes sadly: 'When one discusses this subject with an
educated believer who has reflected philosophically upon his faith, it is
not uncommon for him to say: "This dogma is unthinkable: in Christ
only the man has suffered; to believe the contrary would be to diminish
God".'[3] I hope that educated believers will continue to say that when
they are presented with this 'dogma'. And I would make Galtier's
words my own: 'To make out that fear, disgust and sadness overflowed
from Christ's human nature into his divine nature has always seemed an
impiety; for anyone in our time to want this spectacle to unfold in the
divine consciousness itself, so as to seem moving to us, indicates moreover a profound ignorance of what the Christian life has always been.'[4]
It can be retorted, of course, that Galtier and I (not to mention more
important persons down the ages) have failed to achieve the essential
Christian insight, that we are trying to impose our own 'ideas' of God on
the Christian consciousness instead of listening to the voice of God in
the Bible and in the Church. There is nothing more, at this stage, to be
said about that. Admittedly the thought of an infinite love, absolutely
active and absolutely unchanging, is one which we can attain to only
at the furthest limit of our powers; and it is surrounded with the deepest
mystery. But I believe it to lie at the heart of true religion. Admittedly
we are only babbling when we speak of it. But we must speak as best
we can—and we can at least satisfy ourselves that there are some things
which must *not* be said.

The tendency of our time is against this. The 'impassibility' of

---

[1] Article cited, 585.   [2] Rahner, 177.
[3] Art. cit., 585.   [4] *L'Unité du Christ*, 326.

God is one of the most frequently contested Christian doctrines. It would be possible to point to many modern theologians who in other respects are highly perceptive, fully informed and solidly traditional but who think it necessary to introduce hazard and frustration into the life of God himself. There is a *Zeitgeist* which affects the 'process-theologians' in an obvious way and others who cannot be simply so described in a less obvious way. Without erecting the processes of our human knowledge and our timefulness into laws which must control the life of God, they feel nevertheless that absolute *sameness* must mean restrictedness. So we find Professor Frederick Sontag[1] suggesting that God's perfection is safeguarded provided that his *power* is acknowledged to be unlimited. If we have said this, then, he thinks, we can attribute to him what I may perhaps sum up by calling it an 'expanding freedom', a freedom to do fresh things which will be *for him* a real development. Unless this is granted, Sontag seems to think, God must be 'static' in a restrictive sense. It is clear to him that Professor Hartshorne's view of a developing God has the effect of making him *vulnerable*, and this he very properly rejects. But the alternative which he proposes, it seems plain to me, is still anthropomorphic. I cannot avoid the conclusion that this recurrent failure to grasp what is meant by the 'transcendence' of God in classical theology is a mark of theological decadence.

Let us take one more example of introducing change into God and denying it at the same time. In *Man and Sin*,[2] a generally admirable (if somewhat obscure and highly controversial) book by Father Piet Schoonenberg, there is the statement: 'Despite his transcendence above our world and his immanence within himself, nevertheless God himself operates, communicates himself, enters into relation with his creatures, and is thus himself affected by these relations.'[3] If this meant only that God's creative act and his operations upon his creatures are identical with God's changeless self, it would be quite acceptable, although it would bring us again to the question of God's freedom in these activities. But a footnote to the passage shows that it does not mean this:

'We admit a real relation not only from effect to cause, but also from cause to effect, respectively a passive and an active relation. This is why we would like to call real not only the relation from creature to

[1] *The Heythrop Journal*, Oct. 1968.
[2] Translation from the Dutch (Sheed and Ward) 1965.   [3] 50.

God but also the relation from God to creature. The latter is then a relation of pure perfection (scholastic philosophy, too, admits relations of pure perfection when it conceives of the three persons as relations to each other). God is not "relative" as opposed to "absolute". But he is "relational", "involved" or, better still, "involving himself". In this way he really changes in his perfect outward activity and relation, without, however, any imperfection or dependence.'

Schoonenberg tells us in this footnote that he 'has been led to these conclusions among others by a passage of Karl Rahner's about the activity of God and of Christ' referring to the chapter in *Theological Investigations* with which we have been concerned. It will be seen that he calls in question the Thomist doctrine that there are relations between creatures and God but no relation between God and creatures, the whole point of which is to preserve the truth that God is wholly immutable. The 'relations of pure perfection' which constitute the divine Persons are a red herring here, for they obviously introduce no change into God. We could indeed say that God is related to his creatures if we meant by this only that he 'includes', so to say, his own operations upon them (some theologians, anxious to give God freedom of *choice* and to avoid any *necessity* in the creative act, have spoken of it as if it were something to do with the world but nothing to do with God himself, and we might well wish to insist that this is nonsense by speaking here of a 'relation'—which is in reality identical with God himself). But to say that 'he really changes in his perfect outward activity and relation, without, however, any imperfection or dependence' must mean, in the context, that God adds to himself in some way. And this, again, I venture to say, is really meaningless.

One must be grateful to Rahner for facing squarely the central Christological problem, even if one rejects his thesis, because it has been so often evaded by unphilosophical theologians. A sort of cryptofideism, concentrating on subsidiary or on merely historical questions, has so often passed itself off as Christology. Once upon a time there was a marked tendency to swallow up Christ's humanity in the divinity or at least to make it unreal, not a genuine humanity. In our time, naturally and rightly, the emphasis has been on the genuineness of the humanity, but this has often led to a swallowing up of the divinity in the humanity. The greatest danger for the theologian, I repeat, is to forget *who God is* or (it amounts to the same thing) to interpret the New Testament in a way which makes it simply *contradict* the basic deliverances of the religious consciousness. It may be added that one of the troubles about orthodox Christology is that it has been conducted to so large an extent in abstract terms. The uniqueness of Christ demands an 'experiential' vocabulary—we must stick to the peculiarity of the facts, the essential *newness* of the Gospel (here must lie the answer to the question so pertinently raised by Professor M. F. Wiles: does Christology rest on a mistake?)[1] The interminable Thomist discussions about whether there is more than one *esse* in Christ, or whether St Thomas is consistent in what he says about it, seem to me very largely a waste of time. And the equally interminable discussions about Christ's knowledge (in particular, his knowledge of himself) must also be a waste of time if the disputants do not begin by asking what it *means* to say 'The Word became flesh'.

The answer which I have adumbrated in this chapter may seem not only to evacuate the mystery (as Rahner and his disciples would, of course, say) but also to imperil the genuineness of Christ's human freedom. I have tried to show that 'freedom to sin' is not a positive perfection without which the Word could not be incarnate. But it may still be felt that, in this case, Christ is not really 'one of us'. The answer must be that he is not simply 'one of us'. Either we accept the 'hypostatic union' and allow that the 'assumption' of our human nature has unique consequences, or we reject it—and reject the whole tradition (the story of Christ's temptations is not the story of our human moral weakness but the story of divine power which has abolished this weakness). It has not been my purpose to suggest a new Christology, only to suggest that the implications of the tradition need to be more persistently investigated. There is nothing here, I believe, which has not been said before—and said very much better. One way of substantiating that last statement would be to quote *in extenso* from *Le Pierre Vivante*[2] by Maurice Zundel. I must be content, apologizing for its clumsiness in English, with a single passage:

'God had not to change and could not in any case do so, for it was impossible to add to the gift which he is. It is the creature which had to

---

[1] In *Religious Studies,* March 1970.
[2] *Les Editions Ouvrières,* 1954.

change, to assimilate *in a new way* and by an infinite opening of itself all that this gift, eternally fulfilled, was ready to communicate, once there was no limit opposed to his effusion. That is why the *kenosis* . . . the emptiness requisite for a complete offering of the self to the divine embrace, clearly affects, in Christ, the *assumed* human nature and not the Divinity which unites it to itself . . . the humanity of Christ is emptied of 'personality' ('*je-individu*') by being seized upon, and wholly transported into the Word by this infinite altruism. . . .'[1]

II. ORIGINAL SIN AND THE REDEMPTION

A Christian is not called upon to believe that Christ came into the world only because it was a sinful one. It seems plain enough to me that the Incarnation must be the point in God's plan 'to which the whole creation moves'. But a Christian is called upon to believe that Christ won a victory over sin in his life, death and resurrection. And before we can discuss how this victory was won and what its effects are we must consider the sinfulness of the world into which he came. This means that we must consider the doctrine of 'original sin'. It is a doctrine which has come under scrutiny in a very big way, among Roman Catholics especially, during the past few years. The account of it which was to be found in theological manuals until quite recently, deriving directly from St Thomas Aquinas and indirectly from St Augustine, has been seen to be, in important respects, only a *theologoumenon*.

Recently an article appeared in *New Blackfriars*[2] by the Dominican theologian, Father Timothy McDermott, in which he first discussed St Thomas's view of the matter and then put forward his own. He points out that 'the significance of the term "original sin" is not primarily sin "started on its way at mankind's origin"' but rather 'sin transmitted to each individual at his or her origin' and that St Thomas understood it in this sense. The essential problem, as he says, does not relate to the story of the Fall in Genesis but to the New Testament teaching, in particular in the famous passage of *Romans* (5, 12), insisted upon by the Council of Trent, to the effect that Christ is our only way of salvation and that all men are somehow guilty of sin. As McDermott puts it, 'mankind not only suffers the effect of sin, but shares in the sin itself'.

[1] 96.   [2] Jan.–Feb. 1968.

He goes on to say that this 'must be true even of men who have not themselves committed sinful actions. For babies have not personally sinned, yet need to be baptized (or whatever other grace God may give them when baptism is impossible). So there must be some other kind of sin which you incur simply by being born a man. . . . The tradition is clear that, although the situation cannot be described as personal sin, it can nevertheless be properly described as "sin" and as "guilty".' This, then, was the problem with which St Thomas was faced.

Certainly he realizes what it is. In the passage which contains his essential teaching on the subject,[1] he allows that, although inherited bodily defects may occasion certain defects in the soul, the idea of guilt, which must always be voluntary, seems to be excluded. I quote from McDermott's convenient statement of the general line of St Thomas's thought on this matter:

'without the special grace of paradise, Adam's nature would have reproduced itself such as it was, with all its natural defects, but the grace given to him by God perfected that nature and ensured that when it reproduced itself it would do so with the same perfection as it had in Adam. After the fall, however, when this grace had been lost, the nature was abandoned to its tendency to reproduce itself with defects; only now this tendency—being one of the effects of Adam's voluntary sin— is not simply natural, but also culpable.'

The well-known conclusion of St Thomas's article in the *Summa Theologiae* must now be quoted:

'All men born from Adam can be considered as a single man in so far as they share one nature . . . they are like the many members of one body. Now the act of one bodily member, such as the hand, is not voluntary through the intention of the hand itself but through that of the soul . . . just as the actual sin which is committed by means of the member is not the sin of that member except in so far as that member is something belonging to the man himself, so original sin is not a sin of the person except in so far as this person receives his nature from our first parent, for which reason it is also called a *sin* of nature. . . .'

McDermott makes the usual and unanswerable comment that this

[1] *Summa Th.*, 1a 11ae, Q. 8, a. 1.

analogy of the will working through the hand with Adam working through his descendants cannot be accepted (the main point here, surely, is that we are *not* 'a single man' in Adam). And, as we shall shortly see, he has another objection to St Thomas's line of thought. But he does claim that St Thomas's explanation 'succeeds in giving some sort of sense to a guilt which is not personal without reducing that notion to the totally improper use of the word "guilt" to mean simply misfortune or penalty'. After speaking of the 'intention of nature' which is reproduced at every birth, he expounds St Thomas as follows: 'Mankind is related to the voluntarily warped intention of nature, as the hand is related to the voluntarily warped intention of the person.' It is not easy to see that this makes the word 'guilt' any less improper in such a context. Adam is the only person, on this showing, who can be called 'guilty' in the proper sense. And if we suffer some defect through Adam's guilt, it is surely our misfortune.

Here I shall interpose a brief comment on St Thomas's doctrine about the grace of paradise and the loss of it. Apart from the question of God's attitude to his creatures (which might appear, on the face of it, arbitrary and ungenerous) there is the difficulty that the first man seems to be described as created with grace, or supernatural life, already, so to say, automatically laid on. It is perfectly respectable, theologically speaking, to hold that the possession of grace implies, in any circumstances, a willingness to receive it. The first man (or men), we may say, if we wish, rejected the grace which had been originally accepted.

McDermott's further objection to St Thomas's account refers to the presupposition that we are all connected up, biologically, with a first man. Scientists, by and large, consider it, at the least, highly improbable that the whole human race derives from a single couple. Here it may be remarked that polygenism has not been condemned by the Church, although it was blown upon by Pope Pius XII in the Encyclical *Humani Generis* in so far as it appeared incompatible with the doctrine of original sin. Theologians were quick to point out that, if it ceases to appear incompatible with that doctrine, then it will become acceptable; and this is one of the reasons why reinterpretations of the doctrine have been so frequent of late. McDermott points out that, in St Thomas's account, 'if Adam had not sinned, then every man in turn would have stood as representative of the progeny that came after him . . . it becomes possible to conceive a situation in which only the father of all

Frenchmen sinned, and in which consequently all Frenchmen were in original sin, but no other men on earth's surface . . .', from which he draws the conclusion that 'biological solidarity as such is not sufficient to explain the kind of unity mankind has'. As he points out, some theologians evolved another theory in order to avoid such difficulties, that of a divine decree constituting the first man sole representative of all mankind, making him responsible for the fate of human nature, apart from all questions about biology (Milton's Adam was very conscious of his vast responsibility, and the suggestion is that such a 'decree' would have been a great incentive to correct behaviour for Adam). It is not necessary to argue that this explanation is implausible.

What, then, is McDermott's proposed solution? In briefest outline it is this. Mankind is a unity because the human drama in which we are all actors is working towards a unity, the unity of each one of us in Christ. Our inability to achieve unity by our own efforts is represented by the natural defects described in the book of Genesis. Until Christ, the chief character, makes his appearance the drama is not seen to have a plot. This is the coming of grace; the rejection of Christ by the authorities of his time is the rejection of grace. It follows that the redemption, instead of undoing what happened in the past, undoes an action coincident with it in time.

But this requires a good deal of explanation, and I shall now quote the key sentences of McDermott's account:

'Just as Aquinas conceived of a biological intention of nature pre-supposed to all personal intentions (and therefore in a position to taint them), so we must conceive of an intention of history, which I call its plot, underlying every man's personal life in so far as that life is a role in the total play. . . . Mankind is, so to speak, a collection of actors in search of an author, a collection of limbs in search of a head . . . the way in which God intended to overcome man's divisions was to send his Son as a man to give unified sense to human history . . . each man has personal responsibility for his life in so far as it is individual to him. Amid the welter of events that it contains and will contain he must try to build a self, he bears the responsibility of *selving* his personal history. The plan of God was to provide a "self" for the whole of mankind's history by living himself a personal human life. Without such *selving* of history no individual can selve himself properly, for part of what he is to be is a role in history at large, and there will be no history at large unless history is capable of selving itself. . . . A biologically-conceived grace can only exert influence chronologically forward in time; a grace conceived of on the analogy of a chief character or climax in a play exerts its influence both forward and backward in time . . . the men on the spot at the time when the incarnation of God was offered rejected it. In doing so they spoilt the whole play . . . they abandoned history to its innate defectiveness. But now the defectiveness, which without their fault would have been only natural, is in the light of their fault culpable.'

Here, I think, we have the essential features of McDermott's theory. Original sin is brought about by the rejection of Christ. There is now a 'culpable failure of history to be *selved* in Christ', and the roles which the individual actors play in the drama are affected by this as soon as they appear on the scene. Original sin attaches to them not as personal sin but in so far as they are characters in the drama. Before trying to assess this theory we must notice that it is bound up with a theory about redemption. History has failed, McDermott goes on, with the rejection of Christ, but Christ, being God, could 'accept that rejection and build out of it another course of history—one no longer bounded by the limits of death but incorporating death within it as one of its events'. For 'in rising from the dead, he opened a new life and a new history. . . . This new history, the history of redeemed mankind, of the Church, which we enter into through baptism, is built on rejection and built on the Cross.'

In all this there are undoubtedly valid theological insights. The theme of man's unification and the theme of the new history inaugurated by the resurrection are fundamental for Christian thought. It is good to be reminded that Christ *could* have been accepted, and then the plot of history would have worked itself out in a way about which it is useless to speculate—but it would have been a very different way. The death of Christ was not *prearranged* by his Father. But his death did not nullify his Father's plan. For this was always that we should have life, and have it more abundantly, through the coming of Christ. And so indeed we have. The way in which the plan works out, however, depends on the use which men make of their freedom. History has 'failed', but only in the sense that some men have failed to rise to their opportunities. That is what sin always is, and we are still left asking in what sense *all* men can be said to have *sinned* on this showing. Has this theory of original sin shed any light on that problem?

St Thomas's strong card was that a defect of nature is something which affects us in a most intimate way. We are now deprived when we come into the world of the grace which God meant us to have, and our nature is 'wounded' in consequence. Whether we can really make sense of St Thomas's view about the relation between nature and grace in this matter is a question which does not now concern us. The point is that original sin still seems to be reducible to the *effects* upon us of other peoples' sins. In other words, it is a misfortune. Does McDermott's theory lead to any different conclusion? Instead of appealing to the bond of nature, he appeals to our involvement in history. We are 'guilty' because we are involved in a history which has failed to work itself out. He refers to the situation of a man who is a member of an unjust society, who disapproves of 'the will of the community' but who cannot function in it at all without 'presupposing' this will because he must make use of the facilities provided by the society. 'In such a way', he writes, 'man is involved in the will of mankind or rather in the lack of will of mankind.' He thinks this explanation preferable to that put forward by a good many contemporary theologians according to which original sin is simply the sinful condition of the world which cannot fail to affect all its inhabitants. This, he says, does not properly explain how it can be itself their sin. I cannot see how his own theory avoids the difficulty, and it seems to have difficulties of its own.

It is often said nowadays that we may find ourselves faced with situations in which we *must* dirty our hands, on pain of an attempt to contract out of them, which is itself either immoral or impossible. This seems to me a confusion. There is no situation, however obscure or however heartrending, in which we cannot be guided by conscience— by our desire to promote the good, to make God our aim. If this is so, our involvement in history does no more to make us sinful than our natural inheritance. The actions of those who lived before Christ are not changed in their moral character by Christ's rejection; nor are the actions of those who live after it. What is true, however, is that a weakness of nature or the need to make the best of some very bad job may cause us the most intense regret. We are ashamed of our inability to act or of the necessary consequences of our action. But we must not confuse (as Mr D. Z. Phillips does)[1] regret with remorse. Some men *cannot* face heights; they feel that they *ought* to be able to face them. So, in a sense, they ought, if there is something 'unnatural' about this inability, some defect in nature. Original sin, as so far described, can be responsible for our committing 'material' sins, not for our committing 'formal' sins, for a deliberate turning away from what we have seen to be the good. How, then, can it cut us off from God?

Let us now consider another account of it, one which is chiefly (and rightly) concerned with God's attitude to his fallen creatures. Dom Mark Pontifex, writing on 'The Problem of the Fall',[2] proposes that when men first appeared (that is to say, when certain of the higher animals received spiritual powers, carrying with them the need for moral choice) they were 'at a first stage of spiritual development which should have led them to 'far keener insights into the purpose of life and the nature of the life to come than he possesses as things are'. 'As a result of these higher powers', Pontifex continues, 'his mind and will would have had far greater control over his body . . . he would have been in control of his passions . . . though he would have died, this would not have troubled him, for he would have had sufficient knowledge of the future life to prevent his feeling that he was entering the unknown.' Pontifex implies that death would not have been for him the separation of soul and body as we know it now but a painless transition to man's definitive state. This was God's design for man, but 'as man began to exercise the power of choice, the first generations, perhaps over a long period of years, gradually failed to choose rightly, and, instead of rising to greater powers, began to fall back'. Here the assumption is that 'human nature was very plastic when men first appeared and for some considerable time afterwards, so that it was capable of rapid progress or lack of progress, and would become fixed before long in whatever state it had reached'.

Certain difficulties may be felt already. We are asked to envisage a general refusal to co-operate with God's purposes building up steadily during this period when human nature was 'very plastic'. This may seem at first rather improbable. But on any showing we have to say, if we are Christians, that all have sinned and come short of the glory of God (Romans 3, 23). The prevalence of actual (as opposed to original)

[1] *Moral Practices*, 99–101.
[2] *The Downside Review*, Oct. 1968.

sin, although very mysterious, is certainly familiar enough, and unless we think of sin as always implying an out-and-out rebellion we cannot reasonably object to this proposal. But it is also proposed that man was destined to reach a fixed state after a period of time. And this may seem harder to accept. It may seem easier if we bear in mind that man's spiritual development cannot, in any case, pass beyond a certain stage in this life. He is designed, we may say, to reach some point of development (which we need not suppose to be the same for each individual), but he cannot go beyond it. The present proposal, as I understand it, is that this stage would have been reached in a relatively short time if all had gone well, but that men, by their moral shortcomings and resistances, began to move no longer towards it but away from it. We might describe the situation by saying that they were in the process of exhausting their spiritual capital rather than of increasing it and, instead of reaching the final point of their earthly achievement, they reached a point at which it *could* no longer be achieved, short of some divine intervention.

Pontifex goes on to argue that we cannot expect a divine intervention which would have the effect of inhibiting man's freedom, and that in these circumstances a divine intervention would have had precisely this effect. The decline into spiritual bankruptcy could not have been prevented. But we are asked to remember that 'at once God met the new situation by a new offer to man, suited to the new conditions'. We are told that 'God at once (to put it in our human way) provided a fresh dispensation . . . supernatural life was again offered to mankind and in a form to which he could respond in his new physical and psychological condition.' So 'the Incarnation and redemption took place.' The first thought that may occur to us at this point is that such an intervention (which does not inhibit man's freedom, but offers him, so to say, fresh spiritual capital) could have been made before; 'grace', Pontifex says, 'was now offered again in a fresh form'. On second thoughts we must surely say that since God does not change his plans there cannot be any 'intervention'. Pontifex, indeed, seems to accept that conclusion when he goes on to say: 'I should be very willing to agree that all grace comes from Christ, whether before or after the fall, so that in an important sense there is only one plan for mankind.' Yet he also says: 'We should have to add that grace becomes available to man in a different way before and after the fall owing to the different circumstances.' If the grace of Christ has been rejected at the time of 'the fall', what is the 'fresh form' in which grace is now to be offered? In what way are the circumstances different? We seem to have reached an *impasse*.

Perhaps we can emerge from it by taking another look at the grace which was originally offered and received. It is the traditional belief that this grace was restored (and more than restored) to us by Christ. The grace which Christ gives us is 'sanctifying grace'; it is that intimacy with God to which we are destined. The original grace was also 'sanctifying grace', although it was not yet that peculiar intimacy which we owe to Christ's death and resurrection. When Christ returned to his Father, that definitive grace, to which the whole world-process had been directed, was at last available to all men. All grace is 'in function' of Christ. But the just who lived before him, we shall have to conclude, could not possess this definitive grace in their lifetime, although they will not be deprived of it in the fullness of time (and what is time when one is dead?—it used to be said that they 'sleep' until he awakes them). The *newness* of Christianity seems to force us to the view that we must make these distinctions. And does it really make sense to talk of the retrospective effects of Christ's resurrection? How can an event which took place in time bear fruit in the past? Nevertheless the original grace was a sanctifying one. On Pontifex's theory this original grace had been, by a gradual process of deterioration, totally lost (this, like all grace, came to men through the Word, for he is always the Mediator). The grace of Jesus Christ, the Christian dispensation, is for the future. But this does not mean that contact with God was lost, for he refuses grace to no one who is willing to receive it. After 'the fall' what we may call 'justifying grace' was available to all men.

So we may retain Pontifex's theory about the fall without danger of incoherence if we also hold that there was not, after it, any fresh intervention or any previously unavailable grace. It hardly needs saying that this proviso is clean counter to the view of those who (like Professor John Hick)[1] wish to interpret *o felix culpa!* in a quite literal way. If we do that, we shall have to say either that the Word would not have become incarnate if there had been no sin to be redeemed or that it was part of God's own plan that there should be sin to be redeemed. I can only repeat that it seems to me plainly inconceivable that the

---

[1] *Evil and the God of Love, passim.*

Incarnation should *not* be God's original plan, that the supreme event of the world's history should be motivated by particular circumstances arising from men's failure to co-operate with the plan. Apart from the question of a *change* in God's plan, this notion of an *extra* outburst of divine generosity, although it often leads to impressive-sounding rhetoric, is a lapse into anthropomorphism, a sort of sentimentalism. And to say that sin is a part of God's plan must be to make him responsible for it. Ingenious attempts have been made to show that the 'motive' of the Incarnation, although not itself directly the catastrophe of man's sinfulness, nevertheless includes it, for God knows eternally that man will sin, and the Incarnation is therefore intended as the redemption of sin. But the *timelessness* of God's knowledge has nothing to do with it. God knows man's sin, we shall have to say (unless we make him responsible for it) only because man does in fact sin—and it is nonsense to say that man 'cannot help' doing so. It may baffle the imagination to envisage a situation from which all sin is excluded, but if we are to mean anything by man's moral freedom we cannot deny the possibility of it.

Nor can one deny the difficulties of the view which I have put forward. It is no contradiction to grant that man has an initiative, a 'negative priority', in his rejecting of God, if God is known to us as the *Source of values*. But God's knowledge of these rejections is something which leaves us baffled. How can he not be affected by them, subject to them in some sense, even though his knowledge of them is timeless? Here perhaps we are entitled to fall back on agnosticism. We cannot pretend to see things from God's end, to see through his eyes. But this sort of agnosticism is no justification for attributing to him what we see clearly to be limitations or imperfections. If it is said that we must confine ourselves to anthropomorphic language and that any attempt to avoid it will take us out of theology and into the uncharted and hazardous regions of mere metaphysics, I can only refer to the whole course of the argument which I have been trying to present in this book.

There are other difficulties. Not only is it difficult to imagine a situation from which all sin is excluded, but it is also difficult to image a situation in which the grace originally given has been *totally* lost. It is, however, by no means impossible to *conceive of* it. Pontifex argues that a certain physical and psychological integrity was necessary for the retention of original grace. The gradual deterioration which his theory postulates makes the same sort of appeal to biology as St Thomas does when he seeks to explain the unity of the whole human race. Men are dependent upon one another for the conditions in which they work out their salvation. They are always free to do so, but they will find hazards to surmount for which others are responsible. Is this unjust? Pontifex is content to say here that it is inevitable. But he would agree that the law of human solidarity may present itself as a stumbling block. Is it just that we should be committed to these hazards? Here I must refer to the discussion of evil in *Absolute Value*,[1] in which I argue that our dependence on one another may be legitimately conceived of as a gift of God's beneficence; our misuse of it is not his affair.

Let us now consider the positive advantages of Pontifex's theory. He can speak of the 'guilt' of original sin with more reason, I think, than one can on McDermott's view. It must still be called, strictly speaking, a misfortune, not a sin, but Pontifex points out that it is a situation 'opposed to God's will' and may therefore be described as a 'sinful state' with some justification; it is also 'a state in which man is especially tempted to personal sin'. The theory avoids the unsatisfactory contention that, since supernatural life was not *due* in any case to any-one, God could deprive men of it without injustice. Such an explanation, apart from the fact that God has other attributes besides justice, misconceives the relationship between the natural and the supernatural. It implies that we can get along satisfactorily enough without the super-natural. But if nature is *for* the supernatural, then, when it is cut off from it, it suffers a real deprivation; it is injured in itself. Such an explanation implies furthermore that the loss of supernatural life is a punish-ment inflicted deliberately by God. On Pontifex's theory, 'when man fell, the results that came about were not due to an arbitrary decree on God's part, but were the effect of the working out of the laws that governed man's evolution'. Furthermore the theory offers a picture of man's origin which is compatible with the findings of scientific research. It does not ascribe any highly developed powers to the first men, but allows for the sort of primitiveness which we should expect them to have. At the same time it can account for the possession, before the fall, of original justice, a state in which certain powers of mind and body were present in germ and intended to develop. 'Paradise', Pontifex writes, 'as described in Genesis is a poetic description of man's state, if he had evolved as he should.' There is no novelty about this or about

[1] Ch. 10.

some other features in the theory. But it constitutes, I think, a novel synthesis.

Finally Pontifex claims that the theory fits in with the doctrine of the Immaculate Conception:

'The doctrine tells us that at the first moment of her conception, through the merits of Jesus Christ, our Lady was preserved from any stain of original sin. I should put it like this. Just as Adam, the first man or men, introduced a condition of mankind contrary to God's will, so Christ, the new Adam, introduced a new condition, once more in accordance with God's will, but fitted to man as he existed as a result of the fall. . . . The preparation for the new dispensation began with the conception of our Lady, and she was at once in the new condition of human nature again in accordance with God's will. Thus she was never in the state handed down from Adam. . . .'

Once again, we must avoid any suggestion that God abandoned his original plan and substituted another, and in particular the suggestion that the Incarnation resulted from the fall. But we may say (I think we must say) that his plan is 'a priori adaptable', as Blondel puts it, to the needs of men, in so far as what is best for us at the time will depend on what we ourselves have made of our situation. But the plan itself, the providential ordering with the Christ-event as its climax, cannot, it seems to me, be altered. I should therefore wish to say, as the Book of Sirach (XXIV, 14) has been interpreted as saying, that our Lady was chosen before the foundation of the world, as part of the plan, as the necessary instrument of God's purpose. If what I have said about 'original grace' and the grace of the 'last times' is acceptable, it would seem to follow that it was 'original grace' to which our Lady was destined at her conception—that is to say, more precisely, she was destined to those conditions which would make possible the acceptance of such grace. She is, so to say, a fixed point in the plan. Whether or not things go wrong in the meanwhile, it is part of the plan that she should be conceived in these conditions. Perfect man, full of grace and truth (John 1, 14), could not be born of a mother with a deprived humanity.

It will be obvious that an awkward question arises. What if this original grace had been offered and rejected? We can only say, I suppose, that it would have been offered to some other Jewish maiden.

But all this is a matter of the vaguest speculation. I have only wished to suggest that we may have some clues in an area of theology which is certainly obscure. Such theories must be submitted to the judgement of the Church. But, having gone so far, I shall make the further suggestion that, if there is anything in what has been said here about the doctrine of the Immaculate Conception, the doctrine of the Assumption may come to appear as the natural pendant to it.

My purpose in this chapter has not been to put forward a definite thesis about original sin but only to show how wide open are the questions which arise in this connection and to remove, if possible, any suspicions that this Christian doctrine must be, metaphysically, an absurd one. With the same purpose in view I shall conclude with some reference to Schoonenberg's book mentioned in the last chapter.[1] Anyone who thinks that the Council of Trent canonized a particular theological theory in its declarations about original sin may be advised to read what Schoonenberg has written on this topic. In considering the authority of conciliar pronouncements we have to distinguish between the essential truths which they are concerned to preserve and the presuppositions in terms of which they are expressed. For example, it had just not occurred to the theologians of Trent to refer to the origins of the human race except in terms of 'Adam'. We have also to remember that their purpose, on certain occasions, was to *reject* a particular theological view; if this is not realized, we may interpret their statements in far too wide a sense. For example, the third canon of Trent's decree speaks of original sin as '*origine unum*'. Schoonenberg declares (with a reference to Jedin's history of the Council): 'Through these words the Council intends to reject the theory of Pighius, according to which original sin is numerically one and not multiple because in Adam's descendants it is no reality, but only imputed to them.'[2] And he here quotes from that very level-headed theologian, Father Peter Smulders: 'The formula says: "Original sin is not numerically one in different persons, but its unity lies only in its origin." The Council expresses no opinion concerning the nature of this unity in origin.'[3]

When Schoonenberg, at the end of his book, offers his own suggestions, he admits with perfect candour that they are novel ones (we shall see that McDermott was adapting them in the construction of his own

[1] References will be to *Man and Sin*, the translation from the Dutch.
[2] 175.   [3] *La Vision de Teilhard de Chardin*, 185 (Desclée de Brouwer).

178

special theory). But he gives good reason for thinking that, in the circumstances, this is not necessarily fatal to them: in fine, the theology of original sin has been developed so far on rather narrow lines and without reference to factors which seem relevant to it. In particular it has concentrated on the sin of 'Adam' and left out of account 'the sin of the world', the accumulated effect of man's resistance to God. Schoonenberg's proposal then, which (he insists) is only tentative, is 'to equate the influence of original sin and the deepest influence of the sin of the world—especially of its peak, the rejection of Christ'.[1] Some sentences from the Epilogue to *Man and Sin* will show us the broad lines of this proposal:

'From man's point of view the cross of Christ means the greatest disaster. Only from the point of view of God, to whom nothing is impossible, salvation comes to us through the cross of Christ, in connection, of course, with the Resurrection . . . since Christ's death on the cross, every man enters the world in the disastrous situation of original sin. . . . Everybody enters the world in the situation of perdition, but the opposite, too, is true. Every man enters the world in a situation of salvation, for the Lord has risen and his Spirit fills the earth. The ancient Church derived the necessity of baptism from the disastrous situation of original sin, but we may conclude to that necessity from both situations.'[2]

The tentative hypothesis is, then, as Schoonenberg puts it in the same passage, that 'if the universality of original sin does not have to be ascribed to the chronologically first sin, it may be attributed to this crowning fact of the sin of the world, the rejection of Christ himself'.

In support of this proposal he has argued: 'The church has always taught this strict universality of sin, like everything else about it, in function of baptism. Hence before baptism existed in the history of salvation . . . that universality of sin must not be taken strictly, which makes possible our conception of the fall as a history of sin',[3] that is, as a process which does not reach completion until the rejection of Christ. Schoonenberg continues: 'The sin through which Christ has been excluded from the world and from our existence on earth is the fact which makes the situation of original sin inescapable for all . . . God's grace is communicated to all on account of Christ, who stands now in

[1] 191. [2] 197. [3] 190.

another life, the life of final fulfilment. That is why the road of inter-personal, charismatic communication is closed for all, and it is opened only through a sacrament in which Christ communicates himself. . . .' It will be remembered that this was the basis of McDermott's position, but that after saying that babies need to be baptized he also referred to 'whatever other grace God may give them when baptism is impossible'. This reference to what is commonly known as 'baptism by desire' needs surely to be made in Schoonenberg's account at the point which we have reached. We must say that, in the Christian dispensation, the incorporation into Christ which is effected by baptism is the one way of salvation for all men (and that it must be *offered*, somehow and some-time, to all men). The important conclusion which would follow, if Schoonenberg's proposal should come to be accepted, is that there would be no need to postulate some particular catastrophic event or state of affairs in the earlier history of the human race. It would be possible, as he says, to suggest that 'primeval grace' was not lacking to everyone in pre-Christian times, if there is only a 'gradual universaliza-tion of the state of original sin'.[1]

These conclusions are not likely to be accepted, for the present at any rate, by the majority of traditional theologians. Pontifex's theory seems to have more hope of success. It brings into the picture 'the sin of the world' in that it makes the influence of others and, in general, the effects of environment (not only those of heredity) instrumental in the eventual loss of the original grace, and the catastrophic character of this may seem a necessary explanation of the startling disorders which our situation exhibits, despite the healing influence of Christian (definitive) grace. And one may suggest that Schoonenberg's equation of Christ's rejection with 'the universalization of the state of original sin' makes it in a way too catastrophic if we are to take this as meaning that it was a rejection for which everybody, more or less, was responsible. What is true is that to be without sanctifying grace is to be without the means of salvation and that it is, essentially, this situation which constitutes 'original sin'. (It is perhaps even harder to feel happy about Schoonen-berg's position when he tells us: 'It is possible that Christ's redemption would, in a history of faith, hope and charity, impregnate a certain milieu so thoroughly that human beings would start their existence in full openness for the life of grace, that is, without original sin. . . .')[1]

[1] 189.

At least it emerges that all this, as he says, 'puts original sin clearly in another category than personal sin'.[1] His emphasis (like McDermott's) on our involvement with one another emphasizes the hazards of the human condition. But this, of itself, can only make us 'guilty' in the sense that it may bring us into a situation which is, as Pontifex put it, 'contrary to God's will'. It is only personal sin which can cut us off from his love for us, which is itself unchanging.

12. THE REDEMPTION AND THE RESURRECTION

Original sin is, essentially, the absence of sanctifying grace; but it is the absence of something that *ought* to be there; 'nature' can exist without grace, but it cannot begin to develop as it needs to do without accepting grace. This is presumably what we must understand by the assertion that we cannot avoid sin for long in the absence of grace. A human act, in the proper sense of the expression, will always involve some response to grace or some rejection of it, if the first awareness of God, of Absolute Value, is itself the offer of that personal relationship in which grace consists. So, although original sin does not mean that human nature is totally corrupt, it is true that it is entirely dependent upon grace for its development and that it will become disordered if it fails to develop. In so far as disorders are caused by the 'sin of the world', they do not directly affect that centre of personality in which the life of the spirit and its moral responsibility are rooted, but they do hamper its development in very obvious ways. Redemption is the liberation of personality, which is enabled to achieve its own destiny and to combat 'the sin of the world'.

How is it that this liberation comes about through Christ's death and resurrection? The theological revival of our time has led to the gradual abandonment of certain theories which have held the field for too long. But they are still influential, and before offering any positive reply to the question (which has been answered, in principle, already) it seems necessary to notice what these theories are and to dissociate oneself from them. The first part of this chapter, therefore, will be no more than a clearing of the ground.

When religion and culture, theology and the arts, live happily together, it is possible to use language in a flexible way which, with any

[1] *Ibid.*

luck, will not prove to be misleading. The sort of language which Christians need to use in talking about Christianity is a symbolic language, and if it is taken in the sense in which a materialistic culture naturally takes it, then it will certainly be misleading. And when theologians begin to take their own language in a literal or materialistic sense, a very awkward situation arises. This is what seems to have happened to the language in which the Redemption has been traditionally discussed. Christ, we say, 'paid the price' of sin. To whom, then, we may be asked, did he pay it? And if we accept this question (which takes the words materialistically) we shall be led into strange courses. It has been argued, by Père Louis Bouyer, for example, that when some of the Fathers referred to this price as being paid to the devil, they were obviously not using such language in a literal sense.[1] But when theologians of our time continue to speak of God's 'outraged majesty' and of a compensation provided for him, it is often impossible to suppose that they are not meaning, literally, just what they are saying. The theory of a *quid pro quo* is still in currency as an explanation of God's graciousness to us. It should be clear that we cannot *give* God anything, in the word's ordinary sense, and the notion that God should require 'compensation' is peculiarly repugnant.

So now I must turn to the disagreeable task of showing that such language has still to be reckoned with and sometimes in most unexpected places. In a recent book by a French theologian (of deserved repute) there are the following sentences: 'The value of the reparation immeasurably surpasses the gravity of the offence'; 'When Christ offers himself to the Father, he presents to him a homage which pleases him infinitely more than the sins of men have displeased him.'[2] Perhaps we could write off these sentences as incidental lapses into the language of rhetoric (it is certainly language which has been all too common in the pulpit). But what are we to make of the persistent assertions, still too common to require documentation, that the Father gave Christ a specific *command* to accept crucifixion? Is the suggestion not that this had been *arranged* in advance? There is a great deal in the Bible which, if taken literally, might indeed suggest that it was. But is this not an outstanding instance of the need to realize that we cannot take over, as they stand, all the 'thought-forms' of the biblical writers? It is unthink-

[1] *Le Mystère Pascal*, 298f. (*The Paschal Mystery*, 199f).
[2] J. Galot, *Eucharistie Vivante*, 86, 189.

able that the Father should have *planned* Christ's rejection, but how else can we interpret what is so often said, that he 'permitted' it in view of the peculiar benefits which it was destined to bring to mankind? God brings good out of evil; but there is no sense in saying that he 'permits' it, if this means anything else than that we are free to reject his offers. And this, I have argued, is in the nature of things (which must mean 'in the nature of God').

Let us now turn to the first volume of Mgr (now Cardinal) Charles Journet's treatise which appeared in English a few years ago under the general title *The Church of the Word Incarnate*. (It was described by M. Jacques Maritain as 'epoch-making', and he referred to its author as 'the greatest living theologian'). Journet writes in his introduction: 'If therefore anything be thought to be true in the pages which follow, let it be attributed to St Augustine and St Thomas Aquinas, whose faithful disciple I have tried to be.' And it transpires that he does regard St Thomas's authority as final. He tells us that it is 'imprudent' to depart from it in any matter of moment. We cannot, then, regard him as a speculative theologian, for a speculative theologian tries to penetrate into the meaning of the Christian mysteries (that is what mysteries are for) by studying the Church's teaching, the teaching (that is) of Christ in his Church, without submitting his judgement to a merely human authority. The Church has not identified her teaching with that of St Thomas; it would be foolish to disregard it, but of itself it settles nothing. It is this sort of exaggerated loyalty to a Doctor of the Church which has led so many to a wholesale repudiation of 'scholasticism' and to a general condemnation of the influence of Greek philosophy upon Christian theology which misconceives the whole process of theological development.

The searcher after truth who opens this book, encouraged by Maritain's praise of it, will find these dark sayings on its second and third pages:

'There is a difference between the grace of the first man and the grace of the angels. While on the one hand the grace of innocence had to be lost in order to give place to that of redemption, to which it was ordered only indirectly and materially, the grace of the angels was ontologically preaccorded (both intensively and extensively) to the perfect grace that was to fill the soul of Christ when the Word should eventually become incarnate. Consequently, when man's sin had shattered the harmony of innocence, and the Word had resolved to become incarnate so as to die on the Cross, the plenary grace created at that instant in his Heart became the centre of reference. . . .'

At this point, if not before, our earnest enquirer might reasonably conclude that some language-game was in progress in which he felt unable to take part, and he might have a suspicion that it was not worth taking part in. It seems unnecessary to analyse the passage in detail: when we come to the words 'the Word had resolved to become incarnate so as to die on the Cross' (even if we have been able to find a satisfactory interpretation of 'the grace of innocence had to be lost'), we can hardly fail to conclude that the death of the cross was in some sense *intended* by God.

But perhaps it is unfair to seize upon an introductory passage in which the subject is being treated only in a general way. So let us see what Journet has to say about it in his second volume where he is treating it *ex professo*. This is what we find: 'God, from all eternity, could will, simultaneously and in a single decree, the glory of Christ as Redeemer and the permission of Adam's sin; the first being prerequisite from the point of view of final, exemplary and efficient causality; the second being also prerequisite, but this time from the point of view of material causality, since it was to repair Adam's sin that the redemptive incarnation was decreed.'[1] It seems to me that this playing-off of different kinds of causality is acting as a smokescreen. Does the distinction between them mean anything here? Or are they being used like counters, *in abstracto*, taken out of the contexts in which they have a meaning? If we can think about God at all, must we not ask for a straightforward answer to the question: did God or did he not need 'Adam's sin' as the motive for 'decreeing' the Incarnation? Journet might reply, I suppose, that it would be 'imprudent' to depart from the doctrine of the Thomist school. And we find that he does in fact accept that doctrine of the school according to which God overrules—that is, infallibly directs—our moral actions, as also the doctrine about a compensation for the 'infinite offences' which sin does to God. (This doctrine, commonly known as 'Anselmian', has not the crudity in St Anselm's account of it which we find in recent writers, and in so far as

[1] 99.

184

St Thomas takes it over it is only as part of a rather subtle synthesis).

I must take another example of this kind of thing and treat it at some length. It is with great regret that I take issue with a thinker to whom so many of us are deeply in debt (and whom Mr Martin Green in his *Yeats's Blessing on von Hügel* seem to regard as the only really *humanist* theologian since von Hügel's time). Mgr Romano Guardini, towards the end of a book published in English as *Freedom, Grace and Destiny*,[1] takes up the problem of evil and puts to himself the question: Why did God create people when he foresaw that they would go the wrong way? Instead of replying (as one might have hoped) that the question, in this form, is a meaningless one, that unless God in fact created these people there could be nothing for him to 'foresee' in regard to them, Guardini moves straight to the Redemption for his answer with a warning that, to understand revelation, we must 'transcend the natural-mythological and philosophic-absolute categories and think in personal and historical terms'.[2] One wonders what these 'philosophic-absolute categories' are. Is there to be an *opposition* between 'the God of the philosophers' and 'the God of Abraham, Isaac and Jacob'?

What Guardini goes on to say seems to show that he does mean that. He tells us that Christ 'makes sin His own, not as an act He has committed but as a guilt He has representatively assumed', and takes this as the proper context for discussing the problem of evil. He then writes:

'But how can this happen? Does it not contradict all that is meant by God? Is he not the Absolute, perfect in Being and power . . .? Man is accustomed to taking risks in his work and meeting with failure. . . . Surely, such an idea of God must be rejected by any mature mind?

The challenge of revelation is here seen in its sharpest outlines. Once I assess it, for instance, by standards drawn from my feeling for the religious or my concept of absolute Being, then I start dissociating myself from these points we have been examining, and . . . I end with a radical denial. If I wish to avoid this course, then I . . . must not judge it from outside, with preconceptions derived from the world, whether empirical or rational, but I must place myself inside it and use it to assess the world, including my own experience and thinking. Then I can no longer say that God cannot do this or that because it would

[1]Harvill Press, 1961.   [2] 242n.

contradict the concept of pure divinity. I have to say that according to revelation God does this and reveals Himself in it to me'.'[1]

Is this compatible with the view that man can approach revelation with some genuine knowledge of God which enables him not indeed to dictate, as it were, to revelation, but to explore it intelligently? It hardly looks like it.

Guardini now speaks of human freedom (but why was it not mentioned before?), of God's foreseeing sin and of his continuing love for his creatures, but this is followed by another warning against metaphysics:

'Revelation tells us that this is the mind of God; and the message is so astonishing that as a rule the believer does not comprehend it. But if he does, there is the danger that it will be basically rejected with the verdict that "there just cannot exist a God like that". Such a God contradicts the categories of the spirit, the perceptions of religious experience, in fact everything that man assumes as belonging properly to God. It is the danger of scandal. This is overcome through the act of conversion in faith. . . . What man chooses from his own experience to call 'God' is a side-issue. . . .'[2]

In a footnote he adds that 'natural knowledge of God predisposes us to recognize that He transcends all earthly measures and therefore He alone can declare who He properly is'. If our natural knowledge in fact tells us that there is someone who 'transcends all earthly measures' it puts us in touch with him in a very real and definite way. This can hardly be called a 'side-issue'.

Now we come to something very disturbing indeed. After another paragraph about God's assuming our 'guilt-laden being into his Being through the mystery of representative atonement' Guardini continues:

'Once again, what is the answer to our question? Is not such an attitude on God's part a tragic one? Are we not literally compelled— and here the problem appears at its final, most sacred and decisive level —are we not literally compelled to speak of a 'destiny' in God, and indeed of a tragic destiny? Have we not here a vision of destiny in the full and absolute sense, of which our earthly destiny is but a confused echo?

[1] 243-4.   [2] 245.

It would seem nonsense to talk of destiny in connection with God.
. . . But revelation tells us that He loves, really and truly loves. . . .
Through love destiny enters into the personal sphere. This is precisely
what had happened with God. . . . What leads us to the inner secret
of God's mind is no theory of absolute values and motives but our vision
of Christ's attitude and the development of Christ's life. Surely, His
attitude and His experience have a note of most tragic destiny ?'[1]

I shall not try to work out the exact significance of this rather
rhetorical passage. It must mean, in general, that there is something
'tragic' about the life of God, not just about the sacred humanity of
Christ. And what follows emphasizes this:

'Is there not "destiny" here ? And is not the picture of incomprehensible
failure, as we see it in the life of Jesus, the final expression and concentration of a basic attitude within God Himself? With all the
reverence and discretion which these questions demand, a man feels
himself obliged to say that God really experiences "destiny" in His
relations with the world and in a sense that is unique. His nature is such
that He can experience this. And this capacity for such experience is
His ultimate glory, it is identical with the fact that he loves. . . .'[2]

The earlier passages quoted could be paralleled by a good many
others in the writings of theologians; they seem to set up a certain
unintelligibility at the entrance to theology. The last two passages
bring us back to the question of God's changelessness, his freedom
from limitations, and, in asking us to achieve an apprehension of him as
both infinite and at risk at the same time, they seem to set up an unintelligibility of the most inspissated kind at the very heart of theology.
Perhaps I am pressing Guardini's words too far. But we do not expect
loose language from him—the fact that this is a semi-popular work cannot make any difference in a matter of such tremendous moment. It is
true that he warns us against interpreting this 'tragic destiny' in a
merely human sense. It refers to 'the earnestness of God's love'.[3] But
this makes it no easier, so it seems to me, to conceive of divine *tragedy*.
Does it not encourage an anti-intellectualism which, under the appearance of profundity, is really a sentimentalism? Guardini tells us that
'tragic destiny' in a sense which is 'valid only for God' is 'capable of

[1] 246-7.   [2] 248.   [3] 249.

being understood' but 'only from the inner pattern of revelation'.[1] 'This knowledge', he adds, 'signifies that we have broken through the barrier of human thought. . . .'[2] If we are willing to take revelation on its own terms, it appears, we gain this knowledge, which otherwise seems meaningless. Does revelation, then, not merely transform human thought but contradict it?

I have spent so long on Guardini's book because he was a theologian of standing who has done much excellent work but who here illustrates in so compendious a way just those tendencies in theological thought which seem to me most questionable and are allowed so regularly to pass without question even by those who themselves seem free of them. At the least I think it has to be admitted that the issue is one of the most serious kind and that the difficulties ought to be more frankly recognized and more thoroughly discussed.

We may now turn to a very different approach to the mystery of the redemption. Maurice Blondel, in *Le Sens Chrétien*, speaks of the sacrifice of Calvary as the 'consequence of the divine condescension in a world of free men in revolt against God'. He deprecates 'the constantly recurring idea of the heavenly Father's demands and of his implacable justice in condemning his own son to the punishment which follows upon bad will'. Christ's suffering and death, in other words, are the consequences of the world-order in the particular circumstances which men's sins had brought about for it. As Blondel goes on to say, 'things were so arranged that the creation of supernaturalizable man implied in advance, if one may so speak, a mortal danger for God'[3] that is, for the God-Man. What determined Christ's death, then, was not a 'decree' of God but the blindness of those who delivered him to Pilate. Christ suffered and died because of our sins in that this was the consequence of his living a perfect, fully human, life in the circumstances of the world-order which sin had brought about. This is the price which he had to pay for living among us. And, if he had not lived among us, his power would not be available to us, uniting us with God in that definitive way which was planned 'from the beginning'. But first he had himself to pass from this world to the Father, for that is the law of all human life. His mission was completed on the cross in his final act of perfect surrender to the Father.

When the Redemption is discussed in the language of exchange, of

[1] 248.   [2] 249.   [3] 143.

buying and selling, we must remember that, as Blondel put it, we are using the language of parable or allegory which needs to be 'interpreted, rectified and completed: interpreted, because it could suggest, as it stands, that God wants to buy us . . . as if we were not already his servants and his debtors, whereas what he wants is to make us sharers in his kingdom; rectified, because it suggests that we have something of our own to give in payment; completed, for this mercantile parable, like Pascal's wager, suggests a well-considered calculation rather than an initiative of love and generosity. . . .'[1] Theories of the Redemption, Blondel adds, have tended to concentrate attention upon the negative aspect, upon the removal of obstacles, the *buying back*, so as to put into the shade the positive aspect, the *attainment* of God's grace, which is the fundamental question in any case, even before there is sin to be redeemed. So if anyone asks whether we should have been redeemed if Christ had not suffered (if he had been accepted by his people), the answer must be that he is *himself* our redemption and that the conditions in which his mission was accomplished do not themselves make him the redeemer. And if anyone asks whether we could be redeemed if the Word had not in fact been incarnate, he must be reminded that in this system of thought one does not accept that hypothesis.

The most forthright rejection known to me of those theories of the Redemption which have been criticized here is to be found in the Appendix to a paperback book by the late Father Vincent Wilkin.[2] The three passages which I am about to quote are practically identical with passages in an unpublished paper by that French theologian, Alexandre Durand, of whose work on the act of faith I made use in an earlier chapter (this circumstance is presumably due to the fact that Wilkin's papers were put together by an editor after his death and his notes of Durand's paper discovered among them). The first passage comments on 'penal expiation' as an element in Christ's redemptive suffering:

'The idea here is that Christ reconciled us with God by undergoing in our place the punishment due to sin and exacted by divine justice. . . . All that the texts [of Scripture and tradition] necessitate is some connection between our sins and the sufferings of our Saviour. . . .

[1] 129.

[2] *From Limbo to Heaven*, Sheed and Ward, 1961, 'Note on Theories of Redemption'.

Now, by what right does one lay down that a certain dose of suffering is demanded by the justice of God? If it is said that this suffering is not necessary in itself, but God wished it so, one is driven to ask how in the name of justice could God wish that someone innocent, moreover his own Son, should suffer as a condition of the pardon of sinners? Surely this Shylock conception of a God of vindictive justice, demanding his pound of flesh and apparently not minding whose it is, makes very little sense.'[1]

The passage which follows makes equally forthright remarks about the theory of reparation according to which God pardons us 'in view of the satisfaction by which Christ has compensated the honour of God':

'Considerations of justice are made paramount. The necessity of the death of Christ is based on a justice . . . which has to proportion reparation to the size of the offence . . . [it] implies that Christ did not merit by his life but only by his death, and it is by some sort of divine contract that the merits Christ gained are applied to us sinners.

This emphasis on justice and God's due honour which sin frustrates overlooks the fact that creation and supernatural elevation give nothing to God: man is the entire beneficiary, and sin injures only himself. Wherefore some say it is *as if* God lost or gained something—a dangerous formula which needs only to be pressed to result in the purest Symbolism. . . .'

Guardini spoke of Christ's making sin his own 'as a guilt He has representatively assumed'. The third passage which I quote from this Note emphasizes that Christ did not substitute himself for us: 'Redemption does not take place by such interposition. It is too extrinsic. It is unintelligible', and points out that it does not improve matters much to say instead that Christ communicates his merits to us because he is our representative. The solution is 'still too extrinsic and juridical. . . . A more profound solidarity between ourselves and Christ is required.' It is found in 'his participation of human nature, and our achievement of redemption flows from our participation by grace in his divine nature'. Christ saves us 'by handing on the task to us and making it possible for us to do it'.[2] Here we have the elements of an intelligible theory.

It needs to be developed, in particular, with reference to the need of Christ's living out to the end a perfect human life, a life of perfect

[1] 139.   [2] 142–3.

obedience. Clearly he would not be an example to us if he had not done so, although (I have urged) the suggestion that he shares in our experience of faltering loyalty ought to be rejected (in this respect he *is* different from us, living on a plane towards which we are to be drawn and which is not native to us). But the necessity laid upon him (or which he lays upon himself) does not arise just from these considerations. The metaphysics of the Incarnation must be further explored. Père F. X. Durwell might be a little startled if one described as an exploration of this kind his achievement in two well-known books—they have appeared in English as *The Resurrection* (1961)[1] and *In the Redeeming Christ* (paperback, 1963). But at least they seem to provide the materials for it; we have only to assemble, so it seems to me, certain conclusions at which he has arrived to find the main lines of such a metaphysic. Durwell is a 'biblical theologian'. His conclusions are reached on the basis of the New Testament texts, analysed very closely, and they are stated almost entirely in New Testament terms; he even thinks it necessary—dare one suggest that his tongue is in his cheek?—to apologise when he goes beyond them. The advantages, from my point of view, of relying upon his authority will be very obvious. So in what follows I shall draw upon him extensively with only those comments which will (I hope) show that his work does lead us to a further synthesis, one which is still needed if the redemptive process is to seem intelligible in its actual deployment.

First it should be made clear that Durwell is in agreement with the main conclusions which this chapter has so far reached. In the second of the two books mentioned he tells us that Christ 'did not suffer humiliation, torture and death . . . to throw them into the balance as a counterweight to sin. He did not let himself be destroyed to appease the anger of justice; he did it to accept justice, to submit to glory, to make his own the will of the Spirit and receive his life-giving holiness . . . our redemption lies in God's justice and the reception which we give it. . . . Sin injures God only in the heart of man, closing that heart to God's will to save him. . . . Merit in us is a capacity for, and a receiving of, grace. . . . The reign of God's justice does not lie in any balance—it is precisely a reign in which man is wholly possessed by God's justice. Suffering is redemptive for man when it is an acceptance of God.'[2] Here it is to be remarked that 'justice' in the New Testament

---

[1] Sheed and Ward Inc., London and New York. [2] 36–8.

regularly means not an insistence on God's part that there must be some mysterious compensation for the sins of mankind but God's own fidelity to his promises. In the earlier and more substantial book Durwell discusses the topic of merit at some length and concludes that, although the language of St Paul and that of the Johannine Christ are different, 'the underlying reality is in fact the same': 'the idea of supernatural merit, apart from merely juridical notions, has its reality on the ontological plane. To merit is to place oneself in the moral and physical dispositions suited to the good which God destines us for, is to fit one's being for the possession of God who will crown those dispositions.'[1]

In the second chapter of this work Durwell sums up the conclusions which he has reached in the following passage: 'The Resurrection constitutes the basic, prime and total object of the Passion. Current theology all too often subordinates the first objective to the merits won for mankind; the Resurrection is seen at the end of a sidestream flowing out of the mainstream of the Redemption. Yet our Lord has become so completely one with the race of Adam that what he wished to gain for us he first gained for himself.'[2] We may surely say that there was no question of its happening otherwise. The point has been made clearer in these words: 'The redemption of human nature is a drama unfolding first of all in Christ. It takes place in him as a sanctifying transformation from the state of sinful flesh to the holiness of divine life which is its direct opposite. . . . This transformation was worked out in our Lord's death and glorification as in a single mystery, for death was the end of sinful flesh only in so far as it resulted in glorification, the principle of divine life.'[3] We are told also that Christ's death 'is redemptive in as much as it is his resurrection; we find expiation for our sins in our salvation, and that salvation is the Resurrection. . . . The expiation was not so much a debt to pay as a gulf to bridge, by the painful abandonment of a profane state of life in order to achieve union with God.'[4]

This thesis about 'sinful flesh' and a 'profane state', which may at first be startling, is an essential feature of Durwell's account. It is only because Christ has first achieved a personal victory that he can invite us to share its fruits. Although he is without sin, the flesh which he takes is *our* flesh. He is 'at a distance' from the Father and only through death can he be united with him. Sin dies with the death of the flesh. 'There

[1] *The Resurrection*, 54n.   [2] 56.   [3] 58.   [4] 71.

was no resurrection for the flesh in the Pauline sense of the word. The glory did not reawaken the old life. . . . the new life in its spirituality spells for ever the end of the flesh.'[1]

Christ's immolation is a destruction only in this sense that it is the end of the 'flesh' in the Scriptural sense in which, as carnal weakness, it is opposed to the 'spiritual': 'nothing of the richness of his human life is lost to Christ'. This 'passing-over' into the glory of God is sacrifice, a 'making holy'. So 'Christ's death becomes eternal in the goal which gives it the power to save; in other words, in the divine life'. For 'the death and resurrection are intertwined in their dynamism' and 'Christ need only communicate himself' to those who believe in him 'to extend to them his death, which is life'. And so 'His glory has . . . conferred upon Christ as priest a fullness which he did not have during his life on earth. It has brought his priesthood and sacrifice to perfection and maintains them there'.[2]

Durwell describes the Church as 'the body of Christ *redeeming us*, joined to our Saviour in one special moment of history, in the instant of the Redemption. . . . The identification is dynamic as well as existential, for it is effected by participation in the same action. . . .'[3] This may sound as though our historic actions synchronize with the historic acts of Christ, but Durwell explains that this is not what he means: 'The death and resurrection are not, as it were, prised out of the past in order to be translated into the present; neither does the believer leave his place in the present to be linked to the act of redemption in the past. This action, performed once in the past, remains fixed in an everlasting actuality in the Christ of glory. . . .'[4] Our passing-over from the 'flesh' to the 'spirit' can thus be inaugurated, but it remains for us incomplete, as it once did for Christ. There is, of course, in all this no condemnation of the material body, but an insistence on the need for a 'spiritual' one, that is, on the need to leave the world-without-God and to share in the redeeming of the world. Durwell thus describes the process: 'It is man as a unity who has died in principle in the sacrament [of baptism], and though the body is the last objective of the invasion of grace, its death and glory are the first to be envisaged, since the body of flesh is at the root of the earthly state. . . . There are some who carry their paschal consecration to its final conclusion. Since baptism has united them to Christ's body they wish to have no union other than

[1] 148–9. [2] 149–50. [3] 222. [4] 225.

with that body. . . . Those who remain virgins publish the presence of the Easter mystery in the Church.'[1]

In another summary Durwell writes: 'There is only one resurrection, the resurrection of Christ, and the Church shares in it at the *parousia*. Similarly there is only one judgement whereby man is justified . . . a judgement pronounced in the mystery of Easter, but becoming fully effective only when the Church is wholly caught up in the mystery.'[2] Like other theologians of our time, he sees no reason for talking about souls separated from their bodies and awaiting the final judgement: 'Pauline theology does not provide a single argument to show why an individual believer's resurrection should be delayed beyond death.'[3] And he adds that 'the final resurrection is a universal judgement, the manifestation of the mystery of Christ in the whole Church, the re-creation of the universe'. (It may be well to insist at this point that we cannot usefully speculate on what a 'risen body' may be.)

Finally a brief reference to the conclusions of Father Ladislaus Boros in *The Moment of Truth* will show a close agreement with Durwell's. 'In his death', Boros writes, 'Christ attained the perfect accomplishment of his reality as man with a human body and soul . . . therefore, and precisely in his death, he was able to effect our salvation finally and irrevocably.'[4] It has been his thesis that only in death can we achieve our fulfilment because only then can we hand ourselves over completely to God. 'At the same time', he continues, '. . . he created a fundamentally new situation in the scheme of salvation for all spirits. . . . By its removal from all limitations of time and place Christ's body makes it possible for us to reach our salvation in a growing together with him . . . Christ, even in his body, is henceforth in the realm of being proper to God and has thus become the ultimate fulfilment of the cosmos, the point *omega* of an evolution pressing even further forward into the sphere of the divine.' Boros further suggests that the Ascension and even perhaps Pentecost are to be thought of as aspects of the one redemptive event, making a distinction between relative (clinical) and absolute death so that we can distinguish the death on the cross from the *act* of Christ's death (which is thus coincidental with the act of his Resurrection), and regarding the ascent from the Mount of Olives as the outward sign of the 'inner dimension', that is, the significance and the implications, of the Resurrection; he refers to the fact that 'for the

[1] 277–8. [2] 299. [3] 347. [4] 161.

Johannine point of view, the Resurrection and the outpouring of the Holy Ghost represent but one single process, i.e. the exaltation of Christ'.[1]

Boros agrees with Durwell and so many other theologians of our time in regarding the body of Christ as literally the instrument of salvation: 'there is no such thing as a "double" body of Christ. . . . In the process of salvation we do not become members of a "mystical body", we become in a "mystical and hidden manner" real, actual members of the risen body.'[2] And he also suggests that the Christian's death is at the same time his own resurrection and ascension. For man always 'aims at reshaping in a personal way what he finds present in himself (and as himself) in nature'.[3] And this cannot be achieved until he makes his final, irrevocable, decision.

13. THE RESURRECTION AND THE EUCHARIST

Theories of the Redemption which can be called anti-philosophical have been dying out, we have seen, in the recent past under the influence of the revival of biblical and patristic studies in our century and a certain revival of metaphysical thinking at the present time. Theories of merit which imply that we can persuade God to look on us with favour by supplying him with suitable offerings constitute a very serious menace to religion, and it seemed necessary to dissociate one-self from them. The same considerations apply to anti-philosophical theories about the Eucharist, which is the appointed means by which the power of Christ's Resurrection is made available to us in increasing measure.

Thirty years or so ago, theologians in their discussions about the Eucharist were largely concerned with its sacrificial character. We have moved since then into a fresh atmosphere of thought which has practically abolished the problems which seemed so important at the time, but here too (as with theories about the Redemption) mis-conceptions survive even among theologians and, naturally, among many non-theologians. Something must be said about them at the out-set. Just as there was a marked tendency to think of the Redemption as a transaction effected upon the Cross with the Resurrection following upon it as a separate affair (and primarily as a demonstration of Christ's

[1] 160 and note. [2] 197. [3] 200.

Godhead), so there was a marked tendency to think of the Eucharist simply in terms of Calvary. The Council of Trent laid it down that the Eucharist is the same sacrifice as that of Calvary, differing from it only in its mode; the difference lies in the fact that it is, in the accepted but infelicitous phrase, an 'unbloody sacrifice'. This was interpreted in a number of ways, some of which seem plainly unsatisfactory but have been nevertheless highly influential. Theologians have given the impression that the Eucharist is somehow a *repetition* of Calvary. Since such a suggestion cannot be taken in a literal sense, attempts have been made to show that the Eucharist is the same sacrifice as that of the Cross because Christ repeats or recalls to mind, whenever the Eucharist is celebrated, that interior act of self-offering which he made in dying. There is some new special act on his part which constitutes each celebration as *this* sacrifice. This is an artificial theory, thought up to get round what was felt to be a difficulty. It does not seem to make sense to suggest that Christ repeats anything; his sacrifice was made once for all. Attempts were also made to connect the Eucharist with the sacrifice of Calvary by suggesting that Christ somehow reduces himself to a state of victimhood, although not by a fresh shedding of his blood. This is obviously just as unintelligible. And, finally, it was pointed out that the bread and wine of the Eucharist are consecrated separately and are visible as separate on the altar so that the Eucharist can be said to 'represent' Calvary. The view that the separate elements constitute the essential *symbolism* of the Eucharist is one which has considerable authority behind it, but I must confess that this symbolism has never seemed to me of central importance. In any case it does not succeed in identifying the Eucharist with Calvary in any real sense. It cannot be identical with Calvary merely because it portrays it. A slightly macabre air still sometimes persists in devotional works about the Eucharist. This, one must say bluntly, is all wrong. The Eucharist is essentially triumphant, a thanksgiving for the gift of Christ, for his entire achievement, a uniting of ourselves with him in his risen, consummated state.

Lurking behind all these theories is the view that sacrifice must always mean destruction, and that this element must therefore be present in the Eucharist. And so it was even suggested that the changing of the bread and wine into Christ's body and blood might fulfil the necessary function. Nowadays theologians commonly insist that it is a mistake to begin one's thinking about the Eucharist with some general theory of sacrifice: the sacrifices of the ancient world have to be interpreted in the light of Calvary, not the other way round. This is no doubt true, but we must presumably continue to say that Christ's sacrifice abolished the ancient ones, and we must still find some continuity between it and them. There seems no good reason for repudiating St Augustine's view, which has been adopted by so many Christian thinkers, that a true sacrifice is an action by which we try to unite ourselves with God. It involves, therefore, the abandonment, the destruction, of sin. It does not seem to involve, necessarily, the destruction of anything else.

What, then, is the answer to the question which provoked these unsatisfactory theories? How is the Eucharist the same sacrifice as that of Calvary? The answer must be that Christ's final achievement, his state as the accepted victim, is a permanent state. The act of his death and the act which glorifies him are two sides of a single event; that is what Durwell has shown us to be the Bible's teaching. Sacrifice is for union. When it has reached its achievement, it does not cease to be sacrifice. In the Eucharist Christ's sacrificial act draws us to itself. But this needs a good deal of explanation.

The book which first gave me what I was looking for about this was Eugene Masure's *Sacrifice du Chef*, which appeared in 1932. Since it was so little known in the English-speaking countries, I made a translation of it, *The Christian Sacrifice*, which seems to have put some information into currency for the first time in certain quarters (it is my hope that some of these chapters may prove useful in the same way). If I quote a few passages from it, the view which I have just indicated will be sufficiently explained, and we shall have a convenient background against which later developments in eucharistic theology can be intelligibly assessed. I begin with a passage about sacrifice which does little more than expand what has been suggested already:

'Sacrifice is the expressive, and, if possible, efficacious sign of the deliberate and suppliant return of man to God. . . . Oblation and immolation in an actual ceremony seem to be opposed like joy and grief. . . . But if the first signifies our drive towards God and our meeting with him, and the second the detachment from ourselves and from creatures which, since sin, is painful for us, then it is clear that in principle the movement towards the Creator and the renunciation of our sinful or imperfect attachments are only the obverse and reverse, the positive and negative sides, of a single undertaking, our restoration (namely) to right order. . . .'[1]

Destruction, then, is not an essential, necessary, element in sacrifice, in this account, although in point of fact it is always present for particular reasons.

Masure's book has three parts. At the end of the second part he sums up his conclusions so far in some passages which I shall quote at length:

'Christ, living his unique mystery . . . has passed through its stages in a series of historical events, grievous and glorious, whose sum henceforth constitutes the one true sacrifice. In what does this sacrifice consist? First in the return of the Son to his Father with his religion of adoring love, accomplished in the hard conditions which our sin imposed; then in the acceptance granted by the Father with all the depth of his eternal love to this homage of the Incarnate Son. . . . From his Passion and Death to his Resurrection and Ascension . . . Christ Jesus visibly realized this metaphysic of return and meeting which the ritual and symbolic sacrifices tried unceasingly to delineate and to perform upon their altars. This is the context in which he was established in his own Person the one and only victim. At the same time he was established as the only priest. Henceforth no religion will exist save his. . . . Thus the Christian sacrifice did not lie only in the immolation of the Cross. . . . We must keep the whole, from the kiss of Judas to the Father's welcome. St Paul always bound these moments together as interdependent parts of one same work; and our Liturgy for Paschal time has found admirable formulas for this powerful unity: "the Crucified has risen from the dead and has redeemed us . . ." But once the mystery of Jesus has been historically achieved, can we not enclose it within an efficacious rite, a sacrificial and eucharistic rite which will owe all its value to it and give us all its fruits?'[2]

It may be observed that the notion of the 'efficacious sign', referred to in the passage first quoted, is beginning to assume a fresh importance.

To the question which he has now raised Masure addresses himself in the last part of the book. He writes that 'the Redemption is not a treaty of peace concluded some nineteen centuries ago between God and men, the clauses of which are applied by the church to new-born

---

[1] *The Christian Sacrifice*, 79.   [2] 185–7.

children and repentant sinners without any relation between this ancient contract and our present salvation save a victim's body and blood. Thanks to this sacrament we may communicate with this victim, sharing in all the effects of his mystery, above all in the charity which Redemption has established between God and man on earth, and, through God, between man and man. The visible unity of what was bread and wine shows forth clearly that charity which ought to reign among the faithful who approach the altar; the species are now signs of grace, after being signs of the presence and the immolation of graces' Author and before that of the religion of us men.'[1] (As we shall see, this social aspect of the Eucharist is insisted upon in a special way in our time). Man needs to express himself in outward, symbolic form. The gesture which he makes to intensify his will to worship, his desire to hand himself over to the source of all his good, is made the starting-point for Christ's communication of himself. Our offering of bread and wine is made at his command so that he can return them to us as the sacrament of the new life. Our sign becomes his.

Recent developments in theology have not contradicted these conclusions, so far as I can see, but they have certainly enriched them. First there is Père Louis Bouyer's contention, in *Le Rite et l'Homme* (1962), that sacrifice is fundamentally and originally a sacred *meal*. This view has not gone unchallenged, but it seems to be gaining the field. It is repeated in his *Eucharistie* (1966), a long and detailed investigation into the history of the Eucharistic prayer, the 'Canon'. Bouyer regards theologians of the Eucharist in the first half of the century, Masure included, as producing theologies *about* the Eucharist rather than theologies *of* the Eucharist, because they did not concern themselves primarily with the eucharistic texts.[2] He allows that they were a great improvement on the theologians of the preceding centuries and that 'they have restored to us a much more satisfactory conception of the eucharistic sacrifice, especially in its relation to the sacrifice of the Cross'. Nevertheless, he maintains, we can hardly regard their achievements as definitive because their method was so much at fault. Not only did they pay little attention to the history of the liturgy, but they adopted far too narrow a basis of scriptural texts and often had somewhat arbitrary ideas about the nature of sacrifice and the nature of signs. Certainly it must be agreed that they left much undone, but I

[1] 271-2. [2] 11-12.

do not know that there is anything of importance to be discarded from Masure's account. That this is so may be indicated by some passages from Bouyer's final pages in which he sums up his most important conclusions and which certainly add to our understanding of the Eucharist in important ways.

After insisting upon the Jewish origins of the eucharistic prayer, he writes that 'the community meal in expectation of the Messiah expresses definitively the meaning of all Israel's sacrifices. It tends to become itself *the* sacrifice, that is to say the offering of all human life and of the whole world to the recognized will of God.' At this point he makes his claim that 'all sacrifice, as the comparative history of religions makes clear, is originally a sacred banquet in which man recognizes that his life comes to him from God and develops only in a constantly renewed exchange with him'. 'Such', he goes on, 'was the primary meaning of the Pasch, the feast consecrating the first fruits of the harvest. But the Jewish Pasch was charged with a renewed meaning in becoming the memorial of the deliverance by which God had snatched away his own from the slavery of ignorance and death and transported them to the land of promise where they should know him as they had been known and live in his presence.'[1]

In the pages which follow Bouyer shows how closely the pattern of the Pasch is repeated in the Eucharist. The Jewish memorial rite was not just a remembrance of time past, but carried with it the sense of God's saving presence here and now, and it looked forward to the fulfilment of his promises in the definitive establishment of the Kingdom. It was in fact established when Jesus pronounced the thanksgiving over the bread and the cup and at the same time delivered himself up to the cross, thereby making this meal the memorial of the cross. In Bouyer's words: 'Giving thanks with him, through him, for his body broken and his blood shed, given to us as the substance of the Kingdom, we present before God this mystery which has been accomplished in our Head so that it may have its final accomplishment in his whole body. That is, we consent to the fulfilment in our flesh of the sufferings of Jesus for his body which is the Church in the firm expectation of his Second Coming when we shall all share together in his resurrection. . . . All the substance of this Christian sacrifice is in the unique salvific act of the cross. . . . But the cross has not gained its meaning save by the

[1] 430.

offering which Christ made at the Supper. . . . And the cross is not redemptive for men in actual fact save in so far as they are associated with it by the eucharistic meal, his body and blood . . . in so far as they make their own the Son's own thanksgiving.'[1]

As this account proceeds we meet again the conclusion that the bread and wine which we offer become sacrificial in as much as they become, for faith, what they represent. There is an emphasis on the Eucharist as the community-meal or love-feast, but there is again the conclusion that the function of the Eucharist is to associate us with Christ's own love for his Father:

'As Christ's prayer [at the supper] passed into act in the acceptance of the cross, it passes into act in our communion with the body broken and the blood shed. And so the Spirit of the Son springs up in us. To repeat the eucharistic prayer without communicating in the sacrifice which it expresses and consecrates would have no more sense than to communicate without making our own, through that same prayer, the dispositions which were Christ's when he delivered himself to the cross. They were expressed in his final thanksgiving and his final supplication to the Father for the coming of his Kingdom. Thanksgiving . . . supplication . . . memorial . . . communion . . . the unity of the Eucharist is seen to be unbreakable.'[2]

In this remarkable passage Bouyer has shown how the eucharistic prayer, by commemorating the Last Supper and so repeating Christ's own prayer of thanksgiving and offering, unites us with him, and a little later he adds to this a further precision which is closely in line with our earlier conclusions: 'the saving act, immortalized in [Christ's] glorified body, with the perfect human response which is inseparable from it, becomes, through the Spirit, the principle of our renewed life. . . . This is present, objectively, in the eucharistic celebration, which simply actualizes in us the unique offering consecrated at the Supper, as the body and blood are objectively presented to us in the sacramental elements, so that we become one with him who is unique.'[3]

Working independently of Bouyer, Father Nicholas Lash has reached substantially the same conclusions about the characteristics of the eucharistic prayer. In his book, *His Presence in the World—A Study of Eucharistic Worship and Theology*, he has given even stronger

[1] 431–2.   [2] 433.   [3] 435.

emphasis to the 'community' aspect of the Eucharist. It seems to me that the emphasis is made in his first pages in a way which might easily be misleading. He tells us that the love of God and the love of the brethren are one and the same love so that the fulfilling of the first Commandment and the fulfilling of the second do not occupy 'distinct areas'.[1] This could be taken to mean that the only way of loving God is to perform acts of service for our brother men. It is true that we should love God in man and man in God, that our love for one another is the proof and the test of our love of him and that we are helping them in our worship of him. But this is not the whole meaning of our worship of him. We worship him as a community, not as isolated individuals, but also and fundamentally as individual persons, and this direct personal relationship is something which needs to be emphasized at the present time. The reaction against an individualistic piety, as we have seen earlier, has led to an exaggeration in the opposite direction, to a distrust and a disregard of that 'mystical element' which is the soul of true religion.

A few pages later Lash does say that 'we know our brother in God', but this remark has been preceded by the statement that what Christianity, and so theology, are about is 'the recovery, and the discovery, of human brotherhood that springs from the love God has for us',[2] which might be taken (at this stage) to mean that God, so far as we are concerned with him, is just the means to our loving one another as real human beings. In fact Lash does not mean this, as the rest of the book makes clear. What he is concerned to emphasize is that 'belief in Jesus is, directly and formally, a commitment to brotherhood'.[3] That is undeniably true, but this commitment is also the inauguration of our passage to the Father in the Spirit of Jesus, and loving one another should mean, fundamentally, helping one another to get on with it. I have dwelt upon this fashionable imbalance, although it appears incidentally and only at the beginning of the book, because if it is operative in anyone's mind he will have difficulty in appreciating the many excellent things which Lash proceeds to say about the Eucharist.

The Eucharist, he tells us, in agreement with Bouyer, is a *meal*, a sign of 'covenant-sacrifice'. He rejects the theory that the separate consecrations have, as such, a special significance for 'showing the death of Christ'.[4] And he is right, I think, in rejecting the view that 'offering

[1] 4.   [2] 12.   [3] 13.   [4] 48.

the sacrifice of Christ in the Church' means 'a giving of Christ, or the consecrated elements, to God'. He very properly excludes the whole notion of sacrifice as a giving of something to God. This idea, he says, 'colours many current explanations of the offertory rite'. It is true that we cannot be said to *give* bread and wine to God in any significant sense, but I see no reason for rejecting the idea that we give ourselves to God, using bread and wine to symbolize our offering, and that these symbols of our offering are then transformed into the Christian sacrifice, the body and blood of Christ. For our offering or 'gift' of ourselves obviously means nothing more than our openness to receive God's gift to us. But it is certainly not imperative to insist on this symbolism, and the offertory rite does double duty with the offering which is an element of the eucharistic prayer, the 'Canon', itself. Nevertheless there need be no harm, I think, in anticipating this element of offering and there can be some good. It is true, however, that the offertory rite has sometimes acquired a misleading sort of importance in the course of the recent liturgical revival, and Lash is no doubt right to say: 'There are only four essential elements in the eucharistic liturgy; they are the actions of Christ at the Supper. Food and drink are taken; they are made the centre of a prayer of thanksgiving ('blessed'); they are shared (the "breaking of bread") and eaten.'[1]

More importantly for our purposes, Lash writes that 'the essential meaning of sacrifice is that of a sharing (attempted or realized) of divine and human life, a communion, a union of heart and mind'. He concludes that the Eucharist 'is not a sacrifice followed by a meal denoting communion in that sacrifice; it is a sacrificial meal'.[2] And he adds that 'by the grace of Christ, our self-offering to the Father, expressed and sealed by our sharing in the meal, is a participation in his self-offering to his Father on Calvary'. The argument is further developed as follows: 'The principal agent in the celebration is Christ, because the praise and commitment of the people is the praise and commitment of Christ', the prayer of the president who voices the assembly's covenant-accepting praise and faith is the prayer of Christ, and the food which they share as the language of their brotherhood is the body of Christ;[3] This seems to me a valuable synthesis of findings which have been adumbrated at earlier stages in this account of current eucharistic theology. Here I may remark that if I make no direct

[1] 50. [2] 51. [3] 88-9.

reference to 'traditional' theologians of the Reform it is because I believe that there is nothing of principle in all this from which they would need to dissent. No doubt there are differences of approach and of emphasis, but it is often maintained today that the old controversies are dead, and I hope that I shall not offend if I take it for granted.

But there is one eucharistic topic, once the most controversial of all, which is still controversial, but now (like other theological topics) not just a matter of inter-confessional controversy but cutting across the old divisions. Before turning to what Lash has to say about transubstantiation and Christ's real presence in the eucharist, I shall put forward a few elementary considerations by way of supplying some context for this topic. A child brought up as a Christian may be inclined to think of Christ, at first, simply as God who came to live with us here below, and to think that God no longer lives with us—except in the Eucharist, under the forms of bread and wine. God's presence in all things is a notion which has not yet explicitly arisen. When it does, this simple view of things has to be revised. God is indeed present everywhere, but it is the Incarnate Word who is present in the Eucharist in a special way which has now to be considered. One thing is immediately clear: that the risen body of Christ, to which we are united in the Eucharist, is not subject to our limitations of time and space. He can be present to all of us at all times. But that only emphasizes the need to discover what distinguishes his presence in the Eucharist from his presence in all other circumstances.

Something must now be said about recent discussions of 'transubstantiation'. Some of these caused disquiet in Rome, and the Encyclical *Mysterium Fidei* was issued, followed by much argument about its interpretation as seems to be inevitable with modern papal pronouncements. Father Joseph M. Powers in his helpful book *Eucharistic Theology* describes the Encyclical as 'a well-balanced statement . . . which sets out all the dimensions into a well-focussed unity'. Lash, in an appendix to his own book, seems to me to have shown that the teaching of the Encyclical is obscure at the critical point. I mention these verdicts to indicate that the present position in this matter is a complicated one, and that the comments which I shall now make in regard to it are tentative, intended to suggest simply that no one is committed to a view which involves any absurdity. Christ's presence, then, I think we must say, is in itself not physical and local, but personal and spiritual, and it is not less but more real and objective on that account. To say that our bread and wine are converted into his body and blood is a perfectly meaningful statement. But the particular thought-forms employed by the Council of Trent to express this truth are no longer possible for us; this, I consider, has been made quite clear by Schillebeeckx in his little book *The Eucharist*. What the Council expressed by its use of the word 'transubstantiation' was simply the real presence of Christ in the Eucharist, and we have to interpret the use of the word accordingly. In doing so it is necessary for us to make use of thought-forms which are not those of the Tridentine Fathers.

I can now quote what Lash has to say in an important section of his book which will bring more to a point the proposals which I have just been making: 'a personal relationship (presence) between people cannot be achieved "silently", without communication. Persons become present to each other by disclosing, in word and gesture, that care and concern for each other which constitutes their mutual presence as personal. Therefore if Christ is present to a group of people, his presence is achieved in the very act of disclosure; it does not pre-exist this disclosure as "merely bodily", or sub-personal presence. Christ is "here" because he speaks to us, in his speaking to us; he is not "simply here" so that he can (as a consequence) speak to us.' It will now be clearer, I hope, what was meant by saying that Christ's presence in the eucharist is 'not physical and local, but personal and spiritual'. 'He is present', Lash goes on, 'as "offering his sacrifice" ',[1] for this 'will continue to be present, through its effective commemoration, which commemoration, as effective, draws from the men to whom God in Christ is thus made present in the Spirit the praise of faithful love and service'.[2] And so Christ 'is (objectively) present to the people in the food they share, because the terms of the language in which they recall and realize the presence of his sacrifice is the covenant-supper which he left them for this purpose'.[3]

The importance of this for the ecumenical discussion needs no underlining. But it is perhaps pertinent to mention in this connection that in his last chapter Lash suggests that 'the concept of "validity of orders" is too narrow to form the basis of a judgement concerning the authenticity of a ministry within a particular church' and that, in certain circumstances, a separated community could have its authentic church-

[1] 114.   [2] 119.   [3] 120.

ness and *therefore* its ministry recognized by Rome provided that it in turn recognized 'the primacy of the church (the diocese) of Rome and of her bishop'.[1] And this topic of unity must come to our mind when we read the following statements in the previous chapter: 'We are gathered because we are the body of Christ. We gather to become more fully the body of Christ. Therefore the meaning of the language which we employ to declare what we are doing must be the body of Christ.'[2] But, to return to my first point about the eucharistic presence, Lash also insists that 'Christ is present, in some way, in all the things we share',[3] and this leads him to a discussion of the Church's relation to the world in which the fashionable imbalance which I found in his first chapter is no longer present. This discussion is indeed to be warmly recommended to those who are in danger of succumbing to it.

But is there an incompleteness, and so an imbalance, about Lash's account of the Eucharist? Father Brian Kelly, in an article 'The Eucharist—Sacrifice or Meal',[4] has suggested that there is. Lash's view, he says, 'appears to be that the totality of the external rite is a meal, which meal is at the same time a sacrifice through its signifying Christ's sacrifice on Calvary. There is no question here of a rite, one part sacrifice and the other meal (or communion): the entire rite is meal and, in its entirety, it signifies (and thereby *is*) sacrifice'. Kelly asks why we have to suppose that the rite which expresses our communion with one another must be fully identical with the rite which expresses our desire for communion with God. His own view is that 'sacrifice and sacramental meal are really different' in the Eucharist, and he argues for this on the ground that there was a distinction between sacrifice and communion on Calvary and that in virtue of the identity between the Eucharist and the sacrifice of Calvary the same distinction is to be found in the Eucharist. This carries with it the view that there was a lapse of time between Christ's offering of himself in death and his exaltation or communion with the Father; we have seen reason to reject this view. Kelly also considers that Christ's communion with the Father is incomplete until the members of his body have been drawn into it, but that the eucharistic communion is 'the completion of Calvary' and therefore 'not a sign of the sacrifice of Calvary'. Thus there are 'two distinct elements, sacrifice and sacrament', in the Eucharist.

It seems to me that it is the rite as a whole which constitutes the sign

[1] 192-5.   [2] 147.   [3] 161.   [4] *The Irish Theological Quarterly*, July 1968.

of the sacrifice of Calvary. What Christ ordered us to repeat was a thanksgiving over a meal; and this commemorative thanksgiving effects the Christian sacrifice, his body and blood. And even if there is a certain sense in which the eucharistic communion completes his sacrifice, there seems no reason why this should not also be an element in a rite which signifies it. But the importance of this difference of view lies in Kelly's conclusion that the element of 'offering' is underplayed in Lash's account and the 'community-meal' element overplayed. Certainly Lash puts a great emphasis on the latter element. But does he leave out any essential element in the Eucharist when he writes, in the words which I have already quoted: 'by the grace of Christ, our self-offering to the Father, expressed and sealed by our sharing in the meal, is a participation of his self-offering to his Father on Calvary'? Nevertheless Kelly does draw our attention to the danger of an imbalance which the current emphasis on the 'community' aspect of the eucharist does not always avoid. It is necessary to say something more about this.

To take an example of it, Mrs Rosemary Radford Ruether, in her book *The Church Against Herself*, writes as follows: 'the breaking of the bread, in which community is most perfectly manifest, far from being a cultic act, is, in the most complete sense, an "everyday" act. The event of community, therefore, is not some sacred ceremony, but precisely what is intended to be the centre of our everyday lives. As wayfarers sharing food together, we find the Lord in our midst.'[1] Father Peter Hebblethwaite, who quotes this passage in an article 'The Eucharistic Dilemma',[2] asks very pertinently what is this opposition between 'cultic' and 'everyday' and whether the prime mover in this act is Christ or the community. It seems to me very odd that there should be a widespread enthusiasm for 'desacralizing' the Eucharist. The proper and necessary emphasis on the 'community' aspect along with the realization that we are never out of touch with the risen Christ should have the effect of 'sacralizing' the whole of human life, not that of playing down the awe and reverence which should surround the Eucharist as the act in which Christ is present to us as our spiritual food. It is his appointment and his power, not just our getting together, which constitute the Eucharist. The recent changes in the Roman liturgy have been misapplied in so far as the 'numinous' character of the Eucharist has become obscured in some parts of the world (a disregard

[1] 164 (Sheed and Ward, 1967).   [2] *The Month*, May 1970.

for the dignity and beauty of the liturgy has had much to do with this). Hebblethwaite, however, after giving us Bouyer's view that the eucharist 'is primarily the mystery enacted in our midst, into which we are graciously drawn', writes that 'his absolute verticalism is inadequate, but so also is Mrs Ruether's absolute horizontalism'. He goes on to say: 'We do have to work out the meaning of the Eucharist for our lives, the meaning in human terms for precise communities . . .' I can find nothing in Bouyer's writings to suggest that he overlooks this obvious requirement unless it means that each community has to invent its own eucharistic prayer, and that means, as Hebblethwaite himself points out, that 'the sign of unity would become the means of disunity'.

Finally I would draw attention to certain remarks of Père Yves Congar's in a collection of papers recently published in an English version, *The Revelation of God*. 'How', he asks, 'does Christ draw us to himself, assimilate us to himself and form us into his body by the eucharist? The best approach would seem to be by way of the equally mysterious fact of assimilation in the natural order . . . the conversion of an alien substance into our own. . . .'[1] Congar goes on to refer to another sort of assimilation, that which takes place in knowledge: 'In the relationship between truth and the mind, it is the mind that receives sustenance, but it is truth that assimilates the mind to itself because it is truth that is the active principle.' This familiar consideration, found in the seventh book of St Augustine's *Confessions* (probably with the same application in mind), will be important for the discussion in the next chapter about the way in which the development of grace can be interpreted. And Congar concludes this discussion by speaking of a 'mystical identity with Jesus Christ', telling us that 'eucharistic transubstantiation should be envisaged as the most definite aspect of God's purpose as revealed to us in the Bible'.

This leads him to mention the implications of this eucharistic doctrine for the understanding of the Church. Albert the Great, he points out, 'before the days of competent modern exegetes . . . had observed that the description of the Church as the body of Christ is based on its essential relationship with the Lord's body sacramentally present and active among us . . . It follows that the Church is in no sense a terminus, but a means. She is herself a sacrament, that is an external, physical reality whose effect is inward and invisible. . . .

[1] 174.

The things that are done ministerially in her have their existence in her as an external and physical activity intended to produce an inward and invisible reality of communion with God in Jesus Christ. . . . Sometimes after being sincerely impressed by the labour expended by priests and laymen and by the outward success of their undertakings, one wonders what is their real worth in terms of prayer and of the union with God which they obtain . . . history as well as theology shows that a connection exists between a loss of a full understanding of the Mass and the Church, on the one hand, and consideration of the Eucharist and of the institution of the Church as things existing for their own sake, as terminal realities and objects, on the other.'[1]

At the end of this book Congar writes: 'I find particular pleasure in quoting here a passage from Maurice Blondel. . . . It shows the depth and catholicity of mind of a man who was for long suspect, but whose influence is now becoming important in many spheres of Catholic thought.'[2] The passage which he quotes comes from a difficult treatise of Blondel's on the *Vinculum substantiale* of Leibnitz. A few sentences of it, which speak sufficiently for themselves, will set these reflections in their fullest context:

'Transubstantiation is seen to be the prelude of the ultimate assimilation, the supreme incorporation of all things with the Incarnate Word . . . the spiritual configuration which, without confusion and without identification of substance, is completed in the transforming union which is the normal conclusion of the spiritual life and of sacramental communion. For if the things of earth are destined to be transposed into a new earth and a new heaven, where the Word, Alpha and Omega, the first-born of all creation, will be the sole light, the only food and the universal bond (*vinculum*), in which all things have their consistence, then for spiritual beings the *vinculum* is not a suffocating destruction of identity, but an embrace which unites and yet respects their nature; it has a certain analogical resemblance to that *osculum* of the Spirit which consummates the unity of the Trinity itself.'

14. THE EUCHARIST AND THE LIFE OF GRACE

A philosopher may fail to understand what a theologian is talking about because he lacks a certain vision; and this may lead him to conclude,

[1] 181–4.   [2] 196.

wrongly, that the theologian is talking nonsense all the time. But a philosopher is capable of understanding what the theologian means (or ought to mean) by 'God', and if he does understand it he may conclude, rightly on particular occasions, that the theologian is talking nonsense because he is failing to apply consistently principles of thought which are as much the philosopher's business as they are his own. A theologian who objects to talk about 'supernatural metaphysics' must be presumed to be in a state of some confusion about these matters. In this chapter I shall be concerned specifically with the metaphysics of grace as regards the reception rather than the bestowal of it. What is supposed to happen at our end? Is there any intelligible account of it?

Faith itself, I have maintained, implies a knowledge of God which is not just a bare awareness of him but a union with him, a personal relationship which is meant to grow. What we might call the 'official' means to its growth is the sacramental system, a phrase which will be offensive to some ears. Even when the propriety of sacraments for creatures of flesh and blood is acknowledged, even when it is recognized that God is not tied to sacraments and that these 'official' means do not detract from his generosity but rather help us to benefit from it, there is still the feeling that a certain automatism seems to preside over the whole business in the minds of theologians. It has to be admitted that this has often been the case. In the first part of the chapter I want to show that it is not the case with theologians who are also philosophers. If anything can be called 'automatic' in the sacramental system it is God's fidelity to his promises. This is unfailing, and that is what must be meant by saying that a sacrament is effective *ex opere operato*: the work is God's work, and he works on us if we let him; that is what must be meant by speaking of the effect of a sacrament *ex opere operantis*. And there is a good reason for speaking of a 'system': the sacraments are all means to the building up of a human society in union with God, and their climax is the Eucharist, the 'sacrament of sacraments'.

It will therefore be chiefly important to dispose of any suggestions that grace, God's saving presence, can be *injected* into one automatically in the Eucharist. But first it may be well to consider a circumstance in which the administration of a sacrament (so it might seem from the statements of theologians) is held to operate in such a way. It has been asserted that a man dying in certain dispositions would not save his

soul unless a priest came along to absolve him, or, if he were unconscious, to anoint him. Nowadays theologians are chary of putting forward such propositions in this bald way. Here it is perhaps worth
remarking that if the moment of death is always a conscious one
(which, despite appearances to the contrary, is a tenable view) then
the anointing of an unconscious man before his death need not be a
pointless proceeding. One could suggest that he finds himself, at the
moment of death, with a power to exercise, an opportunity to accept,
which he would not otherwise have had. This notion of a gift which
remains latent for a time—as in the usual account of baptismal grace,
for example—is certainly not without difficulties of its own. But at any
rate it fits in with the principle that grace does not 'take', if I may so
put it, unless and until it is accepted. And that some people should have
opportunities for accepting grace which others do not have does not
contradict the general principle that saving grace is always offered,
sometime, to everybody.

To return to the central question about the Eucharist and the
spiritual benefits conveyed to those who offer it, we find ourselves
faced by an attitude of mind, in the Western Church, at any rate,
according to which (so at least it would sometimes appear) two
Masses are always better, more fruitful somehow, than one. It is now
twenty years since Karl Rahner produced a little book on 'the many
Masses and the one sacrifice' which at the time produced some raising
of eyebrows in authoritative quarters. The discussion of it subsided
into an uneasy lull. But a few years ago another book by him appeared
and was translated into English as *The Celebration of the Eucharist*, in
which his previous conclusions (so far as they concern us) are set out
once more together with a good many fresh ones. He begins by
pointing out that we must ask ourselves what it means to say that
God's glory is increased whenever Mass is celebrated (here I may
mention that he rejects without hesitation the view that there is in each
Mass a *fresh*, distinct, act of oblation on Christ's part). The following passage will indicate his general position on this matter: 'Where the
concrete psychological conditions are such, on a sober estimation, that
growth in inner participation of Christ's sacrificial attitude cannot be
looked for from offering the sacrifice of the Mass, a further celebration
of Mass no longer increases God's honour and glory.'[1] In other words,

[1] 37.

I think we must say, unless the offerers of the sacrifice do participate in Christ's sacrificial attitude, the purpose for which Mass should be offered will not in fact be served. On Rahner's principles, which seem to me to be sound (although I fear that they may seem inadequate to some) it is better to celebrate one Mass, in certain circumstances and with a free choice in the matter, than to celebrate two.

No one denies that it matters to give proper attention to the sacrifice. But people will still feel that it is a good thing for a priest to say three consecutive Masses, in a case where no parochial needs are being served, as he is at present entitled on occasion to do—even though he finds himself functioning, before he finishes, in a rather perfunctory or even mechanical way. At the price of incurring the displeasure of those who take that view (this difference of opinion is usually wrapped in a decent obscurity) I am bound to say that it seems to me not a good thing. Obviously anyone who does what seems right to him is increasing in the love of God by so doing. But is he in fact, in a case of this kind, serving the purpose for which Mass is celebrated? Rahner would say that he is not. There seems to be a material, quantitative, criterion implied which he thinks inapplicable. If priests at clergy retreats and so forth say Mass on soap-boxes in a crowded room, are they really serving the purpose for which Mass is celebrated? Would it not be better for one of them to preside while the others join in with him? Since the Second Vatican Council that is now the common practice on such occasions (which are normal occasions for religious communities). But Rahner thinks, and so do I, that we should regard the present form of concelebration—in which the eucharistic prayer is uttered (in part) by all the priests together—as an interim arrangement. 'A priest', he says, 'does not have to co-consecrate to perform his priestly service in a corporate celebration of the Eucharist, as a member of a college of priests';[1] he also remarks that to many lay people the present form of concelebration 'looks like a new clerical liturgy' and that it obscures the president's proper function. He concludes that 'the normal and ideal form of Mass in which many priests take part will have to be sought in a form of assistance according to a rite which has to be arranged. . . .'[2]

This reference to concelebration might seem to be an irrelevance and of merely clerical interest. But it involves the question of principle with which I am here concerned. The reason why the present form of

[1] 109.   [2] 111.

concelebration is preferred—sacramental concelebration, as it is called, or co-consecration—is that it is thought 'more correct', as Rahner explains, 'because it is a full exercise of the *potestas sacerdotalis*'. If everyone says the words of consecration, that is to say, everyone is fulfilling his full function as a priest. But what does this mean? Rahner tells us that the fruits of the Mass exist 'only in proportion to interior union with Christ's sacrifice, whatever the function occupied or exercised by the individual in the enactment of this sacrifice in the Church'.[1] What, then, is the point of this 'full exercise of the power of the priesthood'? How does it help to serve the purpose of the Eucharist? Is there not some suggestion here that it produces automatic effects?

Rahner again takes a firm stand against such suggestions when he discusses Mass stipends. The stipend, he explains, is the sacrificial offering, presented by those who are entitled and wish to offer sacrifice with Christ in the Church. 'This', he says, 'must be properly explained once more at the present time if in the next generation any idea at all of the meaning and value of the Mass stipend is to survive.'[2] And he observes that 'the poor widow's mite, which is only sufficient for one stipend but is the constitutive expression of *devotio* equally as great as that expressed by the rich man who "orders" a hundred Masses, brings her just as much benefit from her one Mass as the hundred Masses do the rich man'.[3] The transference of stipend-obligations in large blocks, which Rahner calls 'not ideally desirable',[4] seems to me (in the precise and literal sense of the word) a scandal.

Three other points from Rahner's book are important for our topic. The first concerns the theory that the Mass derives a special value from its being offered not just by the participants but by the Church as a whole. Rahner comments: 'There is no corporate subject of supernatural merits independent of the moral achievements of individual human beings. It cannot be proved that acts of that kind are posited in relation to a particular Mass by any human beings other than those who are in some way engaged in the particular sacrifice itself.'[5] The second point concerns the theory that 'a merely finite efficacy is to be ascribed . . . by the will of God to the Mass prior to any relevant disposition of men'.[6] Rahner rejects any suggestion of a positive decree of God's will as a limiting factor, and it is surely fantastic to suppose that God fixes a maximum to the benefits which may accrue from a particular celebration.

[1] 110.   [2] 115n.   [3] 117.   [4] 118.   [5] 42.   [6] 48.

The truth of the matter must surely be that the illimitable grace of Christ is available for us in the Eucharist and that how much we benefit from it depends upon ourselves. The third point concerns another theory which seems to make God's arrangements arbitrary or mechanical, that of an extra-special benefit, *fructus specialissimus*, received by the celebrant in virtue of his celebrating.[1] Such a theory could be excogitated only in a time of theological decadence.

Behind all these questions about the workings of grace lies the question about the way in which grace itself is to be envisaged. If it is considered to be something which we believe to exist because the tradition assures us of it but of which we are ourselves in no way conscious, then we are the more likely to take up with theories which are in fact meaningless. Here it is again Karl Rahner's account of the matter which is probably the most important, or at least the most influential. In an essay first drafted some thirty years ago, to be found in the first volume of *Theological Investigations*[2] (called, somewhat alarmingly, 'Some Implications of the Scholastic concept of uncreated grace') he points out that if, as the tradition holds, grace is the seed of glory, then, since God communicates *himself* to the soul in glory, so he must begin to do so for the soul in grace. Theology in the past has commonly spoken of grace as constituting a created state of being, and this has been called, rather unfortunately, a 'physical accident' of the soul. This state of supernatural elevation has been considered as something which is quite outside our consciousness. Our acts of faith and our desire to serve God have been thought of, Rahner explains, as constituted, so far as we are aware of them, of 'purely natural elements, only *directed* towards the supernatural as their object'. It is thus easy to understand that the faithful, brought up on this sort of theological teaching, can hardly take much interest in a mysterious depth of their being where the 'supernatural' is supposed to be working altogether imperceptibly, and that non-Christians can take no interest in it at all. In another essay Rahner observes that 'it would be good if the teaching of Scripture was confronted point by point' with this scholastic view. It would then be recognized that 'supernatural actual graces are to be qualified as "enlightenments" and "inspirations"', and it would become clear that 'the supernatural act performed by grace is also different spiritually, that is consciously and existentially and not only entita-

[1] 53f.   [2] 319-46.

tively, from every natural act'.[1] This is what emerged from our earlier discussions about the act of faith.

But what has now to be considered is that there is still an unwilling-ness, even among the more enlightened of our theologians, to discuss the life of grace straightforwardly in terms of loving knowledge, know-ledge transformed through love. In the essay in *Theological Investiga-tions* referred to above, Rahner speaks of God's gift of himself to us as a 'quasi-formal communication'. Why does he think it necessary to employ this very rebarbative formula instead of speaking of God's approach to us as the object of our knowledge and love? The reason is that something is thought to be a prerequisite for the exercise of know-ledge and love, namely an ontological unity with God. Rahner describes it as follows: 'This ontological unity is nothing but the pre-supposition and the ontological aspect of the unity of the created spirit with God in the act of immediate loving contemplation, an act therefore which implies the highest degree of unity in the fullest distinction'.[2] This is not perhaps very illuminating, but it does show that this mysteri-ous prerequisite is simply *for* the union of loving knowledge. Rahner also says that the quasi-formal causality is 'one which determines the finite spirit in the direction of the object which it is to know and love'[3] and that 'grace . . . as an entitative supernatural elevation of man can be described in detail only in terms of its definitive unfolding'.[4] What emerges, then, is that there must first be a raising of our being to a fresh level before knowledge and love of God are possible in the super-natural order. It is this state of elevation to which the theologians refer when they speak of 'habitual grace', and we might conclude that this doctrine, even if it may seem unconvincing, need not cause us anxiety.

Indeed it need not in Rahner's account of it. He is not going back on his view that we are in conscious contact with God himself when we perform supernatural acts. He seems only to be saying that God's presence in the soul must be a fact before we can be conscious of it. That is, of course, true of our natural knowledge of him: he is active in us before we are aware of him. Whether it means anything to say that he *must* also be present to us in a more intimate way *before* we can enter into a more intimate relationship with him seems to me doubtful. When we come to know anything the object of our knowledge becomes

---

[1] *Nature and Grace*, Sheed and Ward paperback, 28-9.
[2] Art. cit., 336.   [3] 332.   [4] 334-5.

present to us: knowledge is a presence of the object to the subject. What we know may or may not have been physically present to us (the fly on my nose) before we became aware of it. When we do become aware of it, it presents itself to us, brings about that union of subject and object in which human experience is grounded: this is the fact from which we have to start, and any attempt to get behind it, to discover its pre-history, seems to be doomed to failure. We cannot explain the fact of knowledge by having recourse to the physical model of impact and reaction. The object's activity upon us is not identical with our knowledge of it; subject and object are united, not confused. But the object *directly* causes us to know it: there seems no reason for saying that it must first be present and *then* become known. If this is right, talk of 'quasi-formal causality' is adding a needless complexity. The mysteriousness of 'intentional union' (as the scholastics call the union of knowledge) is found at the very heart of our experience, which, in so far as specifically human, is itself from the beginning a contact with God. There is no harm in talking about 'quasi-formal causality' if this is just a way of saying that God makes a change in us by presenting himself to us, that we become identified with him, *formed* by him, only in the sense that we are '*intentionally*' united with him. But the trouble is that this 'ontological unity' (which is supposed to be the necessary prerequisite for the 'intentional' union, the actual loving knowledge) becomes, for so many theologians, as we shall see, the centre of their interest. And if it is not so clear to them as it is to Rahner that the actual (conscious) loving knowledge is the all-important fact, then their teaching about grace may become obscure and seriously misleading. A concentration on 'habitual' rather than on 'actual' grace may suggest that the language of knowledge and love is inadequate for these purposes. And this must result in incomprehensibility: no other language is available.

That such a danger exists will emerge if I now turn to a report of a meeting held at Chevetogne a few years ago, *The Theology of Grace and the Ecumenical Movement*,[1] by Professors Moeller and Philips of Louvain (the meeting was attended by experts in various theological fields from different Christian confessions). There have been disagreements about the metaphysics of grace not only between Catholics and Protestants but also between Western and Eastern Christians. I am going to pro-

[1] Mowbray, 1961.

pose that the unwillingness to discuss these questions in the comprehensible language of knowledge and love has had a good deal to do
with it and that if the disputants were to use such language that disagreement might be considerably reduced. It may be surprising to
suggest that a philosophical approach to these theological questions
could be generally acceptable to Protestants. But Protestant objections
to such an approach would often prove, I think, to be objections rather
to Aristotelianism than to the sort of reflective analysis of human experience which I have been recommending. And as regards the Orthodox
of the East, the writers of the report remark that 'it is less dangerous
to use only Platonism, and to ignore Aristotelianism, than to do the
opposite; the danger of making grace a "thing", which was not lacking
in the later, decadent scholasticism, goes hand in hand with a too
exclusive use of Aristotelianism'.[1]

The first passage in the report which I shall examine is concerned
with the teaching of the fourteenth-century theologian Gregory
Palamas, whose influence on Eastern Orthodoxy has been profound.
Palamas thought it necessary to make a distinction between God in
himself and the 'divine energies'; God in himself, he holds, is unknow-
able but he is knowable in his 'energies'. I quote:

'The argument of Palamas was that theology provides the most certain
knowledge of God because it is *God* who is the agent in revealing
Himself therein; thus theology, in the context of revelation, becomes
an objective and positive mode of cognisance . . . Palamas wants to
reconcile the impossibility of knowing God, who is beyond all being,
ὑπερούσιος, with the fact that He is communicated in the "divine
energies". . . . The gulf between the creature and the Creator makes it
necessary that the divine energies through which we see God should
not themselves belong to the creation. . . . There is simply a total
participation in the divine energy, that is, in that mysterious mode of
God's presence by which He reveals Himself and acts in the believer.
. . . The East is concerned . . . with what it is in God that makes it
possible for Him to give Himself . . . the East has never attempted a
philosophical explanation of deification. . . .'[2]

First it may be observed that it is indeed God who is the agent in
revealing himself, whether he does this in giving us our first contact

[1] 40. [2] 7-9.

with him (our 'natural' knowledge) or in giving us that knowledge of himself for which natural knowledge is given, the definitive revelation in Jesus Christ. But what I am concerned to suggest is that the paradoxes of the Palamite doctrine (as set forth in the passage quoted) are no longer paradoxes if we recognize that the situation to which they refer is the situation which is familiar to us in our everyday awareness of our environment. There is an ontological gulf between ourselves and everything else. Nevertheless there is communication between ourselves and what is other than ourselves, persons or things, not merely an impact upon our sense-organs but an *awareness* of the other as other. This law of union without confusion, to repeat, is the basic law of our experience. There is no question of finding some link to connect our awareness with its created objects, although it is conditioned by contact on the level of the sense-organs. There is no question of finding a link between our awareness and God of whom we are aware. We know him only as acting on us, but we must say that we do really know him, on pain of agnosticism, not some impossible halfway house between the created and the Uncreated.

The questions which Palamas is really asking and the answers which should be given to them would then take the following form. Are we to say that God as known by us is or is not God? Of course he is, but our knowledge of him is limited. Are we to say that our knowledge of him is God? Of course it is not in so far as it is ours, that is, in so far as it is ourselves knowing God. What we must say is that in knowledge object does not change into subject nor subject into object: there is *union* between them.

The 'historical sketch of the Catholic theology of created grace' which the report goes on to make (in its second chapter) may help to confirm my suggestion. What seems to emerge is that a great deal of talk about 'uncreated' grace and 'created grace' could be eliminated by means of it. St Augustine, we are told, says that 'the divine indwelling is always related to some knowledge or experience' (a topic which the report does not pursue), and that for him 'the idea of a purely created grace has no meaning . . . like St Basil, he speaks only of the contact of the uncreated with the created, and the created element, such as the scholastics distinguished, does not appear in his thought. It is likewise absent in the Early Middle Ages. . . .'[1] The way in which the idea of

[1] 12.

the *habitus*, the habit or state, of grace was excogitated is then very interestingly described. It is not just a question of Aristotelian influence: 'The fact is that the historical development of the idea came primarily as the result of an effort to avoid Pelagianism: St Bonaventure and St Thomas both say that if there were no created grace, one might think that man by his own works gives himself grace.'[1] Even St Albert, who is held responsible for the idea of created grace as an intermediary, bridging the infinite distance between man and God, 'is aware that the soul is directly united to God, and that this union is to be understood in terms of participation'.[2]

It might be more helpful to say that 'participation' is to be understood in terms of 'cognitive union'. This would fit in well with the conclusion reached in the report that the *habitus* is 'an *active tension set up by God at work in man*; and this is not intermittent but continuous; it is like a pattern formed of one unbroken line and not a series of separate figures'.[3] 'At the present moment', we are told, 'theology is moving in the direction of a synthesis between the doctrine of indwelling, and that of created grace, the latter being understood in the light of the great scholastics of the thirteenth century.'[4] It is surely not a question of reconciling these factors, properly understood, but of seeing them as implying one another in our experience.

One finds in this report, as a whole, a certain unwillingness to speak of the knowledge as well as of the love of God, but in the brief synthesis of the Catholic theology of grace which forms the third chapter, a further explanation of the *habitus* is that 'our God-given knowledge and love are poised ready for action.'[5] and there is further emphasis on 'the *vitalism* of the *habitus*' and on 'the *continual presence and activity of God*' therein.[6] The bogy of 'merit' is then properly dealt with by referring to St Augustine's theme that God, when he crowns our merits, crowns his own gifts. This makes it seem all the more a pity that the chapter should end with a paragraph which leaves everything so vague (it is merely typical of contemporary theology in so doing, and is here quoted at length precisely for that reason):

'Certain lines of thought touched on by the scholastics must be further developed before a balanced *De gratia* can be written. The first thing, to be emphasized most strongly, is the personal nature of the relations

---

[1] 17. [2] 18. [3] 20. [4] 23. [5] 25. [6] 26-7.

between the soul and God. St Thomas's language is, perhaps, too abstract; he seems to overlook a number of features of the Eastern tradition. What must be made clearer is that the created *habitus* is simply an *active readiness to receive*, in the sense that the soul does not follow the divine call unwillingly, but submits itself willingly in the course of a living and actual converse with the divine persons. And again, the idea of participation must be further explored, and we must learn to speak . . . of a *quasi-formal union*. Such a union is not merely the effect of an efficient cause, nor of a purely exemplary cause, but is founded in an active presence. It may be doubted whether the term *created grace*, which has never been imposed as of faith, is very fortunate in such a sense. It is no doubt dangerous to abandon such an ancient expression, but terms must be used in the sense they were meant to have when they were coined, and not allowed to keep the secondary meanings that have caused so many ambiguities in discussion. Perhaps one might be allowed to use the expression of Père de la Taille, "actuation créée par acte incréé" applying it, *mutatis mutandis*, to grace. The term "created" is still there, but, applied to the term "actuation", it is meant to express the permanent presence of God, always underlying the activity and continually, as the *quasi-forma*, informing it.'

These last sentences seem to cry out for clarification. In so far as 'grace' means God acting on us, it is obviously uncreated. In so far as 'grace' refers to what we have and are it is obviously created. But if we mean by 'grace' the union between man and God, it does not make good sense to ask whether it is created or uncreated. Indeed, the idea of participation must be further explored. Does it not appear that this paragraph would become convincing if, and only if, the language of knowledge were employed? Rahner's essay is presumably in mind, but the reference to 'quasi-formal union', without reference of any kind to the union of knowledge, is merely mystifying. A footnote suggests paraphrases of the formula quoted from de la Taille: 'God's uncreated act supplies a created actualizing to the creature', or 'the creature is perfected in its nature by an uncreated act'.[1] Now if this is taken to

---

[1] De la Taille's suggestion was, I suppose, the most influential of any made in the generation before Rahner, who tells us, surprisingly, that he was unaware of it when he drafted the essay in *Theological Investigations* (Vol. I, 340, n. 2, where he acknowledges that de la Taille had reached his own conclusion).

refer to God's self-presentation to the creature in the creature's knowledge and love of him, it becomes comprehensible. And this is, in
principle, the explanation of it offered by Père de Letter on several
occasions. It will be sufficient to quote from one of the many articles
which he has written on 'quasi-formal causality'.[1] De Letter points out
that de la Taille and Rahner speak of the 'self-communication' of God
in the same sense,[2] and concludes that there can be 'no basic objection
to conceiving the actuation of the essence of the soul by the uncreated
Act . . . as pertaining to the intentional order . . .';[3] that is, the order of
knowledge, reminding us in a footnote that St Thomas speaks of the
habitual indwelling of God through grace 'ut cognitum in cognoscente
et amatum in amante',[4] even apart from any acts of knowledge and
love. De Letter, too, it will be noticed, is dealing with the problem of
the *habitus*. And before leaving this topic I ought to acknowledge that
there is such a problem. It does mean something to say that a man is 'in
a state of grace' apart from any awareness, explicit or implicit, of his
union with God. He is 'ready', perhaps we may say, for such an awareness. What I have been urging is that God's activity upon us in the life
of grace can be intelligibly discussed only in terms of that conscious
union with him in which (if we accept his offer) it will issue. This union
is not often explicit in fact—that is a topic which must be dealt with in a
later chapter.

The rest of this one will be concerned with the topic of the Trinity.
That should cause no surprise, because the new life which is made
available for us through Christ's victory is precisely a life of union with
the Trinity, recognized as such. The Christian revelation is the revelation of the Trinity. To receive this revelation is to be united in loving
knowledge with the life of God in himself, a union which begins on
earth and is to be achieved in its definitive form after death. Reflection
upon the implications of the Christian life has produced the doctrine of
the Trinity as a result. So it is not illuminating to discuss it as a series of
propositions in abstractions from this life. This, then, is the point at
which to say something more about a doctrine to which only some
scattered references have been made so far in the course of this book.
But I shall make only a few remarks about certain aspects of it. It has
not been my aim to offer a potted treatise on any doctrine, but only to

---

[1] The *Irish Theological Quarterly*, Jan. 1963.
[2] 37.   [3] 44.   [4] *S. Th.*, I, 44,6.

discuss some misunderstandings which can easily arise at important points and to suggest how they may perhaps be obviated.

A passage from Professor Leonard Hodgson's valuable book *The Doctrine of the Trinity* may set the stage for this discussion: 'The Christian life is life "in the Spirit", and as such reproduces in each Christian the same way of life as was that of Christ's on earth. . . . But the reproduction of Christ's life in the life of each Christian is not simply a matter of copying a pattern or example; it is made possible by an initial act of God adopting the Christian to share in the sonship of Christ. Thus he shares his Lord's relationship to the Father and the Spirit.'[1] (And Hodgson concludes, as I did just now: 'Hence the doctrine of the Trinity is the formal setting of the Christian life, arrived at by an analysis of the implications of that life as it has come into existence and continues to exist in the history of the world.') One phrase in this passage may perhaps need some explanation. Christ lived 'in the Spirit'. One cannot deny that before the time of Christ the Spirit was 'at work' upon men, preparing them for the definitive revelation which took place when Christ's mission was accomplished. All the more, then, was he 'at work' in Christ himself. But, as we have seen, the man Jesus had to 'work his passage' to the Father, that is, to the new life of definitive union with Father, Son and Spirit. He had to gain for himself this life 'in the Spirit' before it could be communicated to us.

I shall begin this brief discussion by referring to a misunderstanding which, it seems to me, can easily arise about God's 'indwelling in the soul'; it is regularly described simply as the indwelling of the Spirit, and this may give rise to the notion that our union with the Father and the Son is somehow less real than our union with the Spirit. It may be said that, since the divine Son alone became incarnate (and not the Father or the Spirit), entering into a special relation with our humanity, there is no reason why the Spirit alone should not enter into a special relation with us of a different kind. The reply must be that the Spirit does stand in a special relation to us but that he does not do so *alone*. An 'intentional union' with the Spirit is necessarily also an 'intentional union' with the Father and the Son. To know and love the Spirit would be impossible without knowing and loving the Father and the Son at the same time because they could not be *themselves* without one another. Moreover unless we were 'in touch' with them as they really

[1] 49-50.

are, there would be no doctrine of the Trinity to talk about. Some years ago there was much talk about the 'forgotten Paraclete', and it was quite true that the Spirit had been forgotten. But this was also true of the Father and the Son, for what had been forgotten was that God *is* the Trinity. That is, the true meaning of the new life had been forgotten.

But why should the Spirit's special role be connected in particular with 'indwelling'? Is this not, it might be asked, the result of interpreting New Testament sayings without considering their historical background? Was not this insistence on the sending of the Spirit the only way in which the truth about theChristian life could be expressed at the time? How else could the Trinity have been revealed by our Lord? His disciples had learnt that he was in the Father and the Father in him, and to prepare them for the reception of the new life, for union with the Trinity, it was inevitable that this should be talked about in terms of the Holy Spirit. That is doubtless true, but it does not show that the Spirit has no special role in our life of grace (such a conclusion indeed, as we have seen, would mean that we could not talk about the Spirit at all) or that this role may not be connected in some special way with the 'indwelling'.

That it is so connected is certainly traditional teaching. This teaching has been summarized by Louis Bouyer in the following remarkable paragraphs:

'God, at the origin of everything, of eternal as well as of temporal realities, is Father . . . that is, he possesses his life only in giving it to another. This Other is his Son. The Son is thus himself only in being given, as the Father is himself only in giving himself.

But if the origin of the Son is a primordial gift of the Father . . . the mutual life of Father and Son is again nothing but Gift. In this Son whom his essential love has, as it were, projected into existence, the love of the Father rests and is satisfied. The Son in return loves the Father and loves him with the same love by which he is loved, since everything in the Son proceeds from the Father and reproduces him with perfect fidelity. This gift, by which the Father communicates himself to the Son and in which equally the Son returns to the Father so that their distinction is consummated in the reunion of a mutual love, is the Holy Spirit, Love, the substantial Gift. So in the Trinity it is the Spirit which enables the Son as he proceeds from the Father to be fully himself by enabling him to return to the Father, within that same movement of love which bears the Father towards him.

This is precisely what the Spirit is in us: the gift of the Father's love by which we love him in the Son, by which we become fully ourselves in becoming sons, that is, in returning freely to our source, to *the* Source, the Father.'[1]

This may be at first bewildering, but it should at least suggest that it does mean something to speak of the Spirit as the Gift of the Father and the Son and that the traditional formula for our approach to the Father, '*through* the Son, *in* the Spirit', deserves examination. First we have to remember that the words which we use of the ultimate Mystery are only 'pointers'. We can make no sense of a self-communication between human persons which is itself a distinct reality. And the Father, the Son and Spirit are distinct, although God *is* Father, Son and Spirit. It will be remembered that Rahner has proposed as a formula for the doctrine of the Trinity: 'the one God subsists in three distinct manners of subsisting'. His purpose in proposing it is the removal of a misunderstanding which the use of the word 'person' here can occasion for us today (he is not proposing that this use of the word should be abolished but rather attempting, by means of the new formula, to explain it). When we speak of three persons in ordinary speech we mean three centres of consciousness. 'But', writes Rahner, 'there exists in God only *one* power, *one* will, only one self-presence, a unique activity, a unique beatitude. . . .'[2] And he adds in a footnote: 'We must, of course, say that the Father, Son and Spirit possess self-consciousness and that each is aware of the two other "persons". But precisely this self-communication . . . comes from the divine essence, is common *as one* to the divine persons . . .'. For we must say that 'the Father, Son and Spirit are identified with the one godhead and are relatively distinct from one another'; as distinct 'they are constituted only by their relatedness to one another'.[3] The divine life, communicated by the Father, is 'shared' identically by each of them. The processions are 'moments' in a single eternal, unchanging, act. So, as Rahner says, 'there is properly no *mutual* love between Father and Son, for this would presuppose two acts. But there is loving self-acceptance of the Father . . . and this self-

---

[1] *Le Sens de la Vie Monastique*, 139.
[2] *The Trinity*, 75.   [3] *Ibid.*

acceptance gives rise to the distinction.'[1] We cannot well avoid speaking of 'mutual love',[2] but it will be recalled that Bouyer, who uses the expression, had already explained that the Son loves the Father 'with the same love by which he is loved'. It moves, as it were, in two distinct directions, and as so doing constitutes a third 'manner of subsisting', which is the Holy Spirit. We are still trying to gain some understanding of how it is that we return to the Father *in* him.

Before we can hope to do so, we must look more closely at the Mystery. That these relationships should be 'manners of subsisting', distinct realities which are nevertheless identical with the one God, is what is most mysterious for us. When we speak of 'distinct realities' here, our natural tendency is to think of them as members of a class, instances of the concept 'person'. But they are, as 'manners', totally distinct and cannot be comprehended by any univocal concept. In God there is total distinction and total unity. This baffles us, but we have no right to say that it can make no sense. We can understand something about the two 'processions'. Rahner remarks: 'We must, and rightly so, think of God as of a spirit; there can be nothing objectively real in God which is not also most formally spirit, self-presence, knowledge and love.' And there are only two 'basic activities of the spirit: knowledge and love'. Without taking up with a 'psychological theory' of the Trinity which models it in detail on our human psychology, we must 'connect, in a special and specific way, the intra-divine procession of the Logos from the Father with God's knowledge, and the procession of the Spirit from the Father through the Son with God's love'.[3] (This last formula, it may be noticed, is acceptable to the Orthodox of the East.)

The Father communicates himself as truth—the Word presents himself to us as *uttered* by the Father (so only the Word could become incarnate as God's revelation). The Father also communicates himself as love—and when this communication is extended to us in the order of grace it is the Holy Spirit who enables us to *accept* the Word and so to return to the Father. For the life of grace and the doctrine of the Trinity are not two different subjects: the 'immanent' Trinity and the 'economic' Trinity are one.

To bring all this to a point, although there are no temporal relations in the godhead, there is nevertheless an *order*. There was never an

[1] 106.   [2] Rahner uses the phrase himself (35).   [3] 116.

incompleteness, but we cannot help saying that in a sense the Spirit 'completes' the godhead. We are drawn up into this completeness; we are related to Father, Son and Spirit *as such*. And it is the special function of the Spirit of love to make us complete by uniting us according to our measure with the Word and with the Father.

We cannot hope to plumb the depths of this mystery, although we are invited to penetrate further and further into it. At any rate we learn from the Christian revelation that there is no flaw in the perfect union in which the unity of the godhead subsists; there is not that barrier which separates all human persons from complete union with one another. It is the value to which the value of human love is pointing us, the standard which we are bringing to bear when we recognize its insufficiencies. We are called to a union of knowledge and love with the divine life, to the 'mystical marriage' in which there is still distinction, although now there is no barrier, between finite and Infinite. The marriage of man and woman is the closest approximation to the divine unity in the sphere of inter-finite relations. That is why it is holy—and why its holiness is not appreciated by so many; the human family seems to be its analogue in so far as the union of husband and wife joins them together in their love for their child.

MYSTICAL THEOLOGY: THE CONSUMMATION
OF THE ATONEMENT

15. THE CHRISTIAN VOCATION

The conclusion to which the previous chapters have been leading is that the Christian vocation is essentially a mystical one. I shall discuss in the next chapter the view that the word 'mystical' should be reserved for certain spiritual states of a very special kind. In this one I shall accept the meaning given to it by Père Louis Bouyer in his *Introduction à la Vie Spirituelle*,[1] which seems to me the most useful book on prayer and Christian mysticism written in our time (the question of 'non-Christian mysticism' will also be postponed to the next chapter). Bouyer points out that the adjective 'mystical', which in its original Greek form meant simply 'secret' or 'hidden', came to be used, among Christians, of religious experience only after a long process of continuous development. I quote:

'In Christian language (prepared for to some extent by Philo) it referred in the first place to the profoundest significance of the Scriptures, one which is accessible only for faith. For Clement or Origen, this plenary sense, where all the lines of revelation converge, is "mystical": that is what St Paul calls "the mystery" . . . the Cross of Christ seen in all its consequences. . . . After that, and concurrently with this first Christian usage of "mystical", which will always remain, the word comes to refer, in a sense closely linked with the first, to the profound reality of the sacraments which is veiled and at the same time shown forth by their visible symbols. . . . And finally, the writings of Pseudo-Denis systematizing a third application of the word which had been given to it already by Gregory of Nyssa, its modern, specifically spiritual, meaning became usual . . . the full and personal apprehension on the part of the Christian of what is proclaimed by the

[1] Desclée (Paris), 1960. There is a translation, *Introduction to Spirituality* (New York).

divine Word and given to us in the sacraments: the fulness of the new life, the divine life which we find in Christ who died and rose again.'[1]

Bouyer reaches the conclusion that 'the first act of charity springing from faith in the divine Word, faith nourished by the sacraments, contains in germ the whole of mysticism'. Thus 'mysticism, far from being a way which is singular, equivocal or extraordinary in a pejorative sense, must be considered the normal development of Christian perfection'.[2] That is not, of course, to say that it is in fact common. As Bouyer here points out, the genuinely traditional and solidly theological character of this conclusion was first demonstrated for our time by Garrigou-Lagrange, in his *Perfection Chrétienne et contemplation*. This was a very important achievement, because the disastrous dispute between Bossuet and Fénelon and the general decadence of theology in the period which followed had very largely obscured the traditional doctrine. And it is also necessary to emphasize this achievement because the unpopularity of Garrigou-Lagrange's work as a whole (it is of the 'high and dry' Thomist kind) naturally arouses prejudices against it. The book, despite its 'high Thomist' atmosphere, is still essential reading for anyone concerned with the present state of the question in the theology of the West. It made clear (it is strange that it needed to be made clear) that mysticism has no essential connection with imaginative visions, 'locutions', levitations and psychological manifestations of a sensational kind; indeed the great mystics have always regarded these as, in general, a sort of nuisance which tends to arise at a certain stage of development; or a sort of weakness to which the physical organism is liable in particular circumstances. Mysticism is the loving awareness of God.

Prejudices against mysticism are so strong that it seems necessary, before going any further, to spend some time on them. Even among (otherwise) orthodox Roman Catholics one still finds the attitude of mind according to which 'it begins with "mist" and ends in "schism" ', with the implication that all claims to an experience of God are suspect. Many of them are indeed suspect. An experience which can be produced automatically by the adoption of some technique or by drugs cannot be an experience of God. For the experience of God is the

[1] 302-3.   [2] 303.

result of God's free activity upon us. This does not mean that God's bestowal of his gift (the gift of union with himself) is arbitrary. It means that the consciousness of God's presence cannot be brought about by the mere dictate of the subject. It also requires an *openness* of mind and heart, a willingness to attend to God and to accept his purposes (for one cannot love God without accepting his plan and co-operating with it so far as one at present understands it). False mysticism is to be recognized fundamentally by its aiming at the attainment of some psychological state, to be enjoyed for its own sake, and by its consequent disjunction of the moral life from the mystical. This disjunction has often appeared among the (otherwise) orthodox in so far as they have tended to disjoin the first commandment from the second. The loving awareness of God is not always an agreeable experience—very far from it—and it is incompatible with indifference to one's neighbour.

There are other prejudices which cannot be so briefly dismissed. One of them appeals to history, and for the answer to it I cannot do better than quote at some length from Bouyer's book. 'In the course of the last half-century', he writes, 'it has become quite the fashion, first among Protestants, and then by a process of infiltration in many Catholic circles, to consider the contemplative element in the Christian tradition, and indeed all knowledge of God which tends to claim a central position in it, as a Greek contamination . . . this is a mere prejudice, resulting from a study of words divorced from their contexts . . . Christianity did not have to wait for contact with Hellenism to give to knowledge, and especially knowledge of God, a central position. And this "knowledge of God" was so specifically Christian (biblical and Jewish in the first place) that when the contact was made Christianity refashioned the Greek notions which it took over in its own way. . . . The "knowledge of God" of which the prophets speak is a knowledge which only the Word of God can produce in a man who listens to it with faith . . . it is an eminently personal knowledge . . . which is at the same time a union and a conformation. It is very typical of the Hebraic vision of things that the word "knowledge" is regularly used of the sexual relationship between man and woman. And far from there being in this any depreciation of knowledge, it is very remarkable that, conversely, the knowledge of God . . . is compared to the union of man and woman in marriage. . . . But the aspect of conformation is no less essential to the knowledge of God than the aspect of union. . . .

Because the people of God is the people which knows him, it must become *like* him.'[1]

We are always being told, Bouyer continues, that the idea of a transforming knowledge which assimilates the contemplative to what he contemplates is of Platonic origin. But for Plato assimilation is a prerequisite for knowledge; it is Judaism, not Platonism, which is the origin of the idea of a knowledge which assimilates. It is not by trying to make oneself like God in the first place that this knowledge is gained but by *receiving* the Word. Faith, as Bouyer puts it, 'is the starting point of the only efficacious purification . . . in the soul thus purified by obedience, the knowledge of faith . . . becomes luminous for us . . . and this is what Christian antiquity as a whole called the transition from simple faith to "gnosis" '.[2] So 'it is absolutely false to say that this word "gnosis" was borrowed by the Fathers (Clement of Alexandria and Origen) from the vocabulary of the heretics whom nineteenth-century scholars took to calling "gnostics" as though that term belonged properly to them'. Irenaeus regularly calls them 'pseudo-gnostics,' attributing the true 'gnosis' to the Christian Church. Nor is it true to say that the word, as referring to the knowledge of God, was first used by Greek philosophers; it first acquired this meaning in the Septuagint. It was employed by the first Christians (by St Paul, for example) simply because they were Jews living on the Bible. St John never uses the substantive, but constantly uses the corresponding verb of a knowledge which unites man with the life of love in which the Father and the Son are united.[3]

Equally important are Bouyer's comments on Anders Nygren's *Eros and Agape*, which has been so influential among Protestant theologians: 'According to Nygren, Catholicism betrays its mixed origins, its adulterated Christianity, by the importance which its spiritual tradition gives to mysticism. It is curious to see how many Catholics allow themselves to be impressed by these assertions. The activism of our contemporaries easily persuades them that a religion which does not confine itself to active charity can really be nothing but an adulterated Christianity. To seek God for himself, to find one's last end in union with him, to exalt the experience of this union (so far as it can be achieved on this earth)—all that, they tell us, is a pagan, not a Christian idea.'[4] Bouyer has remarked in an earlier connection that 'a life which

[1] 264-5. [2] 267. [3] 267-71. [4] 289.

does not resolutely preserve in their due place the practices of silence and recollection (necessarily a solitary affair) cannot be a Christian life . . . it cannot even deserve to be called a human life'.[1] The Platonic tradition, unlike Nygren, did recognize that the search for God has the highest possible value in itself. And the answer to Nygren is simply the fact that 'the idea of a "vision of God" in Christ, who transfigures us into his own image, is purely evangelical and owes nothing at all, fundamentally, to any outside influence. . .'.[2] Nygren tries to avoid this conclusion by regarding St John as already contaminated with Hellenism. Even if this could be sustained—and it is becoming plainer and plainer that St John's thought is thoroughly Judaic—there would be, Bouyer points out, an insoluble problem presented by St Paul: 'It is given to us all, all alike, to catch the glory of the Lord as in a mirror, with faces unveiled, and so we become transfigured into the same like-ness, borrowing glory from that glory, as the Spirit of the Lord enables us.'[3]

The fact that faith will pass away, as St Paul says in the same place, 'does not mean', Bouyer concludes, 'that "believing" in the most biblical and Christian sense of the word is opposed to any idea of "knowing" God or even of "seeing" him . . . already in this life, as far as faith tends towards charity . . . it leads us towards a certain vision . . . crepuscular vision . . . it is a knowledge which can and ought in its own way to become as real as, more real than, the knowledge of sense-presented realities . . . it is a vision in so far as it is a knowledge without intermediary, in which we know God by his own presence and his own activity in us'.[4]

Prejudice in regard to the Christian 'gnosis' is even more likely to arise in the English-speaking countries from the perusal of books which try to explain mysticism as a phenomenon which has no essential con-nection with religion at all. The most important instance, perhaps, is Professor W. T. Stace's *The Writings of the Mystics*, since its paperback form ensures it a wide circulation. According to Stace, religious people put their own, illegitimate, interpretation upon the phenomena of mysticism. His own standpoint is not easy to determine. He rejects the God of religion, but he talks about the Infinite and the Eternal. He seems to be what the Fathers called a 'pseudo-gnostic', a sort of Monist. This is a view with which I find it difficult to sympathize,

[1] 220.　[2] 293.　[3] *II Cor.*, 3, 18 (Knox).　[4] 299.

because it seems to be flying in the face of the facts in so obvious a way. But it is quite understandable that for anyone who does not believe in God mystical experience should seem to be just a special sort of awareness of the world as a whole or of one's own 'self'. Stace defines it as 'an apprehension of an ultimate nonsensuous unity in all things'. (It may be noted that this would exclude from mysticism such experiences as those of Aldous Huxley after taking mescalin, for that provoked a special awareness of the *sensible* world). What sort of a unity is this? Is it a unity with a vague something called Nature? Or is it just the consciousness of that unity which is the soul itself? At first Stace seems to hover between these two positions, and what he proves to mean is that subject and object really become *one* in the sense that the distinction between them is abolished. This seems to be the sort of Monism which Professor R. C. Zaehner in *Mysticism Sacred and Profane* calls 'pan-en-hen-ism' ('all-in-one-ism')—the other sort of Monism distinguished by him declares the soul itself to be the Absolute and denies altogether the reality of anything else.

Stace holds that what is common to all the states which he calls mystical is a sense of liberation, of the breaking down of barriers, a reconciliation or unification of some kind. It is quite true that there are various psychological conditions which all share this character. But it is a sheer assumption to conclude that this is the only character, or the only important character, that they possess. Is the soul being liberated by union with the Source of being or is it merely penetrating through the surface of consciousness to its own naked being? Contemplating one's own navel might lead to a locking up of oneself within oneself, a withdrawing of the mind into itself so that nothing else seems to exist, and this might afford great satisfaction and even great excitement. That might be the explanation of the curious states of mind enjoyed by (for example) Marcel Proust. And this direct awareness of the mind by itself may lead to a sense of unity with the world around us. For we are part of nature, and if we pierce to the centre of ourselves our links with nature may become startlingly clear to us. We may feel 'at one with Nature'. Richard Jefferies is perhaps the most striking example of this 'nature-mysticism'. When such a state of affairs is brought about by the use of drugs it may produce, as Zaehner has pointed out, that confusion between the self and the world which is found in madness. This is a 'return to nature' a regression to our origins, which is plainly destructive. It is the soul without God—the very antipodes of mysticism properly so called. Stace, not being a Christian, naturally concentrates on the superficial resemblances between these states which are at bottom so completely different and puts them all together under the general heading of mysticism.

Naturally, too, he misinterprets the statements of orthodox mystics. All mystics, he tells us, speak of the disappearance of the *original* self, the limited self, in their experience. But it should be obvious that Christian mystics (who, admittedly, often use very odd language) never mean that the 'original' self is abolished or literally absorbed into something else. The self, however much transformed, always remains the self—otherwise who or what is undergoing this experience? Stace also says that all mystics describe it as both a fullness and an emptiness and concludes, on this ground, that it is a fundamentally paradoxical affair and beyond logic. But when the Christian mystics speak of emptiness, void, darkness and even nothingness, what they mean is that God as the Source of being is without limitations, empty of particular determinations, the 'ocean' or 'abyss' of being, as they like to say in their more suggestive but at the same time more dangerous language. And when they speak of a loss of personality they mean the loss of self-interest and the absence of anything which separates them from God.

Here I must quote from Père Joseph Maréchal's important book *Etudes sur la Psychologie des Mystiques*, written nearly fifty years ago but superseded only in minor ways: 'We admit to a deep embarrassment in qualifying the writer who in the descriptions of the mystics does not observe, beside the affirmation of negative characteristics, the if possible clearer affirmation of the positive character of ecstasy. . . . The only Catholic contemplatives who at first sight might seem to be describing a void ecstasy, a "lapse into nothingness", are the great German and Flemish mystics of the end of the Middle Ages. Their Dionysian terminology is "negative" in the extreme . . . it would be childish of us to allow ourselves to be imposed upon by these expressions. . .'.[1] The summary of Maréchal's argument here is as follows:

'Two affirmations stand out from the descriptions of the Christian mystics which, according to them, express data of immediate experi-

[1] 242-4.

ence, yet data, on the other hand, constant and universal enough to escape the accusation of being purely subjective and individual illusion. They are:

1. The affirmation of negative characters which radically separate the ecstatic state from the normal or abnormal psychological states of ordinary life; the effacement of the empirical Ego, the leaving aside of imagery and spatiality, the absence of all enumerable multiplicity, that is to say, in a word, the cessation of conceptual thought.

Ecstasy is *negative*.

2. On the other hand, the affirmation that this cessation of conceptual thought is not total unconsciousness, but rather the enlargement and intensification or even a higher form of intellectual activity.

Ecstasy is *positive*.

Now these two affirmations are contradictory on all imaginable hypotheses save one; namely, that the human intelligence is able, in certain conditions, to attain *an intuition which is proper to itself*, or, in other words, that the intelligence, instead of constructing its object analogically and approximately from materials borrowed from the sensibility, can sometimes attain that object by an immediate assimilation.'[1]

Finally, Stace regards Christian mysticism as something which came into Christianity after the time of Christ (he even denies that the writer of the Fourth Gospel was a mystic), and he reveals a strange ignorance of Christian theology, supposing that because God is called a 'person' he must be conceived of as a limited person like ourselves and that the doctrine of the Incarnation asserts a *confusion* of God with man. It is strange that a thinker who abolishes the principle of non-contradiction in the interest of a theory should expect it to be taken seriously: our experience is itself beyond logic in the sense that it is presupposed by logic, but if we prove to be contradicting ourselves then we must have misinterpreted our evidence (we may 'point to' an experience by saying, for example, that it seems to combine the characters of activity and passivity, but we are not saying that these mutually exclusive characters are as such the same; and to talk of a 'higher synthesis' of Man and God or of man and the world means nothing at all). In his book *Mysticism and Philosophy* Stace holds that in addition to saying that the world is

[1] 245–6.

identical with God we must also say that it is not. This remarkable view
has been patiently examined by Professor H. D. Lewis. After making
various attempts to find some tolerable explanation of it, Lewis concludes, regretfully that, according to Stace, the contradiction 'must be
taken in its strictest undiminished form'. Stace is defending an 'essentially contradictory view'. All one can do, faced by this situation, is to
ask, with Lewis: 'Is not this a fatal avowal for any philosopher?'[1]

A determination to separate mysticism from religion (from the worship of God) leads to strange results. Attempts, for example, to make
out that St John of the Cross was not really interested so much in
Christianity as in a mysticism of a Plotinian type or a sort of Hegelian-
ism *avant la lettre* are so plainly in conflict with the facts that one must
call them irresponsible. It is more important to return to the prejudice
that a development of our awareness of God, although possible and
desirable, perhaps, for particular individuals, is no part of a normal
Christian life. For we have still to consider the widespread assumption
that the attempt at personal communication with God (at 'contemplative prayer', as it is commonly called) normally breaks down and that
it is therefore (except possibly in certain rare cases) to be deplored as a
waste of time.

The first thing, I believe, to be said about that is that 'personal communication with God' is so often supposed to refer only to the sort of
ecstatic experience which Maréchal was describing. In fact in its basic
form it is something which, although supremely important, is nevertheless very ordinary. It is the desire for God which God himself arouses
by his loving approach to us. Our business is to keep it, to remember it
even when we seem to have lost contact with it, to give God the chance
to renew it in us, to value it as our most prized possession. It is curious
that this desire is not more widely recognized as presupposing and involving *awareness* of God even when its affective tone is a painful one.
Indeed one might be inclined to say that, the more painful it is, the
more real it is and the less likely to be delusory. Sometimes the desire
is painful because the awareness is so tenuous as to be only an irritant—
like a drop of water on the tongue of a thirsty man. There is normally a
stage in which, for the time being, desire seems satisfied in principle—
yet it does not cease on that account. And finally, according to the
great mystics, there is, at the end of their course, an intimacy with God

[1] *The Elusive Mind*, 315.

in which intense joy and intense pain are commingled because the closer the intimacy the fiercer is the desire for the definitive surrender of death, the definitive vision. But that is not my business here.

I am concerned only with 'ordinary' mysticism. How, in actual practice, is the desire for God to be developed? The tradition tells us that one must pass through an ascetical stage before there is 'illumination'. It is not just a question of 'waiting for the spark from Heaven to fall'. To attend to God is an ascetical business (*the* ascetical business, according to Augustine Baker)[1] for this shift of interest is an exercise of the whole personality. We do not bring it about ourselves in the first instance; God brings it about if we respond (*allow* ourselves to be acted upon). Indeed it may seem at first the easiest, the most 'natural', thing in the world (since it is what we are *for*). But the personality is still undeveloped, immature. We now begin to realize what we are called upon to do—not only to keep up the interest but also to do our best for those around us; we begin to discover our weaknesses as the demands upon us increase. We did surrender ourselves once—such as we supposed ourselves to be. Now we seem to have become different. There are fresh moral dispositions to be formed in the sense that we have to put up our moral sights if there is to be fresh illumination. The 'purgative' and 'illuminative' ways are thus concurrent, intrinsically related to one another. We can separate them in time only if we take them to refer to a stage in which the chief business is the control of our disordered passions followed by a stage in which there is more positive progress in the loving awareness of God. But the dichotomy can never be complete. Attention to God is the general formula at all levels.

How, then, do we manage to *attend*? It is, I think, a mistake to say that we must always try to empty our minds so that God may fill them. This is in any case often impracticable. And then the first thing to do is to ask ourselves why this is so. We find ourselves bored, anxious, depressed, indignant or whatever. How have we got into this condition? Could it have been avoided? If the answer is 'yes', there is something that we can do about it. We can face up to the situation which has thus been revealed to us, admitting our responsibility for it, and in so doing we are not merely removing an obstacle to our attention to God but actually attending to him, for he is present to our consciousness in all our sincere moral judgements. This will be at least a first move in the

[1] *Sancta Sophia, passim.*

right direction. The principle is that we must not try to make a sudden leap into a world of prayer conceived of as separated by some mysterious barrier from the world of our ordinary experience. Rather the world of our ordinary experience has first to be put in order, so that it may expand. We must not worry about our worries, but pass a reasoned verdict on them. If our disturbed state of mind seems to result from circumstances outside our control there is not so much that we can do about it. Trying to abolish it by sheer force of will is likely to make matters worse. What we can do is to remind ourselves that a disturbance of the sensibility does die down in time and that we can encourage it to do so by commonsense methods, which should be obvious enough. We can at least bring our sense of proportion to bear upon the causes of it. It may still remain in the foreground, but if we are doing the best we can with it we are once again attending to God in the only way possible for us. If the result of this exercise seems to be nothing more than some lessening of the disturbance, it would be a mistake to think that it has been without religious value. Value is indivisible.

But if in our attempt to attend to God we do seem capable of 'an act of inattention to everything else', in Abbot Chapman's phrase, what is to be done when, as a result, we find ourselves gazing into a void? Certainly there is no point in gazing into a void. Indeed it is strictly impossible. What is being referred to is in fact a state of mind in which various interests present themselves to us and are rejected one by one (more or less expeditiously) in the hope that the ultimate concern of our lives may somehow come to take a grip on us. What has been over-looked, perhaps, is that since this 'act of inattention to everything else' has been motivated by the desire for God (it is only a means to the growth of this desire), then unless we *continue* to desire him in this exercise (if we are *merely* attempting the 'act of inattention') nothing can be accomplished at all. In other words, what we have to work with is the desire itself and the 'act of inattention to everything else' is what it will lead us to attempt. Once again we have to start with ourselves as in fact we are, not to attempt a leap out of our own existences. God is present to us in our desire for him.

It may be retorted that this is very obvious and that concentrating on our desire for God results, no less, in the state of mind called 'gazing into a void'. The question is now whether this is in fact its only result. The mind may seem to be wholly occupied, so far as it is occupied at all, with purely mundane interests, but unless a willingness to attend to God has been deliberately withdrawn, this state of affairs is not a waste of time. The apprehension of God, normally dim and 'in the background', may not seem to grow clearer, but here we have to bear in mind that this apprehension is so often unrecognized because of the persisting prejudice that a development of it must always be accompanied by feelings of satisfaction; the complaint that it does not 'grow clearer' commonly means just that. 'Gazing into a void' is a description sometimes given of what is in fact a sincere attempt to dwell upon the transcendent origin of our desire, to follow it (as it were) to its source. And, if it is sincere, it cannot go unrewarded. Perseverance in this apparently unrewarding exercise does lead to the growth of the desire, to an interest in God which becomes habitual even in the midst of the most humdrum activities. A little patience will reveal the truth of this claim. So what the 'void' refers to may be in fact God's presence as it impinges upon us here and now. For he is 'void of limitations', beyond conceptual thought. The great mystics say that intimacy with God, as it begins to develop, issues in a 'darkness' and that this is because we are blinded by an excess of light. That may seem puzzling, but we can perhaps recognize that a sort of mere bewilderment is a reaction which is not, in the circumstances, surprising.

But, of course, the 'void' may be an unprofitable one. We may not be ready for the growth of intimacy to which these mystics are referring. If we are in fact engaged in idle thoughts punctuated by mere vacancies that may be a sign that our appropriate course is at the moment what is called 'meditation', by which is meant not elaborate systems such as those evolved in the sixteenth century but simply a firmer grasp of the Christian Mystery (and therefore of the Bible). It is very improbable that prayer will develop as it can and should do unless that basis has been laid. Contemplative prayer in fact develops out of our acceptance of God's revelation and may even be said to begin with that acceptance. But this revelation, although it can be summed up in a few short sentences, cannot be grasped except by a process of personal assimilation. And until the stage has been reached at which the Mystery is seen not as a series of propositions but as a unity, simple but indefinitely rich, the normal preparation for advance in prayer is still lacking. It is a remarkable and deplorable thing that so many well-intentioned Christians, who in the ordinary way would be called educated persons, think it unnecessary to devote any part of their time to the prayerful study of their religion. It must be insisted that this sort of study should always be prayerful. For it is the desire of God that presides over the whole process which I am trying in some sort to describe. 'Meditation' (in the sense given to it by Christian antiquity) is the nourishing of this desire by the Word of God. We cannot *concentrate* on the desire itself, although it must always be at work, until it has been so nourished. These are the principles which must underlie any genuine liturgical reform.

How do we know that this stage has been reached? St John of the Cross tells us in a famous passage of *The Ascent of Mount Carmel*[1] that one sign of it is that we can no longer meditate, but that is because he is thinking of the sixteenth-century systems. We can perhaps sum up what he means by saying that we are now able to contemplate the Mystery, fruitfully, as a connected whole. The other two signs which he proposes to us reduce in effect to this: there must be a desire to 'wait upon God with loving attentiveness' which reveals itself to us as our most deep-seated desire. So we distinguish the 'void' from a mere vacancy by the value which we have come to attribute to it, the attraction which (even in the midst of aridity) we find it to be exercising upon us. More will be said about this later.

But have I already said too much? Is this discussion relevant to the life of the ordinary Christian? Is it not only the business of 'religious'? This is the suggestion which I want to resist. It seems plain that in the latter part of the twentieth century the Christian vocation will be either actively pursued or else simply lost sight of for the simple reason that it becomes less and less possible to believe in God without making up one's own mind on the subject (which means, in the end, relying on one's personal experience). *Honest to God* sparked off so great a reaction because it gave voice to so very large a body of inarticulate opinion in announcing that there is a 'crisis of faith'. Belief in God, obviously enough, is no longer a vital element of Western society as a whole— and has not been for longer than some people seem to realize. It must suffice to quote from the late E. M. Forster's *Aspects of the Novel* (he is speaking of Moll Flanders): 'If we were to press her or her creator Defoe and say, "Come, be serious. Do you believe in Infinity?", they would say (in the parlance of their modern descendants) "Of course I

[1] Bk. II, Ch. xiii.

believe in Infinity—what do you take me for?"—a confession of faith that slams the door on Infinity more completely than could any denial.'[1] Some people will want to make out that when belief in God is widespread it is nothing but a built-in element of certain human societies. But there have been periods in our history when an apprehension of God in Jesus Christ claimed for themselves by innumerable persons has been the animating principle of a culture, and in this sense we can still talk of the 'Christian centuries'. One can only guess to what extent professing Christians were, like Moll, simply following the conventions. But it is perfectly clear that very many were not, and that very many others who would make no claims themselves for this apprehension nevertheless enjoyed it in an inarticulate way, finding it through the witness of their teachers. If such a situation is to come about again, there must be many such teachers. But it is obvious that, whatever happens, people must fend for themselves, if they are to believe, in a way which was not so necessary once upon a time as it is now. Personal, persistent, prayer will be necessary. And unless there is some understanding of its development it will soon be abandoned in practice. What instruction do the future teachers of Christians themselves receive? A theological college has been described to us as 'the most difficult rather than the easiest place in which to pray'. And we heard in this connection of a 'freemasonry of silent, profoundly discouraged, underground opposition, which felt that all that was said and written about prayer was doubtless unexceptionable but simply did not speak to "our" condition'.[1] It would be interesting to know what this teaching about prayer in fact was. Something 'more relevant', we are told, was needed. It is possible that the teaching was not too demanding but not sufficiently demanding.

If to our contemporaries it seems that the door has been slammed on Infinity, if they regard the question of God as simply irrelevant, what answer must professing Christians be expected to make? Presumably they must recognize that an apparent lack of interest in God on the part of so many of their number has been responsible, at least to a considerable extent, for the present state of affairs. They must be expected to set the example of persistent prayer in their own persons and then to urge others to do the same. This does indeed happen. But what is much more noticeable at present is the tendency among them to

[1] 68.   [2] *Honest to God*, by J. A. T. Robinson, 93-4.

adopt that very attitude of mind which should have provoked their strongest resistances. Instead of emphasizing the mystical or contemplative element which is the root of real religion so many of them soft-pedal it, if they do not actually reject it.

But there are hopeful signs. People are beginning to recognize that the social upheavals of our time must be due to some deep-seated cause. The young, who are causing the most significant upheaval, are vaguely conscious of it themselves. A good many of them experiment with what goes by the name of 'mysticism' in various unpromising ways. If Western Christians could learn from their Eastern brethren, who have largely retained the true, theological, contemplative tradition, they could then supply what is so eagerly sought in the wrong places. But their materialism must first give place to a genuine humanism, a revision of values, a metaphysical experience without which the demands for justice among men cannot be interpreted in a true light and cannot therefore be properly met. That is no excuse for failing to act according to such lights as they at present possess. Such action is indeed a necessary condition for that greater enlightenment to which as Christians they are called.

16. THE FRONTIERS OF MYSTICISM

It is time to give proper consideration to the objection that my use of the word 'mysticism' is misleading. Even if my statements about prayer are acceptable as describing what Christians are called to, it may be thought dangerously confusing to refer to it as 'mystical'. Professor David Knowles in *What is Mysticism?* gives frequent warnings against the abuse of the term, and it is necessary to consider his position. It should go without saying that this book is a piece of distinguished scholarship; it is also impressive as a piece of 'spiritual' writing. When I venture to differ from him it will be because theological questions are bound up with philosophical ones and the philosophical views which he accepts in his theologizing seem to me sometimes unsatisfactory.

He offers the following definition of theological mysticism (or 'mystical theology'): 'an incommunicable and inexpressible knowledge and love of God or of religious truth received in the spirit without precedent effort or reasoning'.[1] This presupposes in the first place 'a

[1] 13.

free gift which human nature cannot demand or even imagine, the gift named "grace", which is no more perceptible than the natural assistance of God, though it can sometimes be recognized in its effects'.[1] And the conclusion is reached that 'the mystical way differs in degree and in kind from the common life of Christian practice'.[2] Discussing the rise of Quietism, Knowles writes: 'Mystic doctrine, which of its nature should be reserved for the few who are called to practise it, was a popular topic of discussion in polite circles, and in conferences, as well as in confessionals, and it is not surprising that the true way of the contemplative was falsified, perverted and misunderstood.'[3] Not only is mysticism a rare phenomenon in fact, but it is not agreed on all hands that all Christians are called to it: 'It is not clear that every soul in grace is called to the mystical life in the same way that it is called, and has it within its power, grace accompanying, to reach its allotted measure of virtuous excellence.'[4] These statements would be widely regarded as theological commonplaces (I shall be raising questions about some of them later), and the meaning which Knowles is giving to 'mysticism' is one which would be commonly accepted.

To see more precisely what this meaning is we must first examine in some detail what he has to tell us about St Teresa's 'prayer of recollection'. I must quote in my turn some of the sentences from *The Way of Perfection*[5] to which he refers us:

'You know that God is everywhere . . . we need no wings to go in search of Him but have only to find a place where we can be alone and look upon Him present within us . . . this is a prayer which brings with it many blessings. It is called recollection because the soul collects together all the faculties and enters within itself to be with its God . . . I advise whoever wishes to acquire this habit, which, as I said, we have it in our power to gain, not to grow tired of persevering . . . reckon your time well spent in acquiring this habit . . . I know that, with His help, if you practise it for a year, or perhaps only for six months, you will gain it. You must understand that this is not something supernatural, but something which, with the grace of God, we can desire and obtain for ourselves.'

Knowles quotes these sentences in order to show that this sort of prayer is 'not mystical', for, he points out, 'by supernatural St Teresa

[1] 20-1.   [2] 44.   [3] 116-17.   [4] 135.   [5] xxviii–xxix.

here means prayer that requires a grace higher than that upon which every Christian may rely, an enablement that is doubly supernatural, that is, not only in itself, essentially, but by reason of the way in which it acts, by the direct "infusion" of knowledge and love.'[1] He then warns us that even the 'prayer of recollection', although 'it is not mystical prayer or "contemplation" in any traditional sense of that word . . . is a stage or degree of prayer which cannot be exercised, and should not be recommended, indiscriminately'. And he concludes: 'To many it has neither meaning nor attraction. Others will feel it to be familiar and as it were natural and satisfying.' This is the prayer which I was recommending in the last chapter with the proviso that it may need to be preceded by 'meditation', by a certain understanding of the Christian Mystery, before it can obtain its proper fruit. My contention has been that this prayer, in times when God cannot be 'taken for granted', becomes indispensable if belief in him is to be attained and maintained. Knowles would, apparently, disapprove: 'St Teresa is writing for Carmelite nuns . . . what is possible for such is not possible for all devout persons';[2] still less, then, for those who could not yet be so described.

Knowles then continues: 'Above this, in so far as a line can be drawn, the first light of the mystical life begins to appear,'[3] but before he speaks of it he quotes St Teresa's warnings against attempting to gain it by a mere emptying of the mind: 'Nor must we cause the understanding to cease from its acts.'[4] This would lead to mere vacancy. It is perhaps worth remembering that even in the 'prayer of recollection' the 'understanding' was engaged only in 'looking upon' God present within us. The warning, however, is most necessary. There is all the difference between listening to God (even though this may result in recurrent vacancies) and making the mind a blank. It is certainly the worst sort of error to suppose that nothing more is necessary in order to enjoy God's presence. As Knowles puts it: 'It is only when the prayer of recollection has become settled and pure, maintained through aridities and distractions for long, that it can be regarded as in any sense a disposition for infused contemplation',[5] that is, for the mystical life. The great difference between this and the prayer of recollection is that it is a state which we cannot bring about for ourselves; we can only dispose ourselves for it. It is God's gift and he now, as it were, seizes

[1] 84. [2] *Ibid.* [3] 86. [4] *The Way of Perfection*, xii. [5] 88.

hold of the faculties, which have only to allow themselves to be *acted upon*. Knowles quotes St Teresa's words: 'Here it is not in our power to retire into ourselves, unless God gives us the grace.'[1]

A pointer to what is meant by the 'mystical state' is provided by Knowles's quotation from St Bernard's *Sermons on the Canticle*. It should be sufficient to repeat what seem to me the key-sentences:

'I confess that even to me the Word has come . . . I always failed to mark his coming. I realized that he was there: I remembered that he had been. Sometimes, I could have a presentiment of his coming, but I could never perceive either his coming or his going . . . he moved, he softened, he wounded my heart, when it was hard and stony and sick . . . that my soul might bless the Lord and all that is within me praise his holy name. . . . But when the Word departed from me all these blessings began to droop with cold and fatigue just as if you had withdrawn the fire from under a boiling pot.'[2]

Now I cannot help wondering whether a good many readers may not have said to themselves, at this point in Knowles's book, that they do seem to understand, in some small way, what St Bernard is talking about, although they would not suspect for a moment that they belonged to that very small class of spiritual 'proficients' to which such experiences are said to be reserved. The answer may be that they do not in fact really understand. But I think they might claim that their own experiences, although they may belong to some far lower sphere, are so definitely *objective* that they cannot write them off as illusions or insignificant. When they issue in a profound humility and a sincere desire for greater generosity, the claim seems grounded. They may not be 'mystical' in what Knowles calls the full or traditional sense, but how else can we refer to their peculiar character?

But what I want to suggest as being the real difficulty about this whole account is that it seems to reduce all knowledge of God below the 'mystical' stage to something which I cannot recognize as being really *knowledge* of him at all. It is no part of Knowles's business in this book to discuss our initial awareness of God or even the knowledge of faith. But he does tell us that every human being 'who has come to a belief in God and a love of God' has reached 'the higher level' on which

---

[1] *The Interior Castle*, iv, iii.
[2] Sermon 74 in J. Leclercq's edition of St Bernard's works.

he 'can perform acts which, either explicitly or implicitly, actually or virtually, are directed towards God . . . as a Trinity of Three Persons' (it may be remembered that this language about 'directing' acts was declared insufficient by Karl Rahner), and he adds at once that grace is 'in itself no more perceptible than the natural existence of God'.[1] A little later, speaking of union with the will of Christ, he tells us that the first gift of sanctifying grace 'gives this love, this union, in their essence and with the possibility of full realization'.[2] But, except for some reference to the 'light' which grace gives, no suggestion follows that it can be *consciously* realized until the 'mystical' stage has been reached. The theology of faith (according to the account which I have given of it) seems to be, in this all-important respect, foreign to Knowles's mind. Knowledge of God which has a character of directness, which bears upon the transcendence of God himself and is therefore indescribable, seems to be something which is reserved for a few. My contention has been, on the other hand, that there is *no* genuine knowledge of God which is not, fundamentally, of this kind.

This should not be taken to suggest that I am downgrading those states of spiritual union described (in so far as they can be described) by St John of the Cross, St Teresa and the English mystics (to mention those writers on whom Knowles naturally concentrates for his special purposes). What they have to tell us goes far beyond my own concern in this chapter. But I feel bound to suggest that there seems some danger of downgrading the state of the 'ordinary' Christian and (in general) of discouraging those who seek God. What is happening in the prayer of simple recollection if there is *no* direct awareness of the indescribable, transcendent, God? Knowles may not be wanting to deny that there is some, but such an impression could be easily received. What he does most emphatically reserve for the 'mystical state' is its special *passivity*. The knowledge and love of God are 'infused'. And here again, so it seems to me, the characteristic of passivity must be found, in some sort, in all knowledge of God, for it is always his gift, not just in the sense that our faculties are given to us by him but in the sense that he presents himself to us. What is undoubtedly the case is that there is a knowledge of God which exhibits a quite new *kind* of passivity (as described in the passage from St Bernard). It gives a heightened perception of one's total dependence on God, and of the

[1] 20.　　[2] 21.

overwhelming power of his love such that it appears an absolute novelty. But I believe that those who are familiar with it would admit that there is also in it the element of recognition.

Knowles remarks at one point that he is 'setting aside the endless discussions as to whether any really devout life is "non-mystical"'.[1] But at the end of the book he does say: 'That all Christians are called, at least remotely by the words of Christ and the constant partaking of the Body and Blood of the Saviour, to the perfect following of Christ is not doubtful, and the perfect following of Christ demands, and surely receives, a perceptible illumination and strengthening that is infused and at least in part mystical.'[2] He is speaking of those saints who do not seem to have been 'mystics'. Should we not say that any sincere attempt at the following of Christ may be similarly rewarded? (What is meant by saying that all Christians are called, *at least remotely*, to the perfect following of Christ? The point is, I take it, that this perfect following is in the 'normal Christian economy of grace' but that circumstances of one kind or another in so many cases make it impossible of attainment.)

To bring this more to a point, let us examine some passages in which Knowles is discussing 'contemplation'. When St Thomas, he says, tells us that 'the duty of a religious who is a theologian is himself to contemplate and then to pass to others the issue of his contemplation', this is 'not mystical contemplation in the full sense of those words . . .' Although it is 'luminous penetration of divine truth', and although St Thomas's theological writings 'convey to a mind in harmony with them the overtones of heavenly wisdom', nevertheless 'such knowledge is mystical only in a very broad sense of the term, for if the words in any particular case are based upon an experience of a higher nature, they fail to transmit or express it'.[3] But how can there be 'luminous penetration of divine truth' unless the theologian's mind bears upon God himself? Why are there these 'overtones' unless the reader's mind has been brought into this condition? It is certainly true that 'contemplation', in what has come to be its technical sense, is illuminative in its own right and incommunicable, whereas in the case which we are considering 'the light that is received illuminates a truth that is already known and expressed in words'.[4] But how can such truth have become known in any real sense without an opening of the mind to God? Knowles adds that there is no mystical experience until 'the soul realizes that the

[1] 36.   [2] 136.   [3] 29.   [4] 23.

knowledge of God and divine things is of another character altogether from that of past experience', in other words, until this knowledge is 'infused'. I am not denying that there comes a point at which the 'infused' character of this knowledge becomes for the first time vividly apparent. And this development is supremely valuable. It is the 'science of the saints'. But is not the knowledge of *faith* in fact 'infused' although it is not recognized vividly, but only implicitly (perhaps retrospectively), as such?

So I claim to speak of 'mysticism' and of 'contemplation' not only in the modern technical sense, but in an older, broader, sense. 'Contemplation', writes Louis Bouyer, 'begins from the moment when the presence of God, the act of God upon us, our life in Christ, have so rectified or dissipated everything that stood in their way or obscured them that what was previously the object of a faith which was in some sort detached from us and opaque becomes the object of an experience, no doubt still very mysterious, yet very real, as real as and more real than our sense-experience or our ordinary intellectual activity.'[1] And he also writes that 'no mystical life will be anything else than the fully conscious but fully normal development of our personal apprehension of what the Word of God reveals to us in the Church of Christ, of what is given us by the sacraments: the gift of grace revealed to faith, working in charity'.[2]

I now turn to consider where we are to place the frontiers of mysticism not within Christianity but outside it. In principle the solution must be that authentic mysticism must be presumed to exist outside the visible body of the Christian Church when it exhibits those signs which authenticate it inside that body. Knowles, in accepting this possibility, makes the necessary point that 'a receptive power, the habit of what we call sanctifying grace'[3] must also be presumed (in other words, baptism by desire). He is not disposed to accept 'alleged philosophical mystics' as instances of this. He believes that Plotinus's experience represent 'the extreme limit of the capacity of the Greek genius, seen earlier in similar, though not identical, experiences of Plato and Socrates, to rise above sense-perceptions and the dialectical process to a momentary apprehension or intuition of the God of what is called natural religion, the One absolute Being in whom all other intelligences have their being and their existence'.[4] But an awareness of

[1] *Introduction a la Vie Spirituelle*, 82.   [2] *Ibid.*, 304.   [3] 123.   [4] 124.

God must be an awareness of the God whom Christians worship. And this awareness, I think we must say, will either find some response, in which case some consequences will follow, or it will not, and there will not be these consequences. In view of the teaching of the Platonic tradition, it seems to me very difficult to suppose that it does not originate, in certain of its aspects, from a response to an awareness of God. Speaking still of Plotinus's doctrine, Knowles tells us: 'There is none of that awareness of the nothing of all being as against the true Being of God, and of the new, God-given capacity of loving without any trace of self-love both God and all his creatures to the degree that they bear his likeness.'[1] It should be clear that there are fundamental differences between these experiences and Christian mysticism, but it is important to realize that they have been frequently exaggerated by Christian writers, according to so weighty an authority on the matter as Professor A. H. Armstrong.

It will be useful, I think, to quote at some length from what he has written about this in an article 'Platonic *Eros* and Christian *Agape*', published in *The Downside Review*.[2] Summing up his conclusions, he writes:

'In the modern Christian account of philosophic *eros* with which we started, this kind of love was presented as a desire aspiring to its divine object with which that object had nothing to do except as an object of desire. . . . It was alleged to be a purely human aspiration, which was not God and was not caused by God except as 'final cause' or object and which did not result in love for other men for God's sake. Our examination of the ancient evidence for the Platonic doctrine of philosophic *eros* has shown that Plato, Plotinus and Proclus between them present it as a love which is not simply aspiration or unfulfilled desire . . . [but as] a love which when it reaches fulfilment is productive and creative; a love which moves the lover to work for the love of his human beloved . . .; a love which God is, and which he causes in men in the act by which he constitutes them in being; a love which expresses the divine goodness in uniting all beings and leading them back to their source and in moving godlike men to work for the salvation of those whom it is their mission to help . . . not that all these points of doctrine are to be found in the writings of Plato himself, or in any one of his successors. . . . But I think it has been shown that

[1] 125.   [2] Spring 1961, 105–21.

the pagan Platonists were able to develop all these ideas about *eros* from Plato's original insights without any help from outside the bounds of the Hellenic philosophical tradition. And this is surely enough to make it clear that the conventional Christian account is inadequate and inaccurate and that Origen and the Greek Christian writers who followed him in this were right in thinking that *eros* in the sense in which it was used by Platonic philosophers was a word which could rightly be used for the *agape* of God revealed in Christ.'

Christian thought recognized itself, so to say, in some features at least of Neoplatonism, and we may have some reserves about Knowles's statement that 'many of the characteristic features of Augustine's and Gregory's teaching on contemplation derive from a Plotininian or Neo-platonic source and are therefore alien to the pure Christian tradition . . .'.[1] He is more willing to allow that mysticism may exist among Muslims and Buddhists.

Zen Buddhism (or rather Zen, which is not bound up essentially with Buddhism) is contrasted with Christian mysticism in Father William Johnston's book *The Mysticism of* 'The Cloud of Unknowing'.[2] This is a book which is in many ways helpful and important, and an examination of it will confirm, I believe, some of our previous findings and introduce fresh aspects of our topic. Something must first be said by way of a general introduction to Johnston's aims and procedures. Speaking of the anonymous fourteenth-century author whose work he is to discuss, he tells us that 'his is a doctrine that follows a long tradition stretching from Gregory of Nyssa and the pseudo-Dionysius to the Rhineland mystics whence it later crosses the Pyrenees to reach a great climax with St John of the Cross in sixteenth-century Spain'.[3] In a first summary account, he tells us that

'the mysticism taught is highly introspective, that is to say, even though the metaphor of a cloud in the sky is central . . . the main endeavour of the author is not so much to fix our eyes on an outer world charged with the presence of God in all things, but rather to direct our eyes into the depth of our own soul in the darkness of which "mirror" we find God. . . . The mind is a mirror; void of images and thought but filled with faith, it is in darkness; and in the darkness one sees God. This dark-ness, which wholly fills the mind when, void of discursive reasoning and

[1] 113.   [2] Desclée, New York, 1967.   [3] 1.

conceptual thinking, it is grounded in supernatural faith . . . is the cloud of unknowing. And out of this darkness of faith there arises the "blind stirring of love"—also called "the naked intent of the will"— that darts . . . towards God who, by grace, is in secret and silence in that deeply mysterious part of the soul that is called "the sovereign point of the spirit"'.[1]

This admirable summary is followed by the usual warnings against mere emptiness of mind, and Johnston also emphasizes the warnings of his author that his doctrine is not to be taught in an indiscriminate way but only to those who are prepared for it. There have been 'Zen-influenced attempts' to interpret this doctrine, and Johnston undertakes to deal with them.[2]

In his first chapter, 'The Problem of Unknowing', he begins to speak directly of Zen. It is, he says, essentially concerned with 'the enlightenment or *satori*, about which no one can speak unless he himself has had the experience—and even he can say very little'.[3] This does sound rather like 'the cloud of unknowing', but Zen, we are told, is divorced (according to its best-known exponent, Dr D. T. Suzuki) not only from all religions and even all philosophies, but even from mysticism itself. After disposing forthrightly of Mr Aldous Huxley's attempt to separate all mysticism from religion and to distinguish 'the contemplatives of the Dionysian tradition' from the 'specifically Catholic' ones,[4] Johnston points out that the author of *The Cloud* would have no use for the irrationality into which exponents of Zen are led by their repudiation of conceptual thinking; *The Cloud* has hard things to say about conceptual thinking, but only when this is being compared with the supra-conceptual. As Johnston says, it takes for granted the medieval distinction of wisdom into three kinds, metaphysical, dogmatic and mystical, the first of them giving 'true analogical knowledge of God' and the second being the wisdom of faith which enables the human faculties to 'penetrate deeply into the mysteries of revelation', while mystical wisdom, in Johnston's formula, is a 'supra-conceptual penetration of those mysteries'.[5] At this point I begin to find difficulties about Johnston's account. For he takes what I must call a conventional line about 'true analogical knowledge'. He tells us in this passage that we 'can rise by causality to the Supreme Being' but that 'the mind does not here

[1] 3. [2] 12. [3] 19. [4] *Grey Eminence*, 97. [5] 27-8.

attain directly to God but only through creatures, His effects, so that we can say that God is "unknown"—He is unknown as He is in Himself'. Mystical knowledge, however, he goes on to say, is 'knowledge of God as He is in Himself'. It is natural that a vivid experience of God should be described in these terms, but, if it is maintained that God is in no way directly known in any other circumstances, then one is faced with the impossible task of building up a knowledge of the Infinite out of materials which are finite. God is known 'in the background', indeed, in non-mystical knowledge (in mystical knowledge he seems to enter the foreground and to occupy the whole horizon), but, unless we penetrate to God himself in some sort, we have no solid ground for believing in him. Johnston's conventional Thomism (accepted, it would seem, by Knowles also) is going to cause trouble.

Turning now to the question of techniques in mysticism,[1] he quotes some passages from Ruysbroeck's *Adornment of the Spiritual Marriage* which seems to suggest the explanation of 'natural mysticism', touched on in my last chapter, according to which it is simply a special awareness which the soul may have, in certain conditions, of its own self:

'When a man is bare and imageless in his senses, and empty and idle in his higher powers, he enters into rest through mere nature, and this rest may be found and possessed within themselves in mere nature by all creatures, without the grace of God, whenever they strip themselves of images and activity. . . . This rest is in itself no sin; for it exists in all men by nature whenever they make themselves empty. But when a man wishes to practice and possess it without acts of virtue, he falls into a spiritual pride and complacency from which he seldom recovers. . . . In this natural rest one cannot find God, but it certainly leads a man into a bare vacancy which may be found by all men, how wicked soever they may be. . . . In this bare vacancy the rest is pleasant and great.'[2]

Johnston does not refer to the explanation of this which I have just mentioned. Instead it would appear that he connects 'natural mysticism' with the first of the three kinds of wisdom which he has distinguished, the metaphysical kind; it is therefore a knowledge of God.

To substantiate this, I must now refer to his Appendix on 'Horizontal and Vertical Thinking', in which he sums up his views on the differences between natural and supernatural mysticism. 'Vertical thinking' is

[1] 29–30. [2] Ch. xxvi.

supraconceptual thinking. Johnston remarks that it has been practised by thousands of non-Christian contemplatives in the East and that 'there are clear indications of vertical thinking in Plato (as in the *Symposium* and the *Seventh Epistle*) and even more so in Plotinus and the ensuing neoplatonic thought-stream'.[1] He concludes that 'mysticism taken in the wide sense of the word [that is, as supraconceptual thinking] is an ordinary phenomenon, largely the product of education, temperament, cultural background and personal effort. It is a phenomenon that the world always has known and presumably always will know.'[2] And he goes on to say that this phenomenon is not '*directly* connected with the supernatural gifts that we call faith and charity; indeed (as we have quoted Ruysbroeck as saying) even the sinner can engage in silent supraconceptuality and (at least theoretically) he would see God united with him in the order of nature'.[3] But Ruysbroeck, in the passage quoted above, has said that 'in this natural rest one cannot find God'. What, then, is the object of the sinner's mind when he is engaged in silent conceptuality if it is not simply *himself*? Johnston seems to have neglected this rather obvious suggestion, and to have overlooked what he had himself quoted from Ruysbroeck, because supraconceptuality is necessarily bound up for him with a natural apprehension of God which demands no response on the part of man—it is in the 'order of nature' which has no essential connection with the order of grace. This conception we have already encountered in Knowles's book.

It is curious that Johnston should have himself recognized in principle the objection which I am now making when he is discussing the question of union with God in the doctrine of the author of *The Cloud*: 'The soul's union with God, by the gift of grace', he writes, summing up this doctrine, 'is built upon a natural union existing in the order of nature—and this latter union prescinds so completely from grace that it can be experienced even by the sinner',[4] but in a footnote he adds: 'Some authors speak of "natural mysticism", that is, a mysticism based on this *natural* union with God and prescinding from grace, but I have avoided this terminology because others object to it on the ground that, in Catholic theology, no man can concretely be a "natural mystic" since everyone is either in grace or in sin. . . .' That is to say, man, in his specifically human experience, is always either in the state

[1] 269. [2] 270. [3] 272. [4] 226-7.

of accepting grace or in that of refusing it. Johnston does not seem to realize that, if this objection is to be allowed, it undermines his whole position about 'natural mysticism'. The position for which I have argued is that a 'natural knowledge' of God is not a state in which one can rest but a turning-point at which God's offer to communicate himself to us (in an initial way) must be either responded to or neglected. The 'sinner' who neglects it is not contemplating God in the order of nature. There is also the curious statement in the Appendix: 'It is even conceivable that vertical thinking of some kind could be induced by drugs like mescalin.'[1] Johnston does add that he says this 'very tentatively' and refers to Professor Zaehner's experiment with mescalin which merely plunged him 'into a universe of farce'.[2] But the point is that, in any case, 'vertical thinking of some kind' is a very question-begging expression.

At the end of his Appendix Johnston produces a formula which, in principle, covers, I would say, the whole ground of mysticism, although he does not seem to regard it so himself: 'The Christian mystic (and here I use the word "Christian" for all those who, whether or not baptized by water, are "justified" by supernatural charity and are temples of the Holy Spirit) is he whose love has begun to burn with such ardour that he abandons discursive thinking (which is now distasteful to him, for love so seizes him that he *cannot* think) to plunge down to the sovereign point of the spirit in supraconceptual silence.'[3] It seems to me that anything which deserves to be called a *union with God* is to be explained in this way. And there is one more passage in the book which I want to quote here: '. . . a mind supraconceptually and silently filled with love is different from a mind supraconceptually silent and lacking in love. And it is precisely supernatural love, based on faith, that forms the whole centre essence [*sic*] of the mysticism of *The Cloud*; love is both the point of departure and the goal; take away love and the whole thing crumbles. And it is here that the difference from Zen (and, indeed, from all forms of pantheism) is most in evidence.'[4] The greatest value of Johnston's book (and, I must repeat, it contains much of great value) lies in his insistence on this. It leads him to the use of a certain language about the relation in which love stands to knowledge which seems to me misleading, but the discussion of that belongs to the following chapter in which I shall suggest that a number of

[1] *Ibid.*   [2] *Mysticism, Sacred and Profane*, 226.   [3] 273.   [4] 208.

difficulties (perhaps already apparent) are due to misleading language of this kind, resulting from an incomplete analysis.

Here I shall conclude by considering certain reactions to Johnston's book. In his review of it[1] Professor Knowles, unsurprisingly, gives special praise to Johnston's view of a 'natural intuition' and speaks of supraconceptual thought as issuing, for the non-theist, in an 'intuition of the unity, goodness and truth of all things'. Must one not add that the the nontheist, although he may still thus describe himself, has now in fact become a theist? I find it hard to believe that anyone who uses the language of goodness and truth in this way is really without God's grace. Language is indeed an unsafe guide in these matters, but that would seem to be at least the most obvious interpretation. And it becomes clear that Knowles not only accepts two fundamentally different species of supraconceptual knowledge, a natural one and a supernatural one, but also holds that there is a perfectly valid, though inferior, knowledge of God which is not supraconceptual at all.

Mr E. I. Watkin, in his review,[2] agrees with me in so far as he holds that 'experience of union' with Absolute Being 'cannot be natural, but must be supernatural' if we are to consider the claim to it as valid. He also writes: 'When I regarded the Zen *satori* as bound up with its explanation in terms of Buddhist doctrine, I was uncertain what to think of it. When, however, Dr Enomiya-Lassalle from his personal experience informed me that *satori* was independent of any theological interpretation, it became clear that it is the same purely apophatic experience described by the *Cloud*'. This is not, I think, the only possible conclusion, for the soul's self-awareness is also, presumably, apophatic. But it may indeed be the case in many instances. Watkin has been writing on the subject of mysticism for over fifty years, and is an authority from whom one hesitates to differ. I must confess, however, that what he goes on to say about union with God I find very hard to accept. He speaks of a 'union of the radical will' and is convinced that mystical prayer, the conscious experience of this union, 'depends . . . partly on the subject's environment, particularly his beliefs but pre-eminently on his psychophysical constitution' in such sort that some people may be practically incapable of it: 'some men and women are what I would term more or less transparent . . . others more or

[1] *The Tablet*, January 20, 1968.
[2] *The Downside Review*, 1968, 300–3.

less opaque whose subconscious depths never, or only with great difficulty, become conscious'. Apart from the difficulties presented by this exclusive emphasis on the will, which must be left for later discussion, it seems to me to go against the tradition as a whole (based on the Gospel promises) to say that God will not make himself more clearly known to those who seek him in faith (itself involving some conscious awareness of him). Again, awareness of God (especially perhaps in its painful forms) is so often not recognized for what it is. This is not to deny that, as Johnston puts it,[1] 'people of a certain temperament' will find it easier than others to practise supraconceptual prayer. Watkin is led to the conclusion that drugs 'may render conscious a union with God existing already . . .'.

But the point which Watkin seems most anxious to make is that the prayer with which *The Cloud* is concerned can 'speak to the condition of those who have lost their faith or are in danger of doing so' and 'to atheists or agnostics who are aware of . . . no order of being beyond the material universe'; Johnston, he thinks, puts an obstacle in their way by representing this prayer as bearing upon the Christian mysteries. As we have seen, he recognizes that it is available for those outside the visible frontiers of the Church. But it is true that he seems to regard this as exceptional. Watkin insists that 'it cannot be distinctively Christian but must be common to contemplatives of all religious denominations or none'—otherwise it cannot be 'a stage on the route to Christian faith or its confirmation against secular assaults'. In itself, Watkin holds, it is simply experience of the Absolute and therefore *not* 'a deeper penetration of the Christian mysteries', for although the author of *The Cloud* knows that the Absolute is the Triune God, in the prayer which he describes there is no *experience* of the Christian God as such.

I venture to make a few comments on this. First, it is true that the fact of mystical prayer will not impress our contemporaries as it can and ought to do if we deny that it is possible, in principle, for all men today (this is something which I have been particularly anxious to insist upon), but we must surely maintain that it is always the fruit of grace, wherever it is found, and that we cannot claim to detect its incidence among non-Christians as a regular and normal phenomenon. If the distinction between 'justifying' and 'sanctifying' grace (pre-Christian and Christian, respectively) is sound, it is questionable whether the acceptance of

[1] 273.

justifying grace can have consequences which properly deserve the name of 'mystical', although it is hard to see what else one can call them (Watkin, after allowing that 'metaphysical intuition may indeed introduce a mystical experience', adds roundly: 'Such was the case with Plato and Plotinus'). Secondly, I would argue that 'a deeper penetration of the Christian mysteries' is not extraneous to the prayer of *The Cloud* (which of course presupposes them) for, as Bouyer explains, the mystic 'begins to participate in the vision which Christ has' of them, and this vision 'does not bear on his humanity apart from his divinity . . . but as subsisting in the divinity itself'; and, it it be said that in *The Cloud* there is no awareness (even implicit) of Christ's humanity, a 'profound intuition of the Trinitarian life', as Bouyer goes on to say, is an intuition of 'a unity which surpasses all multiplicity'.[1] It is this intuition, then, I suggest, with which the author of *The Cloud* is concerned.

17. THE LANGUAGE OF THE MYSTICS

Any account of mysticism, as we have seen, must raise questions about the paradoxical character of the mystics's statements, and it is necessary, at this point, to devote a whole chapter to certain formulas which regularly recur in their writings and which, it seems to me, may easily cause confusion or seem merely unintelligible. Father Johnston's book, '*The Mysticism of* "The Cloud of Unknowing",' will continue to be useful in providing us with examples.

'Strangely enough', he writes, 'when the cloud of forgetting has done its work perfectly, man is permitted to remember; and now for the first

---

[1] *Introduction à la Vie Spirituelle*, 305–6. Cf. Knowles, *What is Mysticism?*, 75: 'The great army of Christian mystics (from Cassian to Sister Elizabeth of the Trinity in our own century) are unanimous in their assertion that it is through and in Christ that they attain union with God. . . .' He, like Johnston (73) quotes the author of *The Cloud* in his *Epistle of Privy Counsel* in this sense. Watkin claims that, on Johnston's own showing (256), the author of *The Cloud* refuses to discuss 'the most sublime trinitarian union' and is therefore not concerned with this 'distinctively Catholic and Christian' experience. But what he actually says (62:19) is that he does not 'dare' to speak of it because it is beyond his power to do so. The point seems to be simply that he cannot attempt to *describe* it. Other Christian mystics have been reticent about it for the same excellent reason. It may be said that Christian prayer does not become experientially and explicitly 'trinitarian' until it reaches a summit in exceptional cases, but it would seem that it must always be radically and implicitly 'trinitarian'.

time he really *knows*: no longer is he warped by the ignorance of con-cupiscence. He looks out on the created world and he sees there only God for (writes St John of the Cross) "even as all the trees and plants have their life and root in the grove, so the creatures, celestial and terrestrial alike, have their roots and their life in God" [*Canticle*, St. XXXVIII, 8], and the English author [of *The Cloud*] puts the idea even more force-fully when he says (and reiterates, several times) that God *is* the being of all things—not in the sense of a pantheistic identity but because we share analogously in what He has by right.'[1] What St John and the Eng-lish author are trying to tell us is of the highest importance, and it is most desirable that it should be freed from philosophical language which may be off-putting or even misleading. To say that we 'share analogously' in what God has 'by right', taken in conjunction with this language of 'being', will suggest that doctrine of the analogy of being according to which we can discover the analogical relationship by using the idea of 'being' as a means, as a middle term in a logical demonstra-tion. This is not likely to commend itself to many, and I have argued that we can discover the analogical relationship only in and through our discovery of its terms, only when we already 'see the world in God'. And to say that 'a man looks out on the created world and sees there only God' must mean that he sees it as the self-manifestation of God—it is not God himself, and it does not disappear; we are seeing the world 'in God', but it does not, in any proper sense, 'share' anything with him.

This may seem carping criticism, but it is just because Johnston is drawing our attention to such a vital truth that the utmost care must be taken in explaining it. Two other sentences from the passage on which I am commenting would be still more valuable than in fact they are if the words which I have italicized were omitted: 'So in the final stage nothing is rejected: science, music, poetry, and the beauties of nature are not rejected but seen and loved in God *who is their being*. It is simply that when the cloud of forgetting has purified the soul, it is free to love in liberty of spirit.' Johnston is adopting the language of his author and has warned us against interpreting him in a pantheistic sense, but the interpretation given us in terms of the analogy of being leaves us with a puzzle (I am not suggesting that this, as an interpreta-tion of *The Cloud*, is an incorrect one). In the same way, after pointing out that the formula which so often appears in *The Book of Privy*

[1] 183.

Counsel, 'he is thy being', is again obviously not intended in a pantheistic sense, Johnston refers to the scholastic metaphysic as reaching 'its perfection in a Thomism which asserted that God alone is Being in the full sense of the word', and (he continues) 'that is why it can be said (as that author of *The Cloud* says so often), that He is the Being of all. . . .'[1] As before, the interpretation is correct, but the language remains at least unfortunate. If creatures are to be called 'beings', as surely they must be, we must call God, not a 'being' or Being, but the Source of beings. Here it may be noted that the mystics frequently use language which seems to declare that the 'ground' of the soul is identical with God himself when what they really mean is simply that the soul is an 'image' (or 'reflection') of God. The relationship in which creatures stand to God cannot be described, I have maintained, because it is necessarily unique; it has to be apprehended.

We have seen that Professor Stace was misled by taking the statement of the mystics about absorption in God in a quite literal sense. Johnston quotes passages from *The Cloud* in which we are told that 'the knowledge and feeling of self is an obstacle to perfect union with God and must, in consequence, be destroyed' (82:19) and that this can be done only by 'a special grace full freely given by God' (83:10).[2] In *The Book of Privy Counsel*, he points out, 'the author explains that he has allowed the contemplative to retain the consciousness of his own being only as a concession to weak human nature. In fact, the climax of contemplation is reached only when the consciousness of self is annihilated and one feels God alone.'[3] Moreover, the writer explains to his disciple that he was preparing him for this conclusion by explaining to him 'that God is thy being'.[4] Johnston seems to find no difficulties in any of this, but we must surely regard this combination of vague metaphysics and superficial analysis as definitely misleading. It is really nonsense, and not only paradox, to say that one's own experience can ever be *not* one's own. One can indeed be without advertence not only to one's physical condition but also to the distinction between subject and object. It may *feel* as though subject had literally turned into object. But plainly it cannot do so. We must not expect the author of *The Cloud* to be an expert phenomenologist, and it is no disrespect to him as a spiritual teacher to point this out. The 'self-forgetfulness' on which he is here insisting is perfectly comprehensible as an attention concentrated upon

[1] 221–2.   [2] 190.   [3] 193.   [4] *The Book of Privy Counsel*, 155: 27.

God alone, a pure self-giving which is also a pure self-fulfilment. The language used by mystics which is perhaps the greatest source of confusion is the language which they use about knowledge and love. Johnston's discussion of the doctrine of *The Cloud* in this matter is, at some points, most helpful. Speaking of the darkness of faith, he explains that it is, according to *The Cloud* and to orthodox writers in general, in itself 'an intensely bright light, blinding the mind of the contemplative'.[1] The passage continues:

'But this blinding light enables one to *see* God's truth hidden in the propositions of Scripture and dogma; that is why the author [of *The Cloud*] seems to regard faith as a kind of vision, for in *Hid Divinity* he declares that we hold "in sight of belief" that God is above all things (H.D. 4:9). And in another passage [of *The Cloud*] he writes: "For if ever thou shalt *see* him [i.e. by faith] or *feel* him [i.e. by love] it must always be in this cloud and this darkness (C.17.7)". Here he says that by faith we see the truth of God in an obscure way; and when we have seen it, love brings us to God Himself.'

Some of this is puzzling; we may explain this darkness as referring to the supraconceptual character of the contemplative experience, but this experience seems also to have a positive character (it is a kind of *seeing*), which we should expect to be described in terms of light. Apart from this, however, love does seem to stand here in an intelligible relation to knowledge, although it is not made clear how it 'brings us to God Himself'. And a few pages later Johnston does say quite firmly that 'since love is always based on knowledge . . . and since it cannot be based on natural reasoning and conceptual knowledge, which is useless for attaining to God as He is in Himself, it must, for every Christian, be based on faith . . .'.[2]

In another passage he refers to the 'blind stirring of love' as 'an activity that *includes* knowledge or consciousness of some kind', and he goes on: 'For purposes of analysis it is possible to speak of knowledge and love in contemplation; but the activity the author [of *The Cloud*] speaks of is a blend of both, a completely simple experience arising in the depths of the contemplative's heart: in the last analysis it is indescribable. . . . He has no doubt, however, that its predominant element is love and it is upon this that he puts all the emphasis.'[3] Certainly

[1] 61. [2] 64. [3] 98.

what is important about this knowledge is that it is a *loving* knowledge. And again Johnston writes that 'as the mystical life advances, a certain simplification of the personality takes place, in such wise that the faculties quietly unite in concentration upon God. . . . Knowledge and love seem to be one in a completely simple action. . . . Contemplative prayer is not the activity of one part of men; it is not thinking nor is it loving nor is it feeling; it is the total offering of one's all to God in utter simplicity.'[1] This seems to make good sense.

Elsewhere, unfortunately, Johnston uses different language. Summing up his author's teaching on love, he writes that his intention 'is to stress the superiority of love over discursive reasoning . . . but he also regards it as superior to the dark knowledge of faith, which is not vision and does not pierce the cloud, even though it enables man to see God in an obscure way'.[2] No doubt it is true that the dark knowledge of faith will not develop without love; but it must also be true that love is a response to the dark knowledge which, although not simply vision, is, as we have seen, 'a kind of vision'. The interdependence of knowledge and love is not recognized here. Other passages seem simply to repudiate it. For example, we are told that 'the contemplative must abandon all knowledge, however holy, in order to enter with love into the darkness where God is';[3] the context, indeed, makes clear that in fact this is to be done in order to gain a 'higher knowledge', but it is suggested that this 'higher knowledge' is not an affair of the intellect: on the next page it is baldly asserted that 'God can be *known* by love' (Johnston's italics). In such passages the language used seems to reflect the familiar reduction of intellectual activity to the conceptual sphere in marked contrast to others in which supraconceptual knowledge is spoken of to such excellent effect. Johnston, however, explains later on that he and his author are not to be understood literally when they use this language: 'The author, grounded as he is in scholasticism, knows that strictly speaking the loving power does not know; when he says that love "knows" he means that in its intensity it enlightens the intelligence which is then filled with a wisdom not coming "from without" through the senses but from within . . .'.[4] Love can indeed be the necessary condition for an enlightenment of the intellect, if I may repeat it once more, but it cannot directly enlighten it unless it has received enlightenment itself—in fact, unless it *knows*.

[1] 203.   [2] 118.   [3] 35.   [4] 124.

We are facing once more the Thomist doctrine, which gave us so much trouble about the certainty of faith, that love takes over the function of knowledge in the religious sphere. St Thomas is unwilling to admit that there can be a direct contact between the human mind and God in the present life—his epistemology being, fundamentally, Aristotelian, and his 'intellectualism' being, therefore, a hesitant one. Johnston proceeds to appeal to this doctrine, pointing out that St John of the Cross accepted it (in the *Dark Night*[1] he speaks of 'mystical theology, which theologians call secret wisdom and which, as St Thomas says, is communicated and infused into the soul through love'). And we are then offered the following conclusion: 'Love is superior to knowledge because it goes straight to the essence of God in this life, whereas discursive reasoning cannot know God as He is in Himself and faith sees God only from afar in darkness. Faith, however, is the ground of the contemplative life. . . . The first stage is that of reasoning and conceptual thinking. . . . In the second stage . . . meditation must be abandoned for the silent emptiness of naked faith. . . . In the third stage love (having abandoned discursive knowledge) finds a higher knowledge . . .'.[2] Here it would seem that faith, although 'the ground of the contemplative life', is not, in itself, knowledge of God at all. It is 'silent emptiness'. Certainly it seems to be the case that in the course of this development a stage is reached which is regularly described as a 'silent emptiness'. I have suggested that this emptiness is apparent rather than real. But in any case it is clear that, in this account, contact with God *himself* is not established by knowledge—it is the business of love in the absence of knowledge.

Mr E. W. Trueman Dicken in *The Crucible of Love* refers to the doctrine that 'in the supernatural order God can . . . infuse love and cause it to grow without infusing or increasing distinct knowledge', and he adds the useful comment: 'The accent here is upon the conception of distinct knowledge as opposed to the more truly real but nevertheless unintelligible knowledge of himself which God is able to convey to a soul voided of all that is not God.'[3] I should prefer to speak of 'inexpressible' knowledge and should wish to say that this must be 'infused' as a knowledge which is indistinguishable (phenomenologically) from love. Unfortunately Trueman Dicken makes no comment on St John's doctrine, which he then proceeds to quote, that union is a 'touch'

[1] II, vii, i, quoted by Johnston.   [2] 125.   [3] 361–2.

261

impressed directly on the will; but he does point out that 'as a matter of practical experience, St John of the Cross regards union as a kind of intellectual vision', in which, however, 'nothing is seen, inwardly or outwardly'.[1] Surely we must conclude, if we are to make anything of this, that this 'touch' is impressed on 'the sovereign point of the spirit', that is, upon intellect and will. There must be something which we can only call 'seeing'.

This may seem to be whipping up a storm in a very small tea-cup. But in fact a one-sided emphasis on love and the will (in conjunction with other factors of an anti-intellectualist kind) has resulted in a good deal of obscurantist piety which is a danger to religion and an encouragement to irreligion. It is perfectly true that love is everything—provided that it bears upon its proper object, genuinely apprehended; and it is the apparent lack of this genuine apprehension which is so depressing in our time. What the French call 'the sense of God' seems to be in such short supply. So often the mystics, with the best intentions in the world, have aggravated such troubles by taking up with a faculty-psychology which puts off intelligent people. What has happened, in very many cases, is that mystics who are concerned to recommend highly important practices, and who are not particularly interested in philosophizing about them, simply take over the philosophical notions which are current in their own time. The philosophical notions current in sixteenth-century Spain, to take the most important example, were Thomist ones. The doctrines of the great Spanish Carmelites were simply repeated by subsequent writers; no distinction was made between the way in which they put things and what, fundamentally, they were concerned to teach. Discursive reasoning had usurped the place of intuitive intellect in discussions about man's knowledge of God, and discursive reasoning has no place in contemplative prayer. How, then, is the contact made (for the mystics know that it is made)? The answer, they seem to have thought, is that it is made by the *will*. And again, this is perfectly true, provided that the will has a known object. But, again, that was not appreciated. There was no question of denying that there is an experience of God in prayer, but mystics, tending (at least) to think of knowledge as always abstractive,[2] came to speak of this experi-

[1] 363.
[2] But this is not true of the Greek mystical tradition, which tends to identify knowledge and love.

ence in non-cognitive terms. And thus the 'supreme wisdom' was deprived of philosophical significance.

So the mystics may seem to be saying that knowledge does not matter —whether we have any awareness of God or not is of no consequence. They were all the more inclined to use such language because they were always much concerned (and most understandably) to warn people against relying upon illuminations or satisfactions in prayer of whatever kind (often referred to as 'experiences'), banking on them, as we might say, and using their presence or absence as criteria for interpreting their spiritual thermometers.

At this point I venture upon some further remarks about spiritual aridity. What is called 'the spiritual life' begins, I have been maintaining, with obeying one's conscience—which in fact means obeying God. There is an awareness of the Good as a demand made upon us. This is not necessarily or even perhaps often an exhilarating experience. But it is an experience, and if it is not pushed under the carpet it does produce a certain satisfaction, seldom much talked about but known as 'peace of mind'. This peace persists through all manner of psychical disturbances although it does not occupy the forefront of the consciousness and may never be explicitly adverted to; I have suggested that it needs to be adverted to, not that we may indulge in smug self-complacency but because it is the awareness of God's presence within us, acting upon us. This will not lead necessarily to anything which we should normally call 'satisfaction', but that is because we normally use the word in a restricted sense. With this as a background, it may be easier to understand the aridities which are so regular a feature of the spiritual life as it begins to develop. The mystics often speak of God's 'withdrawing' himself in order to purify the soul—it must learn to seek not his gifts, but himself. It might be better to say that in certain conditions he cannot get at us as he would. For there comes a stage, as we have seen, when we have to 'open up' in a bigger way if God's closer approach is to succeed. This is usually a painful, even agonizing, business, and for the time being, which may in fact be a very long time, it may abolish all joy in his presence. But he is always present, and his presence, in a profound but authentic sense, must always be known if this is prayer at all.

There is a special reason which has not yet been mentioned for that sadness which seems so often to afflict our mystics. It is that 'Love is not loved'. The spectacle of their contemporaries living in inhuman conditions, or devoting themselves to ends which are either relatively worthless or pursued without reference to man's true end, fills them with an excess of pity and horror which takes a heavy toll on their sensibilities. They prefer to speak of their own short-comings, and their lucid awareness of these causes them great distress. But it is their feeling of loneliness, of being cut off from those among whom they live and who seem to have no understanding of their own point of view, which we may reasonably suppose to take the greatest toll (and this will be especially the case when those among whom they live are themselves professing Christians). For as a rule there is little or nothing that they can do about it. They may do their best to think that the motives of their neighbours are, despite all appearances, worthier than their own; they may even succeed in this. But the fact remains that there is, objectively, moral mediocrity or moral ugliness, and this cannot fail to grieve them.

The warnings of the mystics against relying on 'experiences' are, on this showing, intelligible. But it is one thing to issue warnings such as these and quite another to suggest that spiritual joy is something which we should regard as of no particular value. And it would be easy sometimes to misinterpret them in that sense. They have little regard, and rightly, for 'sensible devotion', a state of mental and physical euphoria which may be self-induced or merely sentimental. But when they themselves rejoice in the Lord, it is obvious that this is a reaction to a real encounter with him, the affective aspect of such an encounter, and some faint foretaste of the beatific vision. It would be blasphemous not to value it in the highest possible degree. The notion that we ought not to *desire* this joy (as being something foreign to our earthly condition) is certainly no part of traditional Christian teaching. In the collect for St John the Baptist's birthday in the Roman Missal, to take just one example, it is prayed for in so many words. We may not feel that we know much about it, but we must not be misled by the language of the mystics into thinking that it is not God's purpose for us, or, more precisely, the way in which its achievement is registered by us, even in this world. It seems to be this joy which makes a mystic; it is the essential clue to his whole attitude to life, and it is what he wants most to talk about (provided that it might help others, but only in these circumstances)—if only he knew how to do it. All he seems able to do is to insist that it is the answer to everything and wholly unmistakable. For this too is a darkness in the sense that it is strictly undescribable, but one very different from the darkness which seemed just empty. All that has to be guarded against here is the assumption that it will be always available to one.

Johnston tells us rightly that the value of mysticism 'can never be measured by any psychological process nor can any such process be the norm of its authenticity'.[1] He goes on to say that 'it stems mainly from its motivation . . . the psychological state of silent supra-conceptuality derives its religious value from the motive underlying the whole process'. Again this is perfectly true, as far as it goes: this value lies, as Johnston adds, 'in its being an expression of love'. But this is only the reverse side of the coin; it is the *sine qua non* of the mystical experience. What makes it valuable, if we turn the coin to the obverse side, is that it is a conscious union with God, which is what we are made for. At the end of his book Johnston reiterates warnings against looking for 'sensible religious feelings', and here a footnote reads: 'I speak of sensible experiences and not of "the beam of ghostly light" that is something of another order. Yet even from this must the contemplative be detached: it is futile to strive for it, God being free to give or to withhold it as He wishes.'[2] True again, but a 'beam of ghostly light' cannot be insensible in the sense of imperceptible, and to be 'detached' from it cannot mean to regard it as unimportant. Nor is it futile to do everything we can to promote it: the point is that it is God's action upon us, not ours on him. It is also true, no doubt, that God does not give certain special experiences except to special people (but he surely intends to communicate himself to us according to our measure). Circumstances may indeed hamper us in a vast variety of ways, but we are not called upon to acquiesce in them as though they were, as such, 'God's will'. Johnston makes the gratuitousness of God's operations a distinguishing mark of Christian theology as against neoplatonist systems.[3] This emphasis on God's free bestowal of his gifts, which is constant throughout the tradition, sometimes causes me, I must confess, a certain uneasiness. What it means, of course, is that we cannot dictate to him, that we cannot discern the workings of his providence, that we must leave everything to him without repining; we must be prepared to suffer without knowing the reason for it. The danger is that this

[1] 210.   [2] 266.   [3] 213.

emphasis might suggest that God's plan is less than supremely generous. There is question here not of asserting man's rights but of safeguarding the perfection of God's love.

In *The Crucible of Love* Trueman Dicken has examined in detail the teachings of St Teresa of Avila and St John of the Cross and shown very clearly that there is substantial agreement between them. In the following passage he is summarizing his findings:

'The true goal of Christian life for St Teresa, as for St John of the Cross and for any other sound teacher of the faith, is that of conformity with the will of God. Because God is the uncreated, detachment from the created order is the essential condition for the attainment of that goal. In our spiritual life, therefore, whatever conduces to virtue will be beneficial; whatever brings us into contact with the uncreated must be a foretaste of the end-term itself. This is the implied criterion by which, although she does not so explain it, St Teresa judges the value and the degree of advancement of all the peaks and plateaux charted on her spiritual map. Recollection, quiet, delectable union, are progressive peaks leading us away from the things of sense. Union actually dispenses with all mediation of created things and is a naked contact of the soul with God. For the short time it lasts it is perfection; but because the soul is not yet fully integrated, because it is not free of human frailties and attachments, because it still is not habitually conformed to the will of God, such union comes only from time to time by divine supernatural intervention into its normal climate of life and prayer.'[1]

This divine 'intervention' may puzzle us, and we may need to remember that this 'detachment' leads to a true appreciation of the created world. Otherwise this passage may seem to move smoothly enough to the conclusion that conscious union with God constitutes the perfection of Christian living, and that it is conditioned by a complete conformity with his will (which is in that sense the 'goal' of the mystic's efforts) and is thus of rare occurrence (there may be other reasons, as we have seen, for its rarity). But this is a conclusion which has caused a great deal of controversy, and this chapter will conclude with some discussion of it.

Knowles puts the question as follows: 'Does the authentic mystic attain to a higher level of supernatural virtue than that reached by

[1] 421.

266

active ascetic perseverance ?'[1] The answer, he goes on to tell us, 'based both on spiritual reasons and on the declarations of the mystics themselves, must emphatically be yes, with the reservation that we are speaking of the fully-grown mystic at the term of his life'. His next sentence gives a disconcerting reason for this: 'If Christian perfection is to be found in the union of the human will with that of God . . . a far stronger, closer and more permanent union is achieved when God moves and holds the intellect and will by his direct control in the soul's centre than when an individual acts, with grace indeed inspiring, aiding and moving, but by means of the normal human deliberate conjunction of reason and will.' The reference to both intellect and will as held and moved in the soul's centre is indeed most acceptable, but it would appear that the importance of mystical experience is that it enhances the union of the *will* with God because it is *this* union (and not that of the intellect as well) in which Christian perfection consists. Knowles's question, it now becomes clear, was not whether the mystic state has 'virtue' as its necessary *condition*, but whether the mystic state is the *cause* of 'virtue', union of the will with God's will. It is, of course, true that in a sense a union of will is what really matters. That is to say, if we have done our best, we shall be prepared for full conscious union with God in the next life, even if we have been prevented by our circumstances from attaining mystical union with him in the present life. And it is perhaps this consideration which is in the minds of mystical writers on certain occasions when they say that 'experiences' are not what really matters. But what we are here concerned with is the perfection which Christians are to aim at in this life, which is surely a union or their whole spiritual being, mind and will together, and the fact that circumstances may prevent them from attaining it is not to the point. Knowles, however, regards perfection as confined to a union of will; a union of intellect does indeed occur, but is extraneous to it. It is an 'infused' conformity of the will. This does not seem to me intelligible.

Here it may be noted that the passage last quoted from Trueman Dicken's book is also capable of that interpretation, if we take 'union' there to mean only union of will when 'union' is said to be 'perfection'. It is hard to avoid the suspicion that there is a good deal of confusion in writings of this kind between 'perfection' as referring to moral dispositions or intentions and 'perfection' as human achievement or (it is

[1] *What is Mysticism?* 36.

THE ABSOLUTE AND THE ATONEMENT

the same thing) the fulfilment of God's purposes, the fruit of his own activity upon us, accepted by us. It may also be noted that for Knowles the distinguishing mark of 'infused' knowledge and love is its passivity. As Bouyer points out, 'if God acts in us, this is not at all by way of substituting himself for us . . . but of fomenting an activity which . . . is no less our own in coming wholly from him'.[1] As he also says: 'It is not the case that in contemplation we become inert under God's action. On the contrary, we are then perhaps more really and effectively active than at any of those moments when we seem, at first sight, left to ourselves and to our own efforts.'[2]

Mr Watkin's theory, touched on in the last chapter, may now be recalled: that holiness consists in a union of will which may not be experienced at all if the subject belongs to the class of those who are psychologically 'opaque'. Trueman Dicken quotes St Teresa's remark that there are many souls who become contemplative without knowing it and comments: 'Hence a consciousness of contemplative prayer is certainly not essential to sanctity. . . .'[3] But surely St Teresa means that many do not recognize it for what it is, not that it is itself an unconscious business. I have spoken of conscious union with God (which involves, of course, devotion to his purposes) as the 'perfection which Christians are to aim at in this life'. It is recognized that the language of the mystics on this topic is often ambiguous or even contradictory, and it is on this that there has been so much controversy. Knowles gives us a masterly historical account of it in half a dozen pages. A few sentences from it will suffice for my purpose:

'The whole burden of the writings of Tauler, of Hilton, of St John of the Cross seem to equate the mystical life with the perfect Christian life, with the fullest possible development here below of the eternal life that begins with baptism and ends in the Beatific Vision. And a great school of theologians, basing itself directly on St Thomas and the unbroken series of his commentators and indirectly (but reliably) upon patristic and medieval tradition, has given its support to the mystics in this.'[4]

It is no argument against this, Knowles remarks very properly, to say that such an achievement is rare: Christianity is not an easy religion. But it may seem an argument against it (one which is vigorously

[1] *Introduction à la vie Spirituelle*, 177,   [2] 81.
[3] *The Crucible of Love*, 49.   [4] *What is Mysticism?* 46.

pressed) that the mystics also say with one voice that this perfection 'is purely and absolutely God's work, and cannot be achieved, or even in the strict sense of the word merited by man'.[1] How, then, can it be something which we are to aim at? St John of the Cross says that 'God grants these favours to whom he wills and for what reason he wills'.[2] Nevertheless, as Knowles goes on to say, 'these masters do not cease to invite their readers to press forward to the goal of mystical union'. We must conclude, it seems to me, that what they really mean is that this union is to be expected if there has been the right preparation for it (although there may be circumstances in particular cases which make it impossible), but that the highest states of contemplative prayer (although not what we may call 'ordinary' mystical experience) are reserved for special people.

The conclusion that God *intends* mystical union in some degree for everyone could be supported by many statements of the mystics of which the following from St John's *The Living Flame of Love*[3] (here quoted by Knowles) may be taken as an example: 'It is not because God is pleased that there should be few raised to this high spiritual state, for it would rather please him that all souls should be perfect . . . but there are many who desire to make progress and constantly entreat God to bring them to this state of perfection . . . and when it pleases God to bring them through the first trials and mortifications as is necessary, they are unwilling to pass through them, and flee away. . . .' The fact that these words are addressed directly to Carmelites does not seem to detract from their significance. (It is true that 'religious' are especially bound to heed them, and many religious institutes are in decay in our time because this fundamental form of asceticism is neglected.)

A reference to 'special people' must not be misinterpreted in the sense that some people are called to a life of perfection, the 'religious life', while others are called only to 'salvation'. This was a common view in medieval times. In *The Cloud*, as Johnston remarks,[4] we find time and again the doctrine that 'the meek stirring of love . . . is the substance of all good living, and without it no work may be begun nor ended' (92:14). But it is also constantly asserted by this master that *perfection* is a *special* gift of God in the sense that it is just not intended

[1] 47. [2] *The Ascent of Mount Carmel*, II, xxxii.
[3] Stanza II, para. 27. [4] 112.

for the common run of Christians. Plainly we must here distinguish between perfection in the abstract or absolute perfection and concrete or relative perfection. Everyone has his or her perfection to aim at, and 'the meek stirring of love' is not the perquisite of a privileged class of Christians. Nevertheless, it seems perfectly reasonable to hold that Christians are not all destined to the same degree, the same intensity, of spiritual union. It is hard to avoid the conclusion that perfection in the abstract must lie in the highest degree of union. A 'loving attention' to God, a developing Christian faith which involves not only the performance of his will but also an increasing awareness of him, is, I submit, what Christians should recognize as their supreme aim according to each one's measure. Some may be capable of concentrating on this development of faith in special conditions and without external works —this is their vocation, and it is not to be thought that they do nothing for 'the world' by embracing it. But for those 'in the world' also it must be this development that gives to their lives its ultimate meaning; it must be the mainspring of their activity and the goal to which they would lead other men.

Johnston in the General Conclusion of his book says that his own position 'differs slightly' from his author's. 'I believe', he continues, 'that his contemplation is one way to perfection—and an ordinary way; but I do not believe it is the *only* way.' He gives this reason: 'The early Church, as it appears in the Acts of the Apostles, found room for the highest sanctity in the active life and in the world; one can then wonder whether this intensely experimental gift is completely necessary to reach the summit of perfection.' But he allows that 'ordinarily perfection will demand touches of mysticism and stirrings of love— though not so deep, not so violent, not so uncompromisingly imperative as those described by the author of *The Cloud*'.[1] Knowles rules out 'any suggestion that an entirely "active", non-mystical life of virtue may surpass in excellence the fullest mystical union'.[2] It will be seen that this verdict leaves open the possibility that the fullest mystical union might be equalled in excellence by an entirely 'non-mystical' life (and we have to remember that Knowles uses 'mystical' in the technical sense which has come to be so widely accepted). We find in both these writers a very abrupt contrast between the 'infused' love of God and that love of him which gives value to an 'active' life of virtue (in this

[1] 263-4. [2] *What is Mysticism?* 37.

context what makes the agent virtuous must be his attitude of mind, his motive or intention). 'Infused' love puts you in top mark-bracket. The other sort of love, which does not attain to 'God in himself', can nevertheless equal this in excellence if you keep it up for long enough and with unremitting vigour.

I find all this very puzzling. It seems to me that we are all called to be united with God, to know and love him 'in himself' and that this knowledge is meant to develop. We are all called to perfection in the sense that we are all called upon to do the best we can. If this is our aim, even though we may fail at times, God will give each of us his or her perfection in the sense that he will, in the end, fill us with himself. But, according to traditional theology, there will not be so much of us to fill as there was, to take the supreme example of a Christian person, for our Blessed Lady, Christ's Virgin Mother.

18. BERGSON AND THE WITNESS OF THE MYSTICS

Mysticism, in the sense in which I have tried to explain it, is everybody's business unless we can rule it out with sufficient plausibility as a pathological state. Its incidence outside Christianity is usually difficult to pin down, but its persistent appearance within Christianity is enough to make it a phenomenon which the philosopher cannot disregard. Unless he has already satisfied himself that the question of God does not arise, this phenomenon will be evidence in favour of the theistic hypothesis; in fact, if the mystics are right, it can be more than a hypothesis. The philosopher may very easily receive the impression that it is only a working hypothesis for the Christian whom he happens to encounter. But, if mysticism is not to be written off as a pathological state, it will be hard to believe that the God to whom it witnesses does not make himself accessible to all men and that they cannot share the mystics' certainty. Moreover, the teachings of the mystics, so far from being incompatible with the doctrines of Christianity, seem to be the key to a fuller understanding of these doctrines.

In our time the philosopher who has emphasized most strikingly the significance of the mystics is Henri Bergson. And to consider the main lines of *Les Deux Sources de la Morale et de la Religion* will have the advantage of bringing us back to those aspects of human experience on which I have chiefly insisted as evidence for theism. A few words are necessary by way of introduction to a book which is not so well known, among ourselves, as it deserves to be.

It appeared in 1932, only a few years before Bergson's death; most English works on Bergson belong to an earlier period. Father F. C. Copleston devoted a British Academy lecture to it in 1955 and pointed out, very truly, that Bergson is not consistent in what he says in it about obligation. The fact is that his outlook was expanding as he wrote it, and its interest and importance are largely due to this. It is significant that Copleston seems to have regarded the book as on the whole simply continuing the previous lines of thought; he complains, for example, that Bergson talks about nature's having 'designs or plans'[1] without noticing that this language is provisional—Bergson points out more than once that such expressions are a manner of speaking, not to be taken literally (for instance: 'We do not assert that nature has, strictly speaking, designed or foreseen anything whatever').[2] In 1957, however, Mr I. W. Alexander's *Bergson: Philosopher of Reflection* did make clear the significance of the book. It is a challenge to the view, still popular among us, that Bergson was an anti-intellectualist. 'In the history of ideas', Alexander writes, '*The Two Sources of Morality and Religion* proved as epoch-making as *Time and Free Will*' (that is, presumably, on the Continent). It 'rehabilitated the *via mystica* as a source of knowledge'. He continues: 'Yet the book is not only a treatise. It is the terminal point of a spiritual dialectic, of which each of Bergson's books represents a stage, whereby the mind becomes progressively aware of the transcendent nature of the activity immanent within its operations: psychic in *The Essay* [*Time and Free Will*], cosmic and biological in *Matter and Memory* and *Creative Evolution*, finally spiritual and divinely inspired in the *Two Sources*.'[3] In 1947 the late Norman Kemp Smith in his Presidential Address to the Aristotelian Society had remarked, with reference to the *Two Sources*, that it 'is probably true to say that Bergson has not ever rightly come into his own and that he will not do so until he has been read backwards. . . .'

It will be useful to note a few more passages in Alexander's illuminating book. He quotes Bergson's words 'there is no other source of

---

[1] *Proceedings of the British Academy*, vol. XLI, 263.

[2] *The Two Sources of Morality and Religion*, 56 (53). References are to the translation published by Doubleday and Co., New York, with the page numbers of the eighth French edition, in brackets, following.   [3] 57.

knowledge than experience', and connects him with 'the time-honoured current of non-speculative Christian thinking that runs from St Augustine to Pascal and beyond'.[1] 'Non-speculative', however, could mislead: 'speculation' is not necessarily bound up with the use of a predominantly abstractive method in metaphysics or with theological rationalism; a theologian by co-ordinating his insights and by reasoning on the basis of them may reach results which are properly called 'speculative'. More important, however, is the context of these remarks, the admirable account which Alexander gives of the basic distinction between the 'two sources', the social instinct which is produced by the morality of the 'closed' or static society and the *élan* of the 'open' or dynamic morality. As Alexander here puts it, the former is 'infra-intellectual', the latter 'supra-intellectual', 'a limitless aspiration which brings us into communion not only with the whole of mankind but with the universal creativity that inspires all human efforts'; it is not anti-intellectual, and 'it can and will be expressed in moral formulae' although 'it transcends all formulae as their source and principle'.[2] This brings us to 'the borders of religious experience'. When morality and religion are reduced to abstract formulae they are 'static' and the source of their immobilization is the social instinct: when they are dynamized by the *élan* the source is mysticism. 'This culminating intuition, this mystic intuition, can come into play only at the level of self-consciousness, which alone permits the distinction between the self and its states or intellectual formulations, and enables the self to retrogress to the supra-intellectual source of its activities and seize the virtualities immanent within it.'[3] Here it must be pointed out that the reduction of obligation to social pressures in primitive societies (which, of course, is not *moral* obligation at all) is a schematic arrangement in Bergson's book: he proves to be quite willing to allow that the 'closed' and the 'open' moralities may have been always intertwined.

I am not entirely happy about Alexander's statement that 'the central feature of Bergson's religious thought is the emphasis laid upon the active life'.[4] This could give the impression that he was unsympathetic to the traditional concept of monasticism. As I understand him, his emphasis is on the way in which the soul *in its contemplation* is fully active because acted upon by God, although its contemplation overflows, as it were, into serving others. But Alexander does make clear

[1] 57–8.   [2] 58.   [3] 60.   [4] *Ibid.*

that Bergson was moving towards Christianity at the time when he wrote the *Two Sources*: in the year following its publication he declared, in a rather curious phrase, 'his adherence to the principle of the divinity of the Catholic Church as linked with that of Christ'. It seems that it was his reading of the mystics which brought to full consciousness that groping towards Christianity which had been going on from the beginning. And it is this which gives his book its peculiar excitement and effectiveness (rather like Chesterton's *Orthodoxy* in this). It contains a good many philosophical conclusions, reached in his earlier work, which seem to me obscure or unacceptable; I am concerned only with those which he comes to here, firmly and explicitly, for the first time.

So I shall now quote some passages from the book's first chapter in which the two moralities are contrasted:

'We are fond of saying that the apprenticeship of civic virtue is served in the family, and that in the same way, from holding our country dear, we learn to love mankind. Our sympathies are supposed to broaden out in an unbroken progression, to expand while remaining identical, and to end by embracing all humanity. This is *a priori* reasoning, the result of a purely intellectualist conception of the soul. . . . Who can help seeing that social cohesion is largely due to the necessity for a community to protect itself against others, and that it is primarily as against all other men that we love the men with whom we live? Such is the primitive instinct. It is still there, though fortunately hidden under the accretions of civilization; but even today we still love naturally and directly our parents and our fellow-countrymen, whereas love of mankind is indirect and acquired. We go straight to the former, to the latter we come only by roundabout ways; for it is only through God, in God, that religion bids man love mankind.'[1]

This is the point of transition to the 'open' morality:

'In all times there have arisen exceptional men, incarnating this morality. Before the saints of Christianity, mankind had known the sages of Greece, the prophets of Israel, the Arahants of Buddhism, and others besides. It is to them that men have always turned for that complete morality which we had best call absolute morality. . . . Why is it, then, that saints have their imitators, and why do the great

[1] 32-3 (27-8).

274

moral leaders draw the masses after them? They ask nothing, and yet they receive. They have no need to exhort; their mere existence suffices. For such is precisely the nature of this other morality. Whereas natural obligation is a pressure or a propulsive force, complete and perfect morality has the effect of an appeal.'[1]

When Bergson asks why this appeal is answered, his reply may seem disconcerting: 'Beyond instinct and habit there is no direct action on the will except feeling (*sensibilité*).'[2] But we must not be misled. This is not really anti-intellectualism. The language of intellect had become in-operative for the Romantics, with whom Bergson here allies himself, because the intellect had become, by their time, rationalized, 'the reason reasoning'. What they mean is what used to be meant by 'intellect'—the power of penetrating into things. Bergson goes on to explain what he means, and talks, inevitably, about music. He concludes that 'we should be inclined to say that it ["feeling"] is supra-intellectual', but that this might suggest only a superiority of value, whereas there is involved also 'the relation between that which generates and that which is generated' for it 'can alone be productive of ideas'.[3] That is, we have now met what will be called a little later an 'intuition'.

'No amount of speculation', Bergson continues, 'will create an obligation or anything like it: the theory may be all very fine, I shall always be able to say that I will not accept it . . . But if the atmos-phere of the emotion is there, if I have breathed it in, if it has entered my being, I shall act in accordance with it, uplifted by it. . . .'[4] What, then, of the relations in which Christianity stands to metaphysics on the one hand and to morality on the other?:

'Antecedent to the new morality, and also the new metaphysics, there is the emotion, which develops as an impetus in the realm of the will, and as an explicative representation in that of intelligence. Take, for example, the emotion introduced by Christianity under the name of charity: if it wins over souls, a certain behaviour ensues and a certain doctrine is disseminated. But neither has its metaphysics enforced the moral practice, nor the moral practice induced a disposition to its metaphysics. Metaphysics and morality express here the self-same thing, one in terms of intelligence, the other in terms of will; and the two expressions of the thing are accepted together, as soon as the

[1] 34 (29–30).   [2] 39 (35).   [3] 44 (40).   [4] 47–8 (44).

thing is there to be expressed . . . the emotion of which we were speaking is the enthusiasm of a forward movement, enthusiasm by means of which this morality has won over a few and has then, through them, spread over the world.'

Bergson is still thinking of metaphysics as a system of 'ideas' generated now by charity, which he calls an 'emotion'. It is the 'feeling' which was called 'supra-intellectual'. So it must be awareness in its most radical and penetrating form. I should call it 'metaphysical experience'. Bergson goes on to speak of it as follows:

'True mystics simply open their souls to the oncoming wave. Sure of themselves, because they feel within them something better than themselves, they prove to be great men of action, to the surprise of those for whom mysticism is nothing but visions, and raptures and ecstasies. That which they have allowed to flow into them is a stream flowing down and seeking through them to reach their fellow-men; the necessity to spread around them what they have received affects them like an onslaught of love. . . . If society is self-sufficient, it is the supreme authority. But if it is only one of the aspects of life, we can easily conceive that life, which has had to set down the human species at a certain point of its evolution, imparts a new impetus to exceptional individuals who have immersed themselves anew in it, so that they can help society further along its way. True, we shall have had to push on as far as the very principle of life.'[1]

Bergson is still using the language of 'life', but what he means by it now is clear enough.

In his third chapter he is perfectly explicit: 'The complete mysticism is that of the great Christian mystics.'[2] He speaks of a 'superabundance of life in the soul' and continues:

'There is an irresistible impulse which hurls it into vast enterprises. A calm exaltation of all its faculties makes it see things on a vast scale only. . . . Above all, it sees things simply, and this simplicity, which is equally striking in the words it uses and the conduct it follows, guides it through complications which it apparently does not even perceive . . . Yet effort remains indispensable, endurance and perseverance likewise. But they come of themselves, they develop of their own

[1] 99 (101), 100 (102).   [2] 227 (243).

accord, in a soul acting and acted upon, whose liberty coincides with the divine activity.'[1]

But how is mysticism to be taught to the world at large? Bergson replies: 'If mysticism is to transform humanity it can do so only by passing on, from one man to another, slowly, a part of itself. The mystics are well aware of this.' He describes their procedure as follows:

'This consisted, not in contemplating a general and immediate spreading of the mystic impetus, which was obviously impossible, but in imparting it, already weakened though it was, to a tiny handful of privileged souls which together would form a spiritual society; societies of this kind might multiply; each one, through such of its members as might be exceptionally gifted, would give birth to one or several others; thus the impetus would be preserved and continued until such time as a profound change in the material conditions imposed on humanity by nature should permit, in spiritual matters, of a radical transformation. Such is the method followed by the great mystics. It was of necessity, and because they could do no more, that they were particularly prone to spend their superabundant energy in founding convents or religious orders, For the time being they had no need to look further. The impetus of love which drove them to lift humanity up to God and complete the divine creation could reach its end, in their eyes, only with the help of God Whose instruments they were. Therefore all their efforts must be concentrated on a very great, a very difficult, but a limited task.'[2]

These references to a change in material conditions should not be taken to imply that the founders of religious societies thought about things in these terms; they are Bergson's own reflections, and we shall meet them again. It is the insistence on mysticism as the explanation of the religious life that is important here.

A passage follows about the relation between mysticism and dogma. 'A doctrine which is but a doctrine has a poor chance indeed of giving birth to the glowing enthusiasm, the illumination, the faith that moves mountains. But grant this fierce glow, and the molten matter will easily run into the mould of a doctrine, or even become that

[1] 232 (248). [2] 236 (252-3).

doctrine as it solidifies.'[1] The topic is pursued in the next paragraph:

'What the mystic finds waiting for him, then, is a humanity which has been prepared to listen to his message by other mystics, invisible and present in the religion which is actually taught. Indeed his mysticism itself is imbued with this religion, for such was its starting point. His theology will generally conform to that of the theologians. His intelligence and his imagination will use the teachings of the theologians to express in words what he experiences, and in material images what he sees spiritually. And this he can do easily, since theology has tapped that very current whose source is the mystical. Thus his mysticism is served by religion, against the day when religion becomes enriched by his mysticism. This explains the primary mission which he feels to be entrusted to him, that of an intensifier of religious faith. He takes the most crying needs first. In reality, the task of the great mystic is to effect a radical transformation of humanity by setting an example.'

This, then, is the witness of the mystics in a society which is animated by religious faith. They are 'the imitators and original but incomplete continuators of what the Christ of the Gospel was completely'.[2]

Bergson now turns to the witness of the mystics in the conditions of modern Western society and considers it as evidence for God. Modern philosophers are inclined to shake their heads reproachfully over this— other people's testimony will not do. But Bergson does not claim to produce a cast-iron argument. He begins a new section of his third chapter by laying it down that any answer to the problem of God must be of an experiential nature. Modern philosophers, he says, 'hamper themselves with insoluble problems which arise only if God is studied from the Aristotelian point of view, and if they are pleased to call by that name a being whom mankind has never dreamed of invoking;[3] for Aristotle's God is not the God who is experienced. He then dismisses the suggestion that the great mystics are unreliable because they are off their heads. And he continues:

'Along with the souls capable of following the mystic way to the end there are many who go at least part of the way: how numerous are those who take a few steps, either by an effort of will or from a natural disposition! William James used to say he had never experienced

[1] 238 (254).   [2] 240 (256).   [3] 244 (261).

mystic states; but he added that if he heard them spoken of by a man who had experienced them "something within him echoed the call". Most of us are probably in the same case. It is no use invoking as evidence to the contrary the indignant protests of those who see nothing in mysticism but quackery and folly. Some people are doubtless utterly impervious to mystic experience, incapable of feeling or imagining anything of it. But we also meet with people to whom music is nothing but noise, and some of them will express their opinions of musicians with the same anger, the same tone of personal spite. No one would think of accepting this as an argument against music.'[1]

Bergson then points out that all the mystics use the same sort of language about God, though they were not directly influenced by one another: 'All we want to make clear is that, if external resemblances between Christian mystics may be due to a common tradition or a common training, their deep-seated agreement is a sign of an identity of intuition which would find its simplest explanation in the actual existence of the Being with whom they believe themselves to hold intercourse. So much the more so, then, if we consider that the other mysticisms, ancient or modern, go more or less far, stopping at this or that stage, but all point in the same direction.'[2]

This witness to God, Bergson considers, can be persuasive for philosophers if they have also other grounds for supposing that such an experience can occur. I am inclined to think that, on his own principle, 'experience is the only source of knowledge', the present 'crisis of belief' can be surmounted only if it is recognized that all men are radically capable of mysticism (as Bergson himself frequently insists) and must be encouraged in the direction of it. 'Mysticism' must then be understood in a non-technical sense to refer to that loving awareness of God of which I have written. And I think that the spread of religious communities which make 'the intensification of religious faith' the object of their existence is of the utmost importance in this connection. But, if they are to be of any use, they must concentrate, first and foremost, on intensifying their own religious faith. They must be, at least in the broad sense in which I am using the word, genuinely 'mystical'. To these topics I shall return at the end.

Bergson goes on to say that the philosopher must consult the mystic

[1] 245–6 (263).   [2] 247 (265).

if he wants to know who God is. If he does, he will avoid many false problems:

'The nature of God will thus appear in the very reasons we have for believing in his existence: we shall no longer try to deduce his existence or non-existence from an arbitrary conception of his nature. Let agreement be reached on this point and there will be no objection to talking about divine omnipotence. We find such expressions used by these very mystics to whom we turn for experience of the divine. They obviously mean by this an energy to which no limit can be assigned, and a power of creating and loving which surpasses all imagination. They certainly do not evoke a closed concept.'[1]

That is the sort of context in which the problem of evil needs to be discussed.

It remains to quote a long passage from Bergson's fourth chapter, 'Final Remarks'. What, he asks, is the real significance of our industrial civilization?:

'Now, would it not be possible to shorten the road before us, or even to smooth away all the difficulties at once, instead of negotiating them one by one? Let us set aside the main question, that of population, which will have to be resolved for its own sake, whatever happens. The others arise principally from the direction taken by our existence since the great expansion of industry. We demand material comfort, amenities and luxuries. We set out to enjoy ourselves. What if our life were to become more ascetic? Mysticism is undoubtedly at the origin of great moral transformations. And mankind seems to be as far away as ever from it. But who knows? In the course of our last chapter we fancied we have caught sight of a possible link between the mysticism of the West and its industrial civilization. The matter needs to be gone into thoroughly. Everybody feels that the immediate future is going to depend largely on the organization of industry and the conditions it will impose or accept. We have just seen that the problem of peace between nations is contingent on this problem. That of peace at home depends on it just as much. Must we live in fear, or may we live in hope? For a long time it was taken for granted that industrialism and mechanization would bring happiness to mankind. Today one is ready to lay to their

[1] 262 (281-2).

280

door all the ills from which we suffer. Never, it is said, was humanity more athirst for pleasure, luxury, and wealth. An irresistible force seems to drive it more and more violently towards the satisfaction of its basest desires. That may be, but let us go back to the impulsion at the origin. If it was a strong one, a slight deviation at the beginning may have been enough to produce a wider and wider divergence between the point aimed at and the object reached. In that case, we should not concern ourselves so much with the divergence as with the impulsion. True, things never get done of themselves. Humanity will change only if it is intent upon changing. But perhaps it has already prepared the means of doing so. Perhaps it is nearer the goal than it thinks. Since we have brought a charge against industrial effort, let us examine it more closely.'[1]

The conclusion to which Bergson comes is that 'the mystical summons up the mechanical', for although it 'evokes asceticism', it also promotes the 'spirit of invention', and this spirit from the fifteenth century onwards was informed, despite appearances, by the true Christian ideal. More precisely, the Christian ideal appeared in an aspect which was unfamiliar. The underlying principle was that man 'must use matter as a support if he wants to get away from matter'. But the original 'spiritual impulsion' has been side-tracked in the direction of 'exaggerated comfort and luxury for the few, rather than liberation for all'.[2] So the conclusion is: 'What we need are new reserves of potential energy—moral energy this time. So let us not merely say, as we did above, that the mystical summons up the mechanical. We must add that the body, now larger, calls for a bigger soul, and that mechanization should mean mysticism. The origins of the process of mechanization are indeed more mystical than we might imagine. Machinery will find its true vocation again, it will render service in proportion to its power, only if mankind, which it has bowed still lower to the earth, can succeed, through it, in standing erect and looking heavenwards.'[3]

Bergson's views about the origins of industrialism have been shared by a good many later writers. Whether they afford us ground for hopes about its future I should not venture myself to determine. But I should like to draw attention to a passage in Dr J. V. Langmead Casserley's remarkable (though uneven) and unduly neglected book *In the Service*

[1] 291–2 (314–15).   [2] 308–10 (333–5).   [3] 310 (333–4).

of Man[1]: 'As technology becomes more sophisticated it becomes paradoxically less dominant. Although men are less and less able to do without it, they are more and more able to rise above and forget it. For one thing it requires so much less of their time and attention. The computer revolution must be estimated and valued in terms of the extent to which it sets men free, and men themselves must be judged by the extent to which they are able to make rich and creative use of their freedom.'[2] This is part of an argument, developed at length in Casserley's book, for holding that the Christian Church will have unprecedented opportunities in the new age.

Before making my own final comments on the significance of Bergson's book for our time I shall consider the view that his philosophy is not properly a Christian one. According to M. Etienne Borne in his *Passion de la Verité*,[3] it falls short of being a Christian one in three ways: it discovers the divine too readily in the world of nature, it makes spirit and matter antithetical principles, and it overlooks the dialectic of conversion. For the moment I pass over the first of these criticisms. The second and third are no doubt justified if one considers Bergson's work *en bloc*, but it seems to me that they do not apply to the *Two Sources* in the same way as to the earlier books. What Borne thinks lacking in Bergson's work is not found explicitly in the *Two Sources*, but the whole tendency of the book, as I see it, postulates conversion. Spirit and matter now appear as antithetical principles in so far as one emerges from the other and must struggle to emerge—so that inevitably matter will be described sometimes as holding it down. And in this struggle the dialectic of conversion is implied. Bergson is not concerned to describe it, but he is certainly not postulating a smooth development, a continuous progression which meets with no serious obstacles. The static and the dynamic tendencies in human existence will never come to terms with one another in a definitive way—Borne thinks that Bergson is going against his own principles in admitting this; in fact, I think, he is making it clear what his principles have now come to be. Alexander, in his book on Bergson,[4] has argued that his 'optimism' is compatible with Kierkegaard's insistence on the opposition between Christianity and mere 'philosophy'.

The first of Borne's criticisms is connected very closely with the

---

[1] Regnery, 1967.   [2] 158.   [3] Fayard, Paris, 1963.
[4] *Bergson: Philosopher of Reflection*, 65 f.

third. It seems a rather curious one to come from a Blondelian, even from one who stresses the 'dialectical' strain in Blondel so vigorously. At any rate it is surely very much worse to exclude the divine from the world of nature than to make the discovery of it seem too easy. Borne's view that Bergson's work has an 'antique' flavour, that he is really a latter-day Greek intellectualist, seems to me, again, an unsympathetic reading of the *Two Sources*. It is perfectly true, as he points out, that Bergson has no use for 'negativity' and says that the mystics have no use for it. Nor have they, in the sense that they use the language of negativity only as a way of hinting at absolute positivity. But Borne's insistence on 'negativity' is of a very different sort. What it seems to amount to, in the end, is that awareness of God's absence is a state of affairs which must be accepted, as it stands, as meaningful. He is not of course alone in saying this—Blondel, for example, does seem sometimes to say it too. But to me it makes no sense. It seems to me very clear that you cannot be aware of God's absence unless you have *some* knowledge of who God is. You can wonder whether such knowledge is illusory; you can misdescribe it; you can regard it as a nuisance; you can even find the bare fact of it (unaccompanied by any agreeable emotion) utterly exasperating; you can perhaps lose it altogether. But it is in itself *positive*, and either you have it in some sort or you do not.

It is true that the *Two Sources* is an incomplete witness to the Christian religion in an all-important respect. Bergson emphasizes the newness of Christianity; it marks the decisive stage in the progress of the race. But he says nothing in particular about the acceptance of a historical Revelation, about the response to a fresh *object* which makes all the difference between a vague and intermittent religiosity and the solid adherence to a visible society which is both human and divine and which is the focal point of Christian life and thought. But what he should help us to realize is that Christian life must be a life of thought, not the abstract thought of the 'mere philosopher', but the thought of the concrete individual. The difficulty is that we have no suitable vocabulary for this. 'Thought' suggests a speciality almost as much as 'mysticism'. But to think about the Christian religion is surely necessary if we are to practise it (it is the great lesson which Blondel has to teach us that we must understand 'thought' and 'action' as bound up with one another). We are not all called upon to read theological treatises, but we must all concentrate, so far as we can, upon the central mystery of

Christ, so as to bring ourselves into it. We must be acquainted with it *at first hand* (this is what all the Christian 'existentialists' are saying, from Kierkegaard onwards), so that we may enter into it with all our human powers, consciously and deliberately handing them all over to it. And here the opposition between 'activity' and 'passivity' breaks down.

Bergson treats of mysticism in a pure state; he is concerned, for purposes of exposition, with the finished product, those who have gone all the way. And such persons would be unanimous in declaring that the combination which they achieved of contemplative union with God and unflagging external works can be achieved only at the cost of a most arduous probation which includes, among other things, an abstention, more or less complete, from external works for a considerable period, in some cases perhaps for almost a lifetime. Bergson does not discuss this probation, but he is not to be understood, I think, as rejecting it. In any case, anyone who is impressed by what he has to say about mysticism, and who is attempting to organize his life on the basis of some such view as his, would be guilty of the gravest folly if he supposed himself capable from the start, or at an early stage, of the extraordinary combination to which I have just referred. It is indeed extremely rare, and to assume that one has achieved it without the long probation—the long period of quasi-solitude—which has always proved necessary in the past would be the height of presumption. It is probably true that the earlier stages of mysticism are more easily reached than they used to be. But it is certainly true that the period of probation presents greater difficulties. For one thing, the need for it is not properly appreciated by many religious superiors and the opportunities for it are not sufficiently provided. The theory of it is not properly taught; the necessity of it is not adequately insisted upon. Above all, the spirit of the time is against it.

I refer here to the religious life because it ought to play a most important part in resisting the reduction of Christianity to secular humanism and in giving witness to the purpose of life in the eyes of all men. The sad thing is that the religious, instead of realizing that the spirit of the time calls upon them to be more truly themselves, have in so many cases adapted themselves to it. Those who are largely engaged in external works (preaching, teaching and so forth) seem to have supposed that they are called upon to devote themselves to these in still greater measure whereas in fact it is their preoccupation with them which has made their witness less effective. There is much talk today about a need for Christian groupings not modelled on the existing religious orders. There may well be a place for them. But there is certainly a need for the sort of grouping which the founders of the monastic order in the West intended and brought into being. It seems so obvious that what the Church always needs more than anything else is simply more saints—more people, that is, whose faith in God and his revelation in Christ is the moving power of their lives, whose overwhelming interest is God himself and his purposes for the world. Such persons are always among us, in larger or smaller numbers, in all walks of life. But if they are to increase in our time it seems that they will commonly need, not necessarily indeed to become religious themselves, but certainly to be in touch with the religious at some stage of their careers. Monks and nuns, in particular, so it seems to me, will be increasingly important because the societies which they form must be rallying points, sources not only of spiritual refreshment but also of reassurance, enlightenment and inspiration. It is therefore most necessary that they should be wholly devoted to their own proper business. But I would urge once more that their proper business is also the business of all Christians in their measure; and here I quote the words of the Archbishop of Canterbury in his important Holland Lectures: 'Whereas mental meditation is something in which not every Christian will persevere because the powers of the human mind in concentration and imagination vary so greatly, the contemplation of God with the ground of the soul is, as these old writers insisted, accessible to any man, woman or child who is ready to try to be obedient and humble and to want God very much. Has it not been a mistake in the last few centuries in the West to regard meditation as a norm for all Christians and contemplative prayer as reserved only for advanced souls?'[1]

It is the fact that mysticism (in the broad sense which I have indicated) is distrusted, disapproved or simply neglected that is our fundamental trouble. That has been my submission. To take one example, even those zealous Christians who have been carrying out liturgical reforms seem so often to forget that the purpose of the liturgy is not only to instruct us and to unite us with one another but also to

[1] *Sacred and Secular*, by A. M. Ramsey (Longmans, 1964), 45—in a chapter on mysticism of peculiar value.

unite us with God. There is a great danger that the liturgy will cease to be 'numinous'. If we cannot create beauty ourselves, we can at least preserve the beauty which others have created. And beauty is more profoundly edifying than anything else can be. The Christians of the East have much to teach us about this.

Nevertheless the situation is, I believe, full of hope. Mr Michael Novak in his recent book *Belief and Unbelief* maintains that there is not only a 'crisis of belief' but also a 'crisis of unbelief'. We all know that many Christians have been forced to ask themselves seriously for the first time what, if anything, they really believe. It is, as a rule, only the negative results of this process which appear in the headlines. But the disappearance of conventional Christianity should lead to a revival of genuine Christianity. And, as Novak points out, many secular humanists are being forced to ask themselves whether after all they really disbelieve. Much religious rubbish is being thrown away, and much which is valuable is thrown away with it—but when the fury of iconoclasm has begun to die down it will no doubt come to light again. Churches get emptier: the world may seem hopelessly godless—but the fact is that more and more people are beginning to ask the right questions. I hope that in this book I have not seemed to be saying that they are easy to answer. 'God's absence' indeed presses with an almost intolerable weight upon the present generation, and in some degree it must bear down upon us all in our journey towards him, even when we are sure of him. All I have tried to do is to indicate how it comes about that in fact some people are sure of him.